the Gamblers Bedside Book

edited by
**JOHN K.
HUTCHENS**

the Gamblers' Bedside Book

Taplinger Publishing Company

New York

First Edition

Published in the United States in 1977 by
TAPLINGER PUBLISHING CO., Inc.
New York, New York

Copyright © 1977 by John K. Hutchens
All rights reserved. Printed in the U.S.A.

Published simultaneously in Canada by Burns & MacEachern, Limited, Ontario

---

Library of Congress Cataloging in Publication Data

Main entry under title:

The Gambler's bedside book.

   1. Gambling
I. Hutchens, John K., 1905–
HV6710.G3   1977   795'.01   74–20212
ISBN 0–8008–3123–3

Designed by Manuel Weinstein

ACKNOWLEDGEMENTS

THE EDITOR is grateful to numerous sources and persons for assistance in the assembling of this volume. Three books, in particular, provided invaluable background information reflected in his introduction and the prefaces to various sections. The books are: *The Complete Illustrated Guide to Gambling*, by Alan Wykes (Doubleday & Company), *Play the Devil*, by Henry Chafetz (Clarkson N. Potter), *Sucker's Progress*, by Herbert Asbury (Dodd, Mead & Company). Among those who aided materially were Mrs. Susan Anderl, Librarian of the Special Collections Department, and her staff at the University of Nevada, Las Vegas; Darrell W. Bolen, M.D., Assistant Clinical Professor of Psychiatry at the University of California at Los Angeles, author of a scholarly paper entitled "Gambling: Historical Highlights, Trends and Their Implications for Contemporary Society," presented at Las Vegas in 1974; Miss Patricia Fox, of Washington, D.C.; and, most notably, Miss Bobs Pinkerton, my editor, without whose patience, understanding, and high professional skill this project would not have come to be.

Grateful acknowledgement is also made for permission to include the following copyright material:

BET A MILLION GATES by Lloyd Wendt and Herman Kogan, from *Bet a Million!: The Story of John W. Gates*. Copyright 1948, © 1976 by The Bobbs-Merrill Company, Inc. Reprinted by permission of The Bobbs-Merrill Company, Inc.

ARNOLD ROTHSTEIN by Henry Chafetz, from *Play the Devil: A History of Gambling in the United States from 1942 to 1955*. Copyright © 1961 by Henry Chafetz. Reprinted by permission of Clarkson N. Potter, Inc.

A. R.: WAS THIS THE ONE? as told to Red Smith, from the *New York Times* (October 10, 1975). Copyright © 1975 by The New York Times Company, Reprinted by permission.

TITANIC THOMPSON by Jon Bradshaw, from *Fast Company*. Copyright © 1975 by Jon Bradshaw. Reprinted by permission of Harper & Row. Publishers, Inc.

JAGGERS' SYSTEM by Charles Kingston, from *The Romance of Monte Carlo*, published by The Bodley Head. Reprinted by permission of The Bodley Head.

"MONTE" by Arnold Bennett, from *Paris Nights and Other Impressions of Places and Peoples*, published by A. P. Watt & Son. Reprinted by permission of the Estate of Mrs. Cheston Bennett.

RIEN NE VA PLUS by Alexander Woollcott, from *The Portable Woollcott*, edited by Joseph Hennessey. Copyright 1934 by Alexander Woollcott, © renewed 1962 by Joseph P. Hennessey. Reprinted by permission of The Viking Press.

LAS VEGAS (WHAT?) by Tom Wolfe, from *The Kandy-Kolored Tangerine-Flake Streamline Baby*. Copyright © 1963, 1964, 1965 by Thomas K. Wolfe, Jr.

Reprinted by permission of Contemporary Books, Inc., and Anthony Sheil Associates Limited.

THE PRINCE OF WALES AT TRANBY CROFT by Virginia Cowles, from *Gay Monarch: The Life and Pleasures of Edward VII*. Copyright © 1956 by Virginia Cowles. Reprinted by permission of the author and Harper & Row, Publishers, Inc.

A GAME OF PIQUET by Giovanni Giacomo Casanova, from *History of My Life*, Vol. 8, English translation by Willard R. Trask. Copyright © 1969 by Harcourt Brace Jovanovich, Inc. Reprinted by permission of Harcourt Brace Jovanovich and Penguin Books Ltd.

THE GREAT RACETRACK CAPER by Rufus Jarman, from *American Heritage* (August 1968). Copyright © 1968 by American Heritage Publishing Co., Inc. Reprinted by permission.

A STORY GOES WITH IT by Damon Runyon. Copyright 1931, © 1959 by Damon Runyon, Jr., and Mary Runyon McCann. Reprinted by permission of the American Play Company, 52 Vanderbilt Avenue, New York, with special permission from Raoul Lionel Felder, Esq., New York City; and by permission of Constable & Co., Ltd. (published in *Runyon from First to Last*).

AND SEE HOW THEY RUN by Oswald Jacoby, from *Oswald Jacoby on Gambling*. Copyright © 1963 by Oswald Jacoby. Reprinted by permission of Doubleday & Company, Inc.

HOW TO WIN WHILE LOSING by William Saroyan, from *Here Comes, There Goes, You Know Who*. Copyright © 1961 by William Saroyan. Reprinted by permission of Simon & Schuster, Inc. (Trident Press Division).

THE PLEASURES OF GAMBLING, from *Esquire's Book of Gambling*, edited by David Newman and the Editors of Esquire. Copyright © 1962 by Esquire, Inc. Reprinted by permission of *Esquire Magazine* and Harper & Row, Publishers, Inc.

THE SIN OF BETTING by Charles W. Morton, from *The Atlantic Monthly* (May 1963). Copyright © 1965 by The Atlantic Monthly Company, Boston, Mass. Reprinted by permission.

Contents

◇◇

INTRODUCTION John K. Hutchens 13

HIGH ROLLERS

Bet a Million Gates   Lloyd Wendt and Herman Kogan   25
Arnold Rothstein   Henry Chafetz   32
A. R.: Was This the One?   as told to Red Smith   41
Titanic Thompson   Jon Bradshaw   43

FABLED SPOTS—MONTE CARLO AND LAS VEGAS

Jaggers' System   Charles Kingston   61
"Monte"   Arnold Bennett   64
Rien Ne Va Plus   Alexander Woollcott   70
Las Vegas (What?)
Las Vegas (Can't hear you!
   Too noisy)
Las Vegas ! ! ! !   Tom Wolfe   73
The Pixie April   Ian Andersen   81

AND ELSEWHERE

John Morrissey   Clyde Brion Davis   87
Canfield's Creation   L. J. Ludovici   92
Tex Rickard   Charles Samuels   95

THOSE WERE THE DAYS

In a San Francisco Gambling Saloon   Bret Harte   107
Madame Vestal   Forbes Parkhill   109

9

Elijah Skaggs	*Herbert Asbury*	116
Science *vs.* Luck	*Mark Twain*	120
Alias Madame Moustache	*Harry Sinclair Drago*	122
A Gambler's Pistol Play	*David A. Curtis*	131
The Heathen Chinee	*Bret Harte*	138

ONE THING AND ANOTHER

Phileas Fogg and the Jumping Frog	*J. Bryan III*	143
A Veteran Looks Back	*John Philip Quinn*	148
The Whang-doodle	*from Esquire's Book of Gambling*	150
A Poker Game	*Stephen Crane*	151

HOW TO DO IT

Advice from Nick the Greek	*Ted Thackrey, Jr.*	157
A Professor Beats the Gamblers	*Edward O. Thorp*	166
Omens and Superstitions	*Stearn Robinson*	177

PSYCHOLOGY OF GAMBLING

The Gambler and His Motives	*Alan Wykes*	183
James Pethel	*Max Beerbohm*	190
Fiodor's Last Game	*Anna Dostoevsky*	206

SKULDUGGERY

Shenanigans on the Mississippi	*George H. Devol*	211
Wilson Mizner	*Alva Johnston*	217
A Great Card Swindle	*John Nevil Maskelyne*	227
Canada Bill	*Allan Pinkerton*	231
How to Beat the Horses	*Yellow Kid Weil*	
	as told to W. T. Brannon	241
Fleecing the Fleecers	*J. H. Green*	247
The Rake of Piccadilly	*Henry Blythe*	250
The Prince of Wales at Tranby Croft	*Virginia Cowles*	258

WAY BACK THEN

Egyptians, Greeks, and Romans   Andrew Steinmetz   267
No Way to Win   Seneca   272
The Barbarians   Tacitus   273
A Game of Piquet   Giovanni Giacoma Casanova   274

HORSES

The Great Racetrack Caper   Rufus Jarman   281
A Story Goes with It   Damon Runyon   287
And See How They Run   Oswald Jacoby   297

WELL, WHY NOT?

A Natural Evil   Girolamo Cardano   301
How to Win While Losing   William Saroyan   302
The Pleasures of Gambling   from Esquire's Book of
                                             Gambling   305
The Sin of Betting   Charles W. Morton   309
The Way to the Dairy   Saki   311

Introduction

◇◇

It is a night around the turn of the century, and you are at a table in a gambling casino at 5 East Forty-fourth Street, New York City. You are the guest of Mr. Richard A. Canfield, an honest gambling proprietor who stays in business by reason of handsome handouts to receptive police and politicians. Across the table from you, in a room that reflects Mr. Canfield's highly cultivated taste in art and furniture, is the awesome John W. "Bet a Million" Gates.

Only you and he remain in this draw poker game. Starting with a modest capital investment of $10,000, you have increased it during the evening by $40,000, a streak that commands even Mr. Gates's respect. Now you have just drawn three aces on which you wager $5000. Mr. Gates meets it and raises the bet by another $5000. You go along with it, and having drawn two cards, one of them a fourth ace, you have a distinctly interesting prospect on which you bet $25,000. Mr. Gates, who has drawn only one card, puts up $25,000 to see your hand. He blinks not at all when it transpires that your four aces have conquered his hand, whatever it was.

You awaken from this delightful dream in a euphoric state that will last for several hazy moments. Then, as consciousness takes over, you sigh at the realization that your triumph has melted into air, into thin air. But the dream has been worth the harsh return to reality. For with that dream you are one with all the gamblers who ever tossed a pair of dice or anxiously watched a ball whirling toward its proper slot within a roulette wheel or tensely waited to see if their 40-to-1 shot would emerge from the pack in the homestretch to edge out a candidate for the Triple Crown.

Definitions of gambling are beyond counting. There is the *Encyclopaedia Britannica*'s stately one: "The betting or staking of something of value, with consciousness of risk and hope of gain, on the outcome of a game, or contest, or an uncertain event whose result may be determined by chance or accident, or which may have an unexpected result by reason of the bettor's miscalculation." George Bernard Shaw's definition was expectedly succinct and sly: "Gambling is [that which] promises the poor what property performs for the rich—something for nothing." Wilson Mizner, confidence man, gambler, screenwriter, spoke with more experience. To him gambling was "the sure way of getting nothing for something." Dr. Samuel Johnson called it "the mode of transferring property without any intermediate good" (but a horse player after a winning day might be inclined to send word back across two centuries to the Doctor that he had just experienced a gratifying parcel of intermediate if temporary "good").

We are all aware, are we not, that gambling is a sin? Authorities whose word is not lightly to be questioned have said so. Aristotle found "all gamblers akin to thieves and robbers." Sundry divines, especially in the nineteenth century, have confidently foreseen the gambler's ultimate residence in surroundings illuminated by hellfire. Yet gambling has always been with us, from prehistory to this moment. "The urge to gamble is so universal and its practice is so pleasurable that I assume it must be evil," Heywood Broun once observed wryly. One has a notion that he was close to the heart of the gambling mystique and its lure even for the nongambler who, roaming through the literature of gambling, finds himself in a multitude of places he might otherwise not know and in company not always admirable but frequently irresistible.

At Troy, or so Greek mythology has it, Palamades employed dice (his countrymen said he invented them) to while away time during the long siege. At Thebes the Egyptians challenged one another with handsome ivory cubes (sometimes loaded), and in Rome youngsters played heads or tails with coins while their betters, Julius Caesar and Mark Antony, were venturing a sesterce or two on cockfights. At White's in eighteenth-century London, the Earl of Sandwich assured himself of a place of sorts in history by ordering meat between two slices of bread delivered to his table lest his play be interrupted. In New Orleans, Louis Philippe, the future "Citizen King" of France, introduced craps at the expense of a local aristocrat, Bernard de Marigny, who later gave the name Rue de Craps to a street in that city (a street later, for obvious reasons, renamed).

There was the Mississippi River with its floating "hells of chance." There was the Old West at its gaudiest and most violent; typical of it was that saloon in Deadwood, South Dakota, where Wild Bill Hickok was shot in the back and, falling, dropped the cards forever to be known as the Dead Man's hand, aces over eights. There were such legendary ladies as Poker Alice Tubbs, who maintained order in her resorts with the demonstrable aid of a six-shooter; Madame Moustache, who combined gaming with houses of joy, one of which launched the career of

Martha Jane Canary, later Calamity Jane; Kitty the Schemer, self-pro-
claimed Queen of the Gamblers on the Barbary Coast. Their male opponents were said to lose to them without resentment, so rare was
feminine company in that womanless part of the land.

By general consensus the most wondrous resort of its kind that
America ever knew was Canfield's Club House at Saratoga. With its
$40,000 wine cellar and its cuisine supervised by a chef imported from
Paris, it was for two months a year the gathering place of the top high
rollers and their friends. There were Tod Sloane, the peerless jockey,
with his English valets and a dozen trunks, and the gross Diamond Jim
Brady dining with the gorgeous Lillian Russell, and the merrymakers
reveling in the failure of that tireless busybody, Anthony Comstock of
the New York Society for the Suppression of Vice, to shut down their
elegant haven.

Still touring here and there in the past, one would like to have been
early at the most glamorous casino of all, Monte Carlo, where Prince
Charles Bonaparte won $15,000, which fazed the founding Blanc
Brothers not at all; they quickly capitalized on it by suggesting that
others come and do likewise, which few could attempt with success.
And there was Deauville where Ignace Paderewski, after an unprofitable
go at roulette, moved to a piano and played Chopin's *Funeral March*,
creating a tradition of nonstop music there. William Crockford's glittering nineteenth-century London resort—that would have been worth a
visit, too, if only to see the arrival of one of its star guests, the Duke of
Wellington himself.

All along the way are names little remembered in this day but household words in their own, assuming the household included a chance-
taker. In the front rank of them was John Davis, whom historian Herbert Asbury has called the father of big-time gambling in the United
States, a polished, well-spoken gentleman from Santo Domingo who
created a superb gambling palace in New Orleans much favored by
gourmets for its food and drink. In pre-Civil War Washington his
counterpart, although one of dubious character, was Edward Pendleton, a suave sharper whose stylish deadfall was known to its victims as
the Hall of the Bleeding Heart and whose personnel numbered a group
of charmers euphemistically described as "Lady Lobbyists." They had a
wide acquaintanceship among Congressmen.

For that matter, who now recalls Price McGrath, who learned his
craft on the Mississippi steamers and came to New Orleans to set up
a fancy establishment where even the minor employees wore evening
dress? Or the phenomenal faro dealer, Hamilton Baker, brought from
Virginia City, Nevada, to Saratoga by John "Old Smoke" Morrissey at

a salary of $4500 a month, only to lose his career in a railroad accident that paralyzed him? Or a nineteenth-century New York casino mogul, Jack Harrison, whose integrity—virtually unique in that time and place —was so complete that his profits barely supported him? Or John Powell, a no-less-honest gambler and a devoted friend and house guest of Andrew Jackson?

One and all, rascals and otherwise, they belong in gambling's pantheon, even if some of them turn up only fleetingly in the annals of their profession, and accordingly are not represented in this book at the length awarded certain of their colleagues. Among them was one who achieved fame in his time by improbably cheating his supposedly crafty fellow punters. He was James Ashby, ostensibly a balmy violinist who, at a distance from the table where his partner was playing, sent signals by way of his fiddle. If Texas has a hall of fame its occupants must include two Austin planters who entered upon a poker game in 1853 and, while provincial matters like the Civil War and Reconstruction were going on somewhere, continued playing until 1873, when they died simultaneously. And let there be a small salute to John Dougherty, of the gun-toting, high-gambling Tombstone community, who usually carried $100,000 in cash, would not take on an opponent willing to risk less than $10,000, and once threatened to shoot the governor of the Territory of New Mexico until the governor agreed to let him have a deed to the territory with which to raise a bet.

Larcenous as the pioneers might have been and often were, their techniques could be so dazzling as to invite a kind of admiration from all save the adamantly righteous. Long after the heyday of the Mississippi River reprobates, a veteran recalled with something like affection in an interview in F. B. Lillard's *Poker Stories* the ease with which rich suckers were separated from their assets:

> It was dead easy money, too, all the time. Everyone who traveled had lots of stuff, and everyone was willing to bet, and bet high. Those Southern planters used to lose money just like fun, and were skinned right and left. Occasionally they caught one, and there was a shooting match, but the boys didn't take much chance on being plugged . . .
>
> The fellows had to be pretty slick, I can tell you. I've seen fellows pick up every card in a pack, and call it without missing once. I've seen them shuffle them one for one all through from top to bottom, so that they were in the same position that they were in at first. They'd just flutter them like a flock of quail and get the aces, kings, queens, jacks and tens altogether as easy as pie. A sucker had no more chance against those fellows than a snow-ball has in a red-hot oven. They were good fellows, free with their money as water, after scheming to bust their heads to get it. A hundred didn't bother them any more than a chew of tobacco would you.

Such is the complexity of gambling and its worlds within worlds, its contradictions and its variety of games and gamesters, that the mind falters when contemplating them. For instance, bingo is a full-fledged gambling game with an estimated handle approaching $2 billion a year, but because it is so often played at church socials by benign old ladies posting a dollar or two after much deliberation, the law looks the other way. The profits presumably serve the Lord. Legalized horse racing at the track and at licensed off-track emporia is gladly sanctioned by states and cities reaping a handsome revenue, while the bookmaker, operating on his own, dealing honestly with his customers, providing credit, quick payoffs and other services, is deemed a criminal. Lotteries are a form of out-and-out gambling, but with a distinguished tradition dating back to Colonial days when they were instrumental in founding such institutions as Harvard, Yale, and Dartmouth and in financing the War of Independence. If gambling per se is evil, this momentarily escaped the attention of the Reverend Samuel Seabury who, after winning 500 pounds in an eighteenth-century lottery in New York City, exclaimed with rapture, "I now record to my posterity my thanks and praise to Almighty God, the giver of all good gifts!" Providence, under certain circumstances, can be a welcome partner. Long banned after they became ridden with corruption, state-conducted lotteries have returned, again on behalf of education, beginning with New Hampshire in 1963. Nevertheless they are still games of chance as surely as a pair of dice scampering down a green felt pathway. As elsewhere in life, ends and means can wind up in rather cynical juxtaposition.

As for gamesters, how can one generalize about them? There are the occasional social bettor, the compulsive gambler, the professional who gambles for a living with the cool detachment of a good business-man and, to the dismay of the virtuous, often makes out quite comfortably. Some fine lines have to be drawn. Was President Washington a gambler when he bought a ticket for the first Federal Lottery in 1793? He certainly was, and in a good cause. Not quite so clearly on the side of the angels, the Father of Our Country was an inveterate card- and horseplayer, in spite—or perhaps because—of which he cautioned a nephew that "it [gaming] is the child of Avarice, the brother of Inequity, and the father of Mischief." Were Daniel Webster and Henry Clay headed for eternal damnation when they tried to outbluff each other with a $2000 poker pot between them on the table? No one can be sure, but there they still stand, giants in the annals of American statecraft.

What it comes to may well be a matter of degree. To be sure,

gambling in excess, like alcohol, nicotine, and overindulgence in chocolate mousse, may bring an addict to an unseemly end. A major aspect
of it is that, unlike certain other threats to a happy existence, it is
perversely interesting and variable. It destroyed the career of the great
English statesman, Charles James Fox. The compulsive gambler like
Fox is surely a sad pathological case, as is the compulsive consumer of
drugs, but a recent responsible survey indicates that the compulsive
gambler represents only 1 percent of the 60 percent of all adult Americans who annually place some kind of bet, sociable, legally commercial,
or illegal. The range of casino operators is no less wide, from the
murderous proprietors of the dens in Mississippi River towns to the
refined, scrupulous Canfield and, well within living memory, the
courtly, philanthropic Colonel Edward Riley Bradley of Palm Beach
who at his death was properly eulogized for his exemplary probity.

Clearly there has been an abundance of hypocrisy and inconsistency
in the massive saga of gambling and gamblers. At the risk of playing the
alleged devil's advocate, one is tempted to ask if a foxy Wall Street
speculator is less a gambler than Nick the Greek was. When Canfield,
who never welshed on a bet, took $300,000 in IOUs from Reginald
Vanderbilt, and let him off with a settlement of only $130,000, who
was the more honest of the two? Is a magnetic belt designed to influence the behavior of dice more reprehensible than a stock rigged
to fleece dupes far from the marketplace? Ambrose Bierce was not
merely sardonic when he ventured the idea that "the gambling known
as business looks with austere disfavor on the business known as
gambling," a sentiment echoed by a modern journalist (Blackie Sher-
wood, in the *Dallas Times Herald*): "If you bet on a horse, that's
gambling. If you bet you can make three spades, that's entertainment.
If you bet cotton will go up three points, that's business. Get the
difference?"

The variations run on. Things are not all of a piece. There have
been gamblers as callous as the Roman soldiers who drew lots for
Christ's raiment at the Crucifixion, and as engaging as "Old Q," the
4th Duke of Queensberry, to be met later in these pages. One has to
infer that no easy moral judgments are to be made in a world so
intricate as gambling, to which it may be added that some long-accepted
dogmas are scarcely to be regarded as final. All steady gamblers die
broke, say the sages, but not all steady gamblers do. As gambling historian Alan Wykes has pointed out, an experienced, steady gambler
can stay ahead of the game, and honestly, too, by adhering to the odds
and percentages. Consider the aforementioned "Old Q," who lived to
an affluent old age, or the premier American handicapper of horses,
Pittsburgh Phil (George E. Smith), who left a tidy fortune of almost

$2 million, or Reuben Parsons, the Civil War–period New York faro dealer who retired with $1 million (and, ironically, was trimmed out of it in Wall Street, that headquarters of respectable finance).

In the last decade or two, social scientists have tended to take an amoral view of gambling, a lenient attitude bordering on approval that surely would have been the horror of old-time moralists. Society itself, some of them suggest, with its boredom and frustrations, explains one appeal of gambling as an antidote and a release. The numbers game is frowned upon for its association with police corruption, but Darrell W. Bolen, M.D., psychiatrist and specialist on gambling, views it objectively: "'Numbers' and 'policy' are integral, functional aspects of ghetto society. They are the poor man's nickel and dime avenue of excitement and perpetually renewed hope against a cultural background of despair and poverty from which the prospects of escape are meager." Still unresolved is the question of the effect enlarged legalized gambling would have. Its proponents offer familiar arguments involving revenue raising for the public good and the discouragement of illegal gambling. Its opponents declare just as positively that by making gambling more accessible it would intensify the incidence of compulsive gambling. Dr. Bolen has put it emphatically: "History has repeatedly shown that legislative sanction expanding legal gambling quickly results in mass gambling and greatly increases its illegitimate offspring."

But this question need hardly weigh you down as you turn to a book intended for your pleasure rather than for your sociological edification or spiritual improvement. Quite simply, the editor would like to believe that you will enjoy yourself here as you meet old friends and find some new ones in the course of a long pageant by turns comic, dramatic, sometimes sinister, and, one hopes, more often than not entertaining. Indeed, you yourself are invited to become a member of the cast, as in the comfort of your armchair you drop in at the court of the Emperor Claudius, visit a San Francisco casino with young Bret Harte, marvel as the skulduggeries of the likable Yellow Kid Weil, learn how the twenty-one counter game was developed amid consternation at Las Vegas, join the young Arnold Bennett as he admits to a youthful misadventure at Monte Carlo, sort out as best you can the subtle distinctions involved in games of luck or skill or both, are dazzled by the complicated "Proposition bets" of Titanic Thompson. Vicariously, if foolishly, you may even invest a sawbuck or two in a faro game conducted by Elijah Skaggs (but be careful). They are all awaiting you, and if some of your favorites are absent the editor can only express his regret and submit that, in such a chronicle, certain omissions were inevitable.

Meanwhile, you are entitled to another spell of fantasy. This one finds you in a place along the garish, hypnotic Strip in Las Vegas shortly before the demise of Nick the Greek. It is man-against-man five-card poker, and by mutual agreement you and Nick will play only the hands originally dealt to you.

Suddenly your life savings are on the table. Time stops. Nick looks at you inquisitively, as if doubting your sanity.

"Are you sure?" he asks.

You are sure.

He calls your bet, and you put down your hand, an ace high royal flush. He puts down his, although he is not obliged to, a ten high straight flush.

"Your chance of getting that hand of yours on the first deal was 1 in 649,740," says the old pro. "The chance on my hand was 1 in 72,193. Congratulations."

Pleasant dreams.

JOHN K. HUTCHENS

the Gamblers Bedside Book

High Rollers

They were called high rollers, and for reasons the more striking if we compare the value of their dollar with that of ours. When their respective biographers tell us that John "Bet a Million" Gates dropped $375,000 in an afternoon at the track in 1902, and that Arnold Rothstein once won a record $650,000 on a single stud poker pot, the modern mind tends to blank out. They, with Titanic Thompson, are presented as a mere sampling of the giants who habitually went for the big jackpot or for broke.

Bet a Million Gates

John Warne "Bet a Million" Gates (1855–1911) appears to have had no rivals in his time, and perhaps since then, as an instant plunger on almost any imaginable kind of wager. He began by risking his own life when, as a twenty-one-year-old barbed-wire salesman from the Midwest, he went to the Texas open range cattle country (of all places) to sell his wares. He sold them. A sturdy freebooter dazzled by no one, including J. P. Morgan the Elder himself, he organized the American Steel and Wire Company and prospered in grain and stock exchanges. But the great joy of his life was gambling, in which he prospered variously, as we learn below.

BY LLOYD WENDT and HERMAN KOGAN

HIS FAVORED arena was the million-dollar gambling house owned by Richard Canfield, king of New York's casino operators and a soft-spoken dilettante in the arts and literature. His place, which he had opened in 1898 at 5 East 44th Street, next to Delmonico's and a short distance from Sherry's, provided precisely the right atmosphere for Bet A Million. Its stakes were high, its décor especially designed for men of wealth, with its Chippendale furniture, Chinese porcelains and teakwood floors that cost $400,000.

In his establishment, Canfield served a lunch of cold meats at eleven o'clock each night so that the gamblers need not interrupt their games. If more food was wanted, it was sent up from Delmonico's. Fine liquors and rare wines were served free at all hours and a full supply of dollar cigars was always available.

Gates, his close friends Drake and Ellwood, along with Senator Edward Wolcott, of Colorado, Patrick McCarren, Brooklyn political boss, Phil Dwyer, "king of the race tracks," and Reginald Vanderbilt, were regular customers. Their amazing games captured the imagination of New Yorkers and added notably to Gates's reputation for profligate betting and recklessness.

When Gates and his companions opened the bronze door of Canfield's and stepped into the thickly carpeted vestibule, the Negro door-keeper lost no time in ushering them into the reception room. He knew Gates's reputation for heavy tipping, whether he won or lost. Sometimes the doorman had to wait a long time for his tip, however, for Gates had rare endurance and would often play for three days and nights without sleep.

Dave Bucklin, the manager, was usually at Gates's elbow before he had crossed the reception room. Fawning over him, asking, "And what will your pleasure be, Mr. Gates?" Bucklin would escort him and his party to the casino on the second floor.

Gates's favorite game at Canfield's was faro, which was long popular in the West. He had first learned to play faro when he was a young barbed-wire salesman in Texas. It was a game of pure chance in which the players, seated at an enormous table, bet against the gambling house's banker on cards drawn one at a time from a full pack. For Gates a special limit of $2,500 was set on single or "case" cards and $5,000 on doubles. At the New York gambling house he sometimes won as much as $50,000 in a single evening—and as often lost as much.

Canfield owned another luxurious gambling house at Saratoga and it was here that Gates once engaged in one of the biggest games in faro history.

On a certain afternoon he had lost $375,000 at the near-by race track, but his day was just starting. After dinner in the Club House Restaurant, Gates began to play faro in Canfield's casino. He took the regular house limits of $500 on case cards and $1,000 on doubles. Other gamblers stopped their games and came to watch Gates when they heard he had lost the first six turns.

Then it was suggested, as the crowd grew larger, that the game be transferred to a private room upstairs. Gates agreed, providing the limits were raised to $2,500 and $5,000.

This done, he continued to play—and to lose. By ten o'clock that night, he had dropped $150,000, which brought his day's gambling losses to $475,000.

Again Gates asked to raise the limits. Because of the money involved, he was told by the dealer to make the request for higher stakes to Canfield.

"What limits are you playing now?" asked Canfield.

"Twenty-five hundred to five thousand," Gates replied.

"How high do you wish to go?"

"Five and ten."

Canfield blinked his gray eyes. His regular limits, highest in the world, were almost double those at Monte Carlo.

But he said, "You may have it," adding sarcastically, "Are you sure that's high enough?"

Without bothering to reply, Gates hustled back to the game. He bet $5,000 and $10,000 on each turn of the cards, sometimes parlaying his bets.

By two o'clock in the morning, he had won $150,000. When he finally quit for breakfast after dawn he had $150,000 more, thus cutting his day's gambling losses to $75,000.

On another occasion, after having won $6,500 in a whist game with Drake, Lambert and Jim Hudson, he tried his hand at faro again. In the first deal, he put $250 on an ace to lose and $250 on another card to win. He continued to make similar bets and when the deck was run through in the deal, he was ahead $2,700. On the next deal, he and the bank came out fairly even. He kept buying more chips and losing them. He bet $5,000, then $10,000, on cards to win, cards to lose.

When he finally finished, he was out $18,000, but the dealer, stretching and yawning, remarked, "He's a pretty tough customer to deal for. If he'd had a deal or two in his favor he would have hooked us for $50,000 as easy as catching lake trout with a net."

Another game Gates enjoyed was baccarat, which he usually played in another gambling spot, the House with the Bronze Door, at 33 West 33rd St. This place was owned by a syndicate including Big Bill Kennedy, Billy Burbridge, Gottfried Wallbaum, and Frank Farrell, the last known as the "king of the poolroom syndicate" and one of the founders of the New York Yankees. The establishment was less elaborate than Canfield's, although its decorations had been selected by Stanford White, the brilliant architect. The bronze door cost $20,000 and was found by White in Venice in the wine cellar of a doge's palace. The second-floor bannister, worth a reputed $60,000, was held up by hand-carved figures on which ten Venetian craftsmen had labored two years.

Best of all Gates enjoyed his poker games in his Waldorf-Astoria suite, or, if Dellora [his wife] were in the city, in a private dining room.

On every previous trip to New York, whether for a brief or prolonged stay, he had arranged at least one robust poker session in his suite. Even before he had acquired his nickname, his Waldorf-Astoria games, which usually had started on the Chicago–New York train, were reported in the newspapers as "million-dollar" affairs. They rarely reached such amounts, but they were steep enough, with limits sometimes at $1,000, and occasionally with no limit at all. Losses or winnings of from $75,000 to $250,000 were not uncommon.

Although the poker sessions continued to be exciting, the most notorious of the games played in Gates's suite had been a climactic draw-poker contest that lasted for five days and nights, involved a dozen players, and saw at least $2,000,000 change hands. But its notable moment came in a deal in which Gates's primary opponent was Joe Leiter, the Chicago speculator, who had engaged with him in a running card game throughout 1899, playing aboard trains and in Gates's Michigan Avenue mansion. In one Chicago–New York trip, Leiter was said to have lost $200,000.

Midway in the five-day game Leiter found himself at the table with Gates, Loyall Smith, John Drake, L. N. Hueston and Sam Wallace. All but Wallace were veterans, but young Wallace was a worthy addition to the card-playing clique. An aide to Charlie Schwab, Wallace had gambled on the West Coast since he was twelve, at which young age he had run away from his native Chicago. During the Klondike gold rush, a syndicate of gamblers had sent him to Alaska with $50,000 and a pact to share half his winnings. A year later, he returned, paid the syndicate $100,000 and used his $50,000 to get into the steel business, where he promptly lost his money. Undaunted, he took a job in one of Schwab's mills as a laborer at ten cents an hour and gradually worked his way into Schwab's favor.

Wallace began the deal after each player had dropped an ante of $1,000 into the pot. The deal passed twice for lack of openers. Each time the pot was sweetened with five-hundred-dollar blue chips. When Gates finally was dealt three fours, $12,000 in chips lay on the table.

"I'll bet five thousand," said Gates.

Wallace dropped out. Smith, Drake and Hueston shoved in their bets.

Leiter hesitated. He stared at his cards, then at Gates.

"I guess I'll give you all another guess," he remarked. He raised the bet to $15,000.

Gates frowned, studied his cards—three fours, a ten and a seven. He decided to stay with Leiter and moved $10,000 in chips to the center of the table. Smith also stayed, but the others threw in their cards.

As the players called for cards, Gates kept his eyes on Leiter. Gates discarded his seven. "Give me one," he said to Wallace. He tossed in a $100 white chip before picking up the card, a nine of clubs, dealt to him.

Smith also asked for one card. Leiter sighed. "I'll stand pat. Don't see how I could help these."

After Smith saw his cards and, with an oath, tossed them aside, Gates and Leiter tensed themselves for the showdown.

Leiter fingered his pile of chips. "John," he said softly, "when a man has reached your age he should quit his bad habits. There is only one way to break a man of playing poker and that is to make it too expensive for him. It will cost you just $30,000 to see my cards."

Gates peered at his cards, puffing on his cigar for what seemed a full minute. Leiter waited for his move. Then Gates, with a shrug, said, "Joe, I guess you've got them. I quit."

Showing his openers, he flipped his cards away. Leiter, chuckling, pulled in the huge stack of chips. Unable to mask his delight, he showed his cards. He had won a pot of nearly $100,000 by a magnificent bluff—a pair of sevens, an ace, a trey and a king.

Later when a *New York Tribune* reporter was apprized of the session—supposedly by Smith, who went on to win $250,000—he gasped in print: "It was the most sensational poker game in all history." For Gates it was also a mighty disaster, said the newspaper, for when the game finally ended he had lost close to $1,000,000.

Gates was not always that unlucky or so easily bluffed. Usually he won at poker, especially in the high-flying years after 1901. In the Waldorf-Astoria he also held his own baccarat games, at which he was successful. The biggest game in the hotel's history, according to Albert Crockett, was staged by Gates in the dining room with John Lambert, Ike Ellwood and Loyall Smith. When the chips were counted at the end they totaled more than $1,000,000.

Besides the "regulars" like Lambert, Ellwood, Smith and Drake, other industrialists sat in on the games sometimes; such men as Herman Frasch, the sulphur magnate; Henry Clay Frick, one of the few men Gates was known to call "Mister"; Hermann Siecken, the "coffee king." Once, just before the United States Steel Corporation was formed, Gary too had sought entry into the dangerous circle, but Gates quickly froze him out. Gary approached Louis, the waiter assigned to the room where a big game was in progress, saying, "Tell Mr. Gates that Judge Gary is here and would like to join him and his friends." Without looking up from his cards when he received the message, Gates replied, "Tell Judge Gary the game is going to be so high it will be 'way over his head."

Throughout the games, the gamblers drank Scotch or brandy, but not to excess, and smoked costly cigars. When players dropped out for a while, there was expensive food at a near-by table. Sometimes all play was stopped while the men sat down to a dinner arranged by Louis, who usually contrived a menu including buffet Russe, green-turtle soup, terrapin or wild duck served in wine sauce, with crêpes suzette for dessert. Gates often stuffed himself with fifteen to twenty helpings of the "fancy pancakes," as he called them, sputtering between mouthfuls, "These are pretty good, but they'll never be 's good as the flapjacks Dell makes."

Now the public figure of Gates the Gambler, "Bet A Million," obscured all others.

Even while he planned systematically toward some grand move to combat Morgan, whirling about in a dozen endeavors toward this end, the concept of "Bet A Million" dimmed that of him as a builder, a man of ambition or simply an angry man bent on vengeance.

His wild wagers at the poker tables and race tracks and faro layouts stimulated many stories, true and false and exaggerated, about his gambling habits. They helped affix more firmly the nickname he deplored, although he found those which Wall Street foes called him just as irritating—"Farmer Gates" and "Moonshine" and "Barbed Wire."

The newspapers and Broadway bons vivants told and retold stories of Gates the Gambler. Some said he had once put up $1,000—or was it $5,000, or $10,000?—while waiting at a railroad station, on whether a train would come first from the East or the West. He bet $1,000 to $10,000 on the speed of raindrops on windowpanes. He flipped coins for $10,000 a throw. It was accepted as gospel—and Gates never took the trouble to deny it—that he had once settled a controversy with Charlie Schwab over $30,000 which American Steel and Wire owed by tossing a coin. "Tell you what I'll do," Gates, according to the oft-repeated tale, said when neither could reach an agreement on payment, "I'll flip you for the money. Double or nothing. If I lose, I'll owe you $60,000. If I win, I owe you nothing." Schwab agreed, the coin was tossed, and Gates won.

Another perennial story involved a young man—he was, in various versions, a salesman, a politican, a steel executive—who called on Gates in the Waldorf-Astoria brokerage office when one of the regular Saturday-afternoon bridge games was being planned. Needing a fourth hand, Gates invited him to sit in.

Cautiously he asked what the stakes would be.

"Just a little game," said Gates. "Just one a point."

The young man played carefully for although he was fairly well fixed he was in no position to be very far behind with stakes so high. When the game was over, he had 330 points.

"You'll get your check Monday," Gates said.

When it arrived, the check was for $33,000. The man rushed to Gates's office.

"Mr. Gates," he said, "I can't take this check."

"Why not?"

"I thought the game was for a dollar a point. I can't afford to play for $100 a point. If I'd lost, I'd have had to sell everything I own to pay."

"Ah, cut it out." Gates laughed. "We played the game, didn't we?

You won, didn't you? You got the check, didn't you? Well, what are you kicking about?"

Some men scoffed at tales of the high bets and longed to sit in just once so that they might boast of playing with the famed Bet A Million. Once, on a business trip to Alabama, Gates, Drake and several Birmingham industrialists arranged a poker game in his private railroad car. As play got under way, a stranger pushed his way inside.

"Which one's Bet A Million?" he demanded to know. "I'm gonna play a poker game with him."

Chewing his cigar, Gates looked at the intruder coldly. "All right," he snapped, "we can accommodate you. Pull up a chair."

With a grand gesture, the visitor drew out his wallet. He counted out $500 in tens and twenties and tossed them on the table.

"All right, John," said Gates, nodding to Drake, "you see the gentleman's money. Give him one blue chip."

Despite dozens of similar stories, Gates's favorite involved the gambling exploits of another—a Negro waiter in a Palm Beach, Florida, resort hotel.

Each year the waiter had served Gates when the promoter spent a few weeks' vacation at the resort. He was expert, skilled, gracious, and the envy of the other waiters because of Gates's deserved reputation as a tipper.

But one morning Gates was surprised to find another waiter at his table. He stared about the dining room until he saw his regular man working glumly in another section.

He summoned him and asked, "What's the matter? Don't you like serving me any more?"

"Yessuh, ah shore do, but you ain' mine any mo'. Ah done los' you."

"Lost me? What do you mean, lost me?"

"Well," explained the unhappy waiter, "las' night we had a little crap game an' ah kep' losin' an' losin'. Then ah run outa money. Well, ah put you up . . . an' ah' los' you too."

◇◇◇

Arnold Rothstein

Even in an era given to gaudy homicide, the murder of Arnold Rothstein was a sensationally memorable one. Who killed him? Henry
Chafetz, in Play the Devil, does not profess to know. Others had their
suspicions but, for realistic reasons, weren't talking. Even without that
bloody last-act finish at the old Park Central Hotel in 1928 the Rothstein career, as Mr. Chafetz recounts it, was an epic in big-time plunging and assorted forms of chicanery.

BY HENRY CHAFETZ

◇◇◇

THE MYSTERY of the life and death of Arnold Rothstein will probably
never be solved, though his story starts conventionally enough—in
gambling terms. Arnold's father was a successful cotton converter in
New York and hoped that his son would, in time, step into his shoes.
The boy was possessed of an inner drive that could not be contained
within the confines of conventional business. Arnold Rothstein began
gambling at an age when most boys are still happily shooting marbles.

Honest John Kelly and Richard Canfield shaped him, gave him a
deep-rooted knowledge of the law of averages and a proper respect for
playing fair at dice and cards (he often said crooked gamblers were
fools). Though he won fantastic sums, no one ever caught Arnold
Rothstein cheating. From Kelly and Canfield, too, he learned the social
value of dressing well, carrying himself with calm and composure in
public, and being soft of speech. Behind this veneer was a temperament
ideally suited to his calling. He was keen and quick in action, had a
tireless energy that allowed him to gamble all night and be fresh and
bright in the morning, and he never touched liquor. His drive came
from an overwhelming confidence in his intelligence, rendering him
impatient of lesser minds, and a tigerish quality that made friends and
confederates wary about dealing lightly with him.

At seventeen Rothstein was an old hand at stuss. He next fell in
love with roulette, then dice and poker. Whenever he could he played
the horses and he was no mean hand with the cue stick. In 1909, in a
thirty-two-hour game against one Jack Conway, champion pool player
of the Philadelphia Racquet Club, he won $4000 plus $6000 in side

bets. He was reluctant to stop but the poolroom proprietor, John J. McGraw, maverick manager of the New York Giants, called off the match lest the men collapse.

Rothstein opened his first gambling house in 1910 on West Forty-sixth Street. The most notable evening in its short life was when "Bet-A-Million" Gates's son celebrated his return to Broadway after an appendicitis operation by dropping $40,000 at the roulette and faro tables. Like most gambling-house proprietors in the Tenderloin, Rothstein shut his place when the police got tough after the bumping off of Herman Rosenthal in 1912. Until public indignation died down he stayed in business by shifting his gambling operations from one hotel to another and patronized practically all the big floating crap games along the Great White Way.

The police learned in 1919 that a high-rolling crap game was going on in one of Rothstein's joints and raided it. Three cops were shot at and two wounded from behind a doorway and Rothstein, alleged to have thrown the slugs, was indicted on a charge of felonious assault. The case was later dismissed. Thereafter Rothstein stopped carrying a gun but hired bodyguards to protect him. That same year, when his name was linked to the World Series scandal by Ban Johnson, president of the American League, Rothstein threatened to sue Johnson. "My friends know," he said indignantly, "that I have never been connected with a crooked deal in my life, but I am heartily sick and tired of having my name dragged in on the slightest provocation whenever a scandal comes up." It is doubtful that his friends would have defended his honor so unreservedly. No one gave particular credence either to a statement two years later that he had done with gambling in favor of devoting himself to real estate and his racing stables.

Rothstein was celebrated and rubbed shoulders equally with the respectable and the criminal. At one time August Belmont ruled him off Belmont Race Track, but he was later reinstated. According to the gambler, he had paid Belmont a visit and convinced him that his big winnings were due to his having a good head on his shoulders and that his moral code was superior to many a businessman's.

"The majority of the human race are dubs and dumbbells," in Rothstein's philosophy. "They have rotten judgment and no brains, and when you have learned how to do things and how to size people up and dope out methods for yourself they jump to the conclusion that you are crooked."

Every big-time bettor in the East knew that he could place a bet on anything at any time with "The Brain," and Rothstein, as one-man depot for huge and diversified bets, could set the odds to suit himself by gambling both ways at various prices. To big businessmen, politicians, newspapermen, and people in the theater Arnold Rothstein was a man who gambled on sure things and they courted him for tips.

Rothstein cleaned up $500,000 on the first Dempsey-Tunney heavyweight championship fight, won $800,000 on the horse Sidereal when it came in as a last-minute entry at good odds at Aqueduct on July 4, 1921. He made money in financial deals and in real estate, owned two office buildings on West Fifty-seventh Street, a hotel on West Seventy-second, and subleased a thousand furnished apartments at a profit. The full magnitude of his operations, legal and illegal, was to emerge and take shape for the public after November 4, 1928.

A few minutes after eleven that night the police found Arnold Rothstein in a state of collapse in the Fifty-sixth Street service entrance of the Park Central Hotel. Despite his request for a doctor to attend him on the spot and send him home in a taxi, they took him to Polyclinic Hospital, where it was found that a bullet fired from a .38-caliber pistol had entered his abdomen. He had $6500 in his wallet.

At 2:15 Monday morning The Brain was given a transfusion and, though he was conscious, he refused to give any information beyond his name, age, and address. "I got nothing to say," he kept insisting. "Nothing. I won't talk about it."

Ace detectives from police headquarters and agents from the district attorney's office began to turn New York City upside down to find the person who had shot Rothstein. Within twenty-four hours they learned that he had lost $340,000 two weeks before in a record-breaking high-spade game and was said to have refused to pay $303,000 of it because he believed that he had been cheated.

As the police began unraveling the story, they found that it had begun months before. Rothstein's customary good luck had soured and he had ruinous evenings in a number of gambling houses and picked a number of losing horses to put his money on. Despite this he had been gambling with six men constantly since September in a series of houses, apartments, and hotel rooms rented by an operator of floating games named O'Reilly. They started by rolling dice, after a week switched to draw poker and then to stud. Early in October stud began to seem tame to these big-action boys and they started high spade, a game played by cutting a deck, the holder of the highest spade winning.

The last night he played in the apartment of ex-convict Jimmy Meehan, in the Congress apartment house on Fifty-fourth Street between Broadway and Seventh Avenue. At the game, besides Rothstein and Meehan, were two gamblers from the West Coast, Joe Bernstein and Nathan "Nigger Nate" Raymond, George McManus, a book-maker, big-time gambler, and floating-game operator who was running the game that night, the brothers Meyer and Samuel Boston, who used a Wall Street address for their gambling and stock-market ven-tures, bookmaker Martin Bowe and Edward "Titanic" Thompson, who was called Titanic because when he gambled he played every dollar he owned and when he lost he sank like his namesake. "Nigger Nate" was a particularly unsavory character, involved in a disgraceful baseball bribery case on the Coast. That spring he married a film actress in an airplane over northern Mexico with Jack Dempsey and the Tijuana concessionaire, Gene Normile, as witnesses.

Rothstein started by winning $60,000, then dropped $340,000 to his pals. "I'll probably have to sell an apartment house to meet these losses," he said, "but I have this and that will help wipe out some of it."

"This" was $37,000 he laid on the table for the winners to split. "That's all I have," he explained, "You'll have to wait for the rest of it." He gave them IOUs for the rest, which they willingly accepted, and mentioned several million dollars' worth of collateral. "I'm Roth-stein, that name ought to be good for the money."

When a week went by and Rothstein did not make good, the winners began hounding him in his customary haunts. He stalled them off by saying that he had overinvested in real estate, that he was not able to get a fair price if he sold any of his buildings at once, and that he was temporarily short of cash. As days passed they began to trail him around the clock. Restlessness turned to concern when Rothstein suddenly broadcast his suspicions that the game had been crooked and to announce that he would not pay off. Broadway laughed at the idea of Rothstein taken for a sucker, but not the gamblers he accused.

Harsh rumors began to circulate: a Chicago gang was said to have been hired to collect or, failing that, rub him out; he was reported to be marked for death at the earliest possible moment. Detectives picked up news that his death had been fixed for Saturday night, November 3, twenty-four hours before he was shot.

The police quoted Rothstein as saying, "I'm not going to give them a cent, and that goes for the gamblers and the gorillas. I can be found at Lindy's if they're looking for me." To show his contempt, he let his bodyguards go. On the night of November 4 he was at Lindy's.

He came in around 10:15, saw some friends, and sat down with them for coffee. Almost at once he was called to the telephone and came back to the table. "McManus wants me over at the Park Central," he told his friends, and left.

George McManus had lost $51,000 on the last night of play. As a friend of Rothstein and the other gamblers, he now undertook to get The Brain together with his "creditors" to give him one last chance to settle his losses. Apparently Rothstein refused again. At 11:07 a bellboy saw him, tottering and barely able to hold himself up against a wall, and called Lawrence Fallon, the house detective. Fallon sent for an ambulance and its doctor discovered the wound, pay-off for Rothstein's $303,000 welsh.

Just as the wounded man was being loaded into the ambulance, Patrolman William Davis, sent to check on the call for the ambulance, arrived riding on the running board of a cab. The taxi driver, Al Bender, had seen Davis hotfooting it and stopped him to show him a revolver. Bender had been driving slowly past the Seventh Avenue side of the hotel when the gun hit the pavement. It was a Colt Detective Special, which, despite a two-inch barrel, packed a deadly punch.

This weapon, so tiny it could be palmed, killed Rothstein. Except for one undischarged bullet, its chamber was empty. Five unexploded shells that the killer had ejected from the revolver before he tossed it away were found on the sidewalk. No dent indicated that the gun had been dropped from a height. Thinking that it might have been thrown from a car, detectives questioned Bender and he recalled that a sedan was just picking up speed ahead of him as he saw the revolver.

The trail led to the two-room hotel suite where Rothstein had gone —No. 349. Two days before, it had been reserved in the name of "George Richards." The gentleman showed up and registered, giving as his address Newark, New Jersey. He said that he would probably want the rooms till Sunday, moved in, and paid each morning for that day.

In No. 349 detectives found: two whisky flasks, one half full, a number of racing-form sheets, poker chips, glasses in various parts of the room, some of them used. On the back of a chair in one corner was a topcoat with George McManus's name on the label in its inside pocket.

"Nigger Nate" Raymond was the first of the suspects to be picked up. Two hours' grilling elicited evidence that corroborated certain police suspicions. Raymond, who had known Rothstein about ten years, heard on September 29 that a high-stake game was slated for Meehan's apartment and that Rothstein would be there. He maintained that he went into the game with $5000 in cash he had borrowed to play, lost it early in the game, and went out and borrowed $10,000 more. By the end of the night Rothstein owed him $219,000. He admitted having asked for it several times and said that he had seen Rothstein in front of Lindy's the night of November 3 and he had said, "I'll give you some of that money Monday." Raymond firmly denied having been at the Park Central, though he had heard that George McManus was.

Rothstein died at 10:15 Tuesday morning and an autopsy showed that the bullet was slanting downward, apparently fired by a person standing on his right as he sat, perhaps talking to someone in front of him.

It was election day and, had he lived, he would have won $500,000 he had laid on Herbert Hoover, but his death voided his winnings—and his losses.

On November 26 Detective Johnny Cordes received a telephone call from George McManus, who told him that he would give himself up if the detective came early next morning to a barbershop on upper Broadway. He was duly arrested and the police were chagrined to learn that while they had been hunting him he had been living in a Bronx apartment rented by the Dutch Schultz gang as a hideaway. On December 4 he was indicted for murder in the first degree along with "Gillie" Biller and two other men identified only as "John Doe" and "Richard Roe." They were said by the District Attorney to have been in No. 349 the night Rothstein was shot.

Justice Aaron J. Levy of the New York Supreme Court allowed McManus to go free on $50,000 bail. This was not usual practice under such an indictment and there were overtones of pressure by political boss James J. Hines. Nor was McManus fingerprinted, as required for all homicide suspects.

A year after his arrest McManus was brought to trial for the killing of Arnold Rothstein. The jury could not reach a decision, so a directed verdict for acquittal was placed before Judge Charles C. Nott by McManus's lawyer, James D. C. Murray, on grounds that the evidence was inconclusive and weak. Minutes later McManus walked out of the courtroom a free man.

Several days after Rothstein's death, United States Attorney Charles H. Tuttle asked and was granted permission to examine the Rothmere papers, the Rothmere Realty Corporation, Mortgage Corporation, and Brokerage Company being three of Rothstein's many businesses. From these papers federal agents learned enough to seize millions of dollars' worth of narcotics and lay bare a hookup to major cities, including Boston, Chicago, Detroit, Philadelphia, and San Francisco. As a result they pulled two raids simultaneously on December 27, 1928, one in a New York City hotel, one in a Buffalo railroad station, and captured five million dollars' worth of dope. The next night they seized several millions more in Chicago and made a huge haul December 18 on a Jersey City pier. The trail led to France, Belgium, Italy, Holland, sources of cocaine, heroin, and morphine smuggled into the U.S. Rothstein was the financier in this vast illegal trade.

An attorney engaged by Mrs. Rothstein asked District Attorney

Joab H. Banton to take instant custody of all of Arnold Rothstein's files, ledgers, and personal account books lest many prominent people blow their brains out if their names were made public. Curiously enough, the district attorney waited until employees and other persons associated with Rothstein could examine the papers on the grounds that this was necessary to the management of Rothstein's legitimate businesses and to safeguard his estate. By the time Banton did take possession of the papers, ten or twelve other people had beaten him to the punch. According to Leo Katcher, he said, "There are more than 40,000 papers, but we believe that some of Rothstein's records might be missing." Katcher commented that the D.A. was "one hundred and ten per cent right." Some papers were missing.

"Fats" Walsh, George Uffner, and "Lucky" Luciano went to Rothstein's office the day he died to collect all papers pertinent to the illicit drug trade.

Quite unexpectedly the district attorney surrendered Rothstein's private papers to different persons asserting claims to the dead gambler's estate. When Tuttle objected and obtained a court order for federal authorities to intervene, his men could find no papers. Somehow they had all—a carload of them—vanished. Several days later Tammany district leader Nathan Burkan, one of the attorneys to whom Banton planned to release the papers, announced that he had found a few of the papers in safety deposit boxes. The amount was small but the contents startling.

Rothstein was a super-fence for expensive goods, especially jewelry. He was involved in a $300,000 robbery in 1922 when gunman Eugene Moran robbed Mrs. Hugo A. C. Schoelkopf. The night of the robbery Moran dropped the loot with a fence named John Mahan to turn over to Rothstein. The Brain sent it to dealers in different parts of the world. Mahan was arrested but assured soft treatment if he recovered the stolen gems. In three months they were rounded up through Rothstein, turned over to Mahan, and returned to Mrs. Schoelkopf.

Rothstein was also behind huge bond robberies, having at one time recovered and returned $25,000,000 worth in an agreement that gave him 10 per cent of the bonds for himself. Big bucket shops and rum-running were also among his operations. He guaranteed bail money that ran into millions over the years for hoodlums and gunmen, slick con men, and gamblers. Finally, his innocence was palpably disproved and justice was shown to be blind when it declared him guiltless in fixing the 1919 World Series.

The Partridge Club, which flourished before World War I in the

Hotel Imperial, was ostensibly run by lawyer, sportsman, and man-about-town George Young Bauchle, but was actually just another of Rothstein's gambling houses. Supposedly select and private, for gentlemen only, the term "gentlemen" was given a wide and loose interpretation. Anybody could gamble who planked down the thirty-dollar entrance fee, which entitled him also to an excellent champagne dinner. The district attorney tried but failed to establish the fact that it was nothing more than a high-class gambling joint.

The Park View Athletic Club on West Forty-eighth Street was a Rothstein business where trained personnel helped patrons build up their muscles. There were also private rooms where a man could strengthen his muscles by rattling and tossing dice and shuffling and dealing cards.

A number of Rothstein's gambling clubs were run in partnership with local politicians who kept the police from annoying the games. Often they were in the political clubhouses, with the gambling conducted by an outside proprietor who gave a share of the take to the political leader.

When the war ended and the immigrant Negroes, Latins, Irish, and Jews, in Jimmie Hines's 11th Assembly District lost their jobs, they turned to him for help. For this he needed money and he got it by renting the top floor of his clubhouse to Arnold Rothstein for five hundred dollars a month plus a share of the house's take. It worked out fine all around.

Money was the seat of Rothstein's power. He acted as banker to the underworld, staking big-shot racketeers who could not go to banks for loans. Rothstein himself could borrow from the banks, with his real estate holdings and bonds as securities.

So explosive was even the small amount of material available that every official who took custody of the files arrived at the painful decision to withhold them from the public: too many careers and reputations would be endangered. Many people believe that most of the papers have never been destroyed and that someday they may be "found" and their contents revealed.

There were legitimate holdings. Rothstein owned hotels, apartments, night clubs, race horses, and backed Broadway plays. But he likewise owned judges and politicians, retained a body of expert lawyers, had many members of gangland on his payroll who looked to him for backing in rumrunning, narcotics vending, bond robberies, and such ventures. Among others associated with him were Owney Madden, Eddie and Frank Costello, Frankie Yale, Larry Fay, Waxey Gordon, Frankie Marlow, Philip "Dandy Phil" Kastel, Albert Anastasia, Irving

"Little Itch" Halper, Thomas "Fats" Walsh, Robert Arthur "Dapper Dan" Tourbillion, George Uffner and Charles "Lucky" Luciano. Jack "Legs" Diamond and his brother Eddie, who led a mob of thieves, hijackers, narcotic peddlers, and gunmen, were also financed and "protected" by Rothstein. Rothstein took a shine to Legs soon after he graduated from being a sneak thief and petty larcenist and became a gun gorilla. Rothstein made Diamond his bodyguard and often lent him to big winners to take them home safely from his gambling joints. Stanley Walker says, "Did Legs take him home?" was the standing but grim jest at police headquarters when a gambler was found bumped off, his pockets emptied.

Rothstein had, inevitably, many enemies who complicate and becloud the question: Who killed Arnold Rothstein? McManus was running the game that night and, as the "house," he was bound to keep the game on the level and see that debts were paid up. When Rothstein stalled the winners, it was up to him to see that they got their money. Dead, Rothstein could not pay. Some who professed to know claimed that the killing of Rothstein was a result of the bloody war between Legs Diamond and Dutch Schultz wherein members of the rival forces were liquidated by lead poisoning. Dutch, protected by Jimmie Hines, was thrusting into the Diamond mob's Manhattan territory. Hines and McManus were close friends and McManus was a member of Hines's political club.

The press clamored and the public waxed furious over the police department's wishy-washy handling of Rothstein's murder. However, the consensus up and down Broadway and in the political clubrooms was that the case was too dangerous and inconvenient, too deep in local politics, for the police to deal with.

Mayor Jimmy Walker removed Police Commissioner Joseph Warren and appointed Grover Whalen in his stead in an effort to appease the public. Whalen promptly opened an investigation at which a number of police officers and detectives were heard. Some were demoted and some fined for "dereliction of duty." That was all.

Rothstein was "King of the Gamblers," somehow romantic to the average man, even after the partial revelations of his private files. He would be remembered as both sinister and romantic after the hubbub died down. In time even that memory would fade and his history would be summed up in The World Almanac's "Memorable Dates" for 1928: "Arnold Rothstein, N.Y. gambler, died of shots Nov. 6; killer never found."

A. R.: Was This the One?

And this is a longtime acquaintance of Rothstein's, Phil Bieber, talking to Red Smith, *The New York Times* columnist, in the issue of October 10, 1975. The last word on the murder? It seems entirely probable.

AS TOLD TO RED SMITH

"A.R. CAME to Broadway from a highly respected family. His father was a well-to-do cotton converter but Arnold's urge was for action, preferably with an edge. His cardplaying, racing operations and betting on games dazzled the imagination. He financed bookmakers, gambling houses, loan sharks and even narcotics merchants late in life, charging usurious interest. It was said he would rather get a dollar cheating than earn a thousand honestly.

"He raced horses under the name, Redstone Stable (English translation of the German Rothstein). In great secrecy, he and his trainer, Max Hirsch, brought a nice colt named Sidereal to top form. On the day of the race A.R. planted agents at the track with instructions to bet. No limits, just bet. Rothstein didn't appear. Sidereal opened at 50 to 1 closed at even money and won with ease. The killing in excess of $650,000, was one of history's greatest.

"On Forty-sixth Street east of Broadway during Mayor Hylan's administration in the mid-1920's the largest dice game in the country was operating. The owners were my brother, Isidor, Bill Dwyer, Marty Madden (brother of the then-little-known Owney Madden) and George McManus.

"Gamblers came from every corner of the country. H. L. Hunt, the Texas oilman, would arrive in a private railroad car with 10 or more friends. Sam Rosoff, the original Nick the Greek, Arnold Rothstein, Frank Keeney, Remy Dorr and other highrollers crowded the place. The game started at midnight. Some fellows would arrive early to play cards for high stakes until the dice game opened. George McManus, a superior card player, often hooked up with A.R.

"On one such occasion Rothstein lost $20,000 and told George he would settle in a few days. This was not unusual, and his credit was good. However, he often delayed payment on purpose until he was dunned. Then he would say he was still short but if the fellow needed the money he could borrow from a loanshark at 15 or 20 per cent. If the proposition was accepted he would pay off, subtracting the interest. When he tried to pull that on McManus, George told him: 'Cut the bilge, Arnold. Pay me what's coming.'

"George McManus was a tall, handsome man with slick black hair and smiling blue eyes. He was popular and easygoing, except when he was drinking. Then he was curt and mean. As a precaution he had a companion called Gil, a quiet quick man completely loyal to George. McManus arrived at the club one evening and it was clear he had been drinking. He asked for Rothstein and was told he was playing poker in the Park Central Hotel. George and Gil went there.

" 'Arnold,' he said, 'I want to see you.'

"Noting Mac's condition, A.R. rose and placed his hands on George's shoulders, easing him toward the door. 'Relax now, George. I'll see you at the game later and straighten you out.' Leaving McManus at the door he turned back toward his seat.

"George laughed. 'Just so you don't forget,' he said, 'take this with you.' He drew a gun and shot Rothstein in the behind.

"McManus loved the Keystone Cops of the silent movies, who were always shooting fugitives in the bustle. In the movies it was fun. The bullets that tore Rothstein's pants glanced off a bone and cut through some of the essential plumbing. Gil grabbed George and hustled him away. The players rushed for exits. Rothstein, bleeding heavily, staggered to a staircase and made it to the street where he collapsed. Two days later he was dead.

"In hiding, McManus drew money for his share of the dice game and proceeded to get his defense in order. He had many well-placed friends. When details were arranged, he went to the barbershop in the Park Central, telephoned the district attorney and told him where he was. When Officer Johnny Cordez arrived, McManus was getting a haircut and shave. 'No hurry, George,' Johnny said, 'I'll wait.' They walked out quietly together.

"George was tried and acquitted but the ordeal took something out of him. He was never the same likable George McManus. He was seen only occasionally and soon afterward we learned that our friend was dead."

Titanic Thompson

The king of the proposition bet (the bet that appears to be surefire to the hapless party who accepts it) had to be Alvin Clarence Thomas Thompson, the famous "Titanic" Thompson, who would wager on just about anything with anyone, and almost always win, sometimes honestly. As Jon Bradshaw demonstrates, there is not likely to be such another life as his. The wonder, as you will see, is that he held onto it through so many years.

BY JON BRADSHAW

IN THE early part of the century the professional gambler was still a romantic figure—a fallen man, perhaps, and evil, if the melodramas of the period are to be believed. He was a freebooter, a man who took the long chance at a time when the country still believed in dark horses. Titanic Thompson was at the heart of that belief. In 1932 he was forty years old and had achieved a kind of mythical status in his profession. Reverent tales of his gambling prowess are still told along the Vegas Strip. He was a master of the cunning proposition, a crack shot, a scratch golfer, a champion bowler, a good pool player and an expert at craps and all forms of cards, particularly poker. He had won more than a million dollars in places as far afield as San Francisco, Chicago and New York. In the early Thirties Titanic and Nick the Greek Dandolos were reputed to be the shrewdest gamblers in the country.

In a photograph of Titanic taken about that time, he is standing next to one of his favorite cars—a 1930 Pierce-Arrow. Posed languidly beside a robust girl, a rifle under his arm, he appears insouciant and boyish. They look as though they have just committed a particularly amusing crime. The girl wears a cardigan and long skirt, Titanic wears a double-breasted suit and hat; there is a more than passing resemblance to Bonnie and Clyde.

* * * *

To the end of his life Titanic remained a backwoods Southern boy. Even in what he liked to regard as his sophisticated days, when he

43

favored yellow polo coats and drove nickel-plated limousines, he seemed somehow out of context, inconvenienced, like a farm boy made to slick his hair and wear his Sunday suit. Fashion was not Ty's métier. Gambling had taken him off the farm and into some of the country's largest cities, but he rarely dallied in them. He disliked cities; he thought them stiff, uncomfortable and cold. He preferred the slow country towns of the South—towns such as Grapevine, Texas, Lafayette, Louisiana, Marked Tree, Arkansas, or Monett, Missouri, where he was born in the winter of 1892.

He was christened Alvin Clarence Thomas, though he rarely used the name once he left home. His people were itinerants and soon after he was born they drifted south into Arkansas, taking up farming in the foothills of the Ozarks midway between the hayseed towns of Eureka Springs and Rogers. But his father was not a farmer; he would rather gamble. Ty's mother often told him his father had been gambling up in the hills the night that he was born. He had come home for a time, apparently, but disappeared when Ty was five or six months old.

During his boyhood the family moved constantly from one rented farm to another. It was a kind of flight, this constant moving, a long retreat. The farm he remembered most clearly was one of about forty acres, crisscrossed with creeks and springs, in the woods above the White River. There, in a three-room log cabin, Ty lived with his mother, his stepfather, two half-sisters and two half-brothers. His stepfather, one Willie Hendricks, was a hard-working silent man with none of Ty's father's vices. They did not get on.

*   *   *   *

As a boy Ty spent most of his free time alone and, despite his poverty, led a relatively carefree life. A loner, he developed a talent for solitary pursuits. He fished the White River for bass and catfish and trout and perch. His grandfather gave him a shotgun before he was ten and Ty became an expert marksman. With Carlo, his pet water spaniel, he hunted squirrel and rabbit and possum and coon. He claimed an ability to hit quail on the wing with rocks and often hunted them that way. He was good with animals; he had not only taught Carlo to retrieve game, but had trained him to dive to the bottom of the river to retrieve small rocks. Thus his boyhood passed —splitting railway ties when necessary, hunting and fishing when he could slip away. And so it might have remained; but he had also learned the more seductive arts of gambling.

Excepting his stepfather, most of the men in Ty's family gambled, particularly his grandfather and uncles who worked a farm on the other side of the river. They gambled at mountain games—shooting at targets with a .22, rock-throwing, pitching to the crack, penny-ante poker, coon-can, checkers and dominoes. Ty was always good with his hands; he had an excellent memory and, curiously, was clever with numbers. Before he was fifteen he could beat his older relatives at their own games easily. He liked to practice tricks such as pitching coins into a small box at a distance of twenty feet and learned to get ten to fifteen in the box in a row. Tricks of this kind, his propositions, were to earn him a great deal of money when he was older. "All I ever wanted to do was gamble," he said, and that longing was intensified by what he came to see as the romantic flight of his gambling father.

Fortified with thoughts of his father, Ty began to look on gambling as a way out, as a means of exit to the world that lay beyond the river. He wanted to gamble. He was good at gambling—too good; his own people refused to gamble with him anymore, though it never deterred him from asking. He had become an opportunist, though he had few opportunities. Disgruntled, Ty continued to work at home, but he spent more and more of his time alone with his dog in the woods.

On summer weekends, during his fifteenth year, Ty began to encounter strangers, or what he called "city folk," in the woods. That summer, he remembered, they often drove up from Fayetteville, the only city in the area, to that part of the White River noted for its fishing. They favored one fishing hole especially; it was fifteen feet deep with a sandy bottom. Ty often saw them there. Accustomed to a wooden fishing pole, he admired their expensive casting rods and had set his heart on getting one when he was older. He had not anticipated an opportunity would come so soon.

One Saturday, having spent the morning with Carlo hunting in the woods, Ty encountered a stranger at the fishing hole. They began to talk and the stranger said how much he admired Ty's spaniel. They talked some more and the stranger offered to buy the dog. Ty refused, explaining he could never part with Carlo for money. Then, with shrewd timidity, he suggested the gentleman might make a bet instead. Since the gentleman, he said, seemed taken with the dog, he would be willing to bet the dumb brute could retrieve a rock from the bottom of the fishing hole, which was twenty foot deep, at least, and in order to avoid any accidents, such as bringing up the wrong rock, he would be more than willing to mark the rock with an X; the gentleman could throw it in any part of the pool he liked. Ty would bet the dog, he said, against the gentleman's fishing rod.

The stranger instantly agreed. Picking up a rock about the size of a small ball, Ty marked it with his knife and handed it over. The stranger smiled. Looking out over the pool, he lobbed the rock into what seemed to be the deepest part. At a word from Ty, Carlo sprang into the water and swam out toward the ripples, a moment later sinking from sight. The man and the boy waited silently. Nearly thirty seconds elapsed. Suddenly the dog broke the surface, its front paws flailing at the water, the rock clenched firmly in its mouth. The stranger swore. Paddling to the shore, Carlo shook himself and dropped the rock at Ty's feet. Grinning, Ty picked it up, showing the stranger the carved X.

"Well, I guess I'll just take that there rod, mister," he said.

The stranger drew back. "Now, boy, you should know I was foolin' with you. Just foolin,' that's all. But it's a damn good trick. That's some dog you got, I'll tell you that."

Ty looked at the man. He was not grinning now. His .22 was under his arm and he slid back the bolt. "Tell you what," he said. "You hold that rock up in the air and I'll make another bet with you that I can knock it outta your hand."

The stranger looked suspiciously at Ty. Ty lifted the gun. The stranger handed over the casting rod.

"That dog of mine was good at that trick," Ty conceded later. "He was very good. But I ain't one for taking chances. A few days before I'd covered the bottom of that hole with dozens of marked rocks. That slicker never had a prayer."

Ty's triumph over the stranger, and he thought it a triumph, was the first indication of a personal gambling credo he defined when he was older. "To be a winner," he explained, "a man has to feel good about himself and know he has some kind of advantage going in. Smart is better than lucky."

When Ty turned sixteen he weighed 180 pounds, stood 6' 1" and was "as strong as a wild razorback hog." The time had come, he reasoned, to leave home, as his father had before him. His mother, who disapproved, made few efforts to detain him, only extracting a promise that he would not take up with whiskey or tobacco, a promise Ty was to keep.

*   *   *   *

[Soon Ty was working] the small towns of Missouri, going as far north as Kansas City. "In those days," he recalled, every little town had a poker game or two. It was illegal, a course, a twenty-dollar fine if you was caught, but once you got to a town you always checked at the pool hall and chances were the game was being held in the back room or down the street at the hotel." Before Ty turned nineteen he had picked up a sound if eccentric education.

"It used to be that people would bet anything on anything," he said. "They bet pitching half dollars to the crack or put a dime down and pitched to that. They bet on pool and poker and dice and pitchin' horseshoes and on card games most people never heard of. It used to be that people really loved to bet. And so did I."

Thus, in one or another of those Southern towns, Ty learned to shoot craps, how to place the six and the ace in the middle, false shake them and roll them straight out so that he could not crap. He learned the odds on every proposition—the true odds on how many coins will come up heads or tails should you throw a handful into the air at once, how many throws of the dice it takes to obtain a specific number, the odds on securing a pair in a five-card hand, of drawing the highest spade, or the price on getting aces back to back. He learned how to scuffle, how to cheat and to connive, learned all the card cons—playing to the light, how to mark cards or use spotted edges to change the suit, the art of signals, the use of pig-joints or thumpers, dealing seconds, cold-decking, anything that gave him "the advantage going in." He practiced such dodges by the hour. "I learned to beat people at their own game," he said. "And if I couldn't beat 'em, I'd find someone who could." He was to beat the checker champion of Missouri, for example, by installing a better player in a peekhole in the ceiling, who signaled the correct moves to Ty through the use of a thumper wired to Ty's leg. And, should emergencies arise, he always carried a gun, which he kept on the floor next to his chair when playing.

"I learned to play any game you could name for any amount of money you could count. And I never made bets on even chances." To that end, he began carrying his own horseshoes, bowling ball, pool cue, throwing rock (made to order—beveled on top, flat on the bottom), his own rifle and pistol. "No sense takin' a chance on somebody else's," he said. "Might be rigged. I learned to do things pretty good or else I didn't do 'em. I aimed to do everything a little better'n the other fellow. And those were the things I bet on, that's all." At eighteen, his apprenticeship was over.

In the winter of 1910 Ty arrived in Kansas City. On his first night in town he fell in with some gamblers who steered him to a black club where he became involved in a crooked game of five-card stud. But he was used to such things now and played on. Toward dawn when the game ended he had won fifteen hundred dollars. That morning over breakfast one of the losers, in answer to Ty's now familiar question, said that he had played with a gambler by the name of Thomas a few months before in a saloon in Oil City, Louisiana. A slicker with diamond rings, the man recalled, played stud. After breakfast Ty purchased a brown-striped suit and a brown derby hat and caught the southbound train.

Oil City, a boom town on the Texas-Louisiana border, was crowded with drillers, roughnecks and roustabouts. It had the rude and heady air of any gold-rush town and those who struck it rich by day celebrated at night in the noisy saloons and poker rooms. In 1910 most of Oil City's streets were still unpaved. It was a clapboard town cluttered with banks, saloons and general stores. Inside one of the main-street saloons he found the man he had spent more than two years searching for. Sitting at a table next to the bar dealing cards was a slim, well-dressed man in his early forties with fast and graceful fingers, two of which were covered with diamond rings. Ty joined him.

"It'll cost you cash to play in this game, son," the man said. "Twenty-five dollars cash." Ty paid and the game began.

I have heard more than a few sentimental versions of that encounter, depending on to whom Ty told it over the years. The other players either dropped from the game or his father, recognizing an unusual opponent, asked them to leave the table; his father dubbed him "The Derby Kid" or one of the other players did; they played head-to-head for six or maybe fifteen hours; Ty won consistently or beat his father on the final hand; his father was an excellent player or second-rate; his father lost $5,000 or $2,500. But all accounts agree that he lost and that somewhere toward midnight, or perhaps it was dawn, the older man rose from the table and said, "You're a winner, son. That's all I care to lose today."

Smiling, Ty counted up the chips and pushed them back across the table. "You never had a chance to beat me," he said. "I'm giving you your money back." The older man looked at Ty, a derisive smile on his face. "Son, nobody ever gave me back my money," he said.

"Maybe not," said Ty, "but I have my reasons."

The two men spent the next few weeks together. "But, other than gambling, we had little in common," Ty recalled. Ty spent most of his time in the crowded saloons fleecing the resident oilmen at cards and dice. Toward Christmas he drifted back to Missouri. He never saw his father again. Thirteen years later Ty heard the old man had died in Denver or San Francisco. The rumor was never definitely confirmed.

In the spring of 1912 Ty turned up in Joplin, Missouri, shortly after the White Star liner *Titanic* hit an iceberg in the North Atlantic. In one of the downtown poolrooms he beat the boys at poker and took the local shark, a man called Snow Clark, for five hundred dollars at straight pool. Giving Clark an opportunity to get his money back, Ty offered him a double-or-nothing bet that he could jump across his five-by-ten-foot pool table without touching it. The bet was promptly taken. Taking a running start Ty dived headfirst across the table, landing safely on the other side. He retired to count his money. Across the room, one of the sweaters who had lost a bundle on side bets asked Snow Clark the stranger's name. "Don't rightly know," said Clark, "but it must be Titanic. He sinks everybody."

* * * *

In the period between 1912 and the end of the First World War, Ty became famous in the netherworld of gamblers and confidence men for the success of his improbable propositions. Not that he sought notoriety in any way, since it was "hard to get somebody to take your proposition," he said, "if they knew your reputation." But by changing the common hustle into a pure and elegantly constructed con, Ty earned an envious respect among his fellow gamblers. Tales of his feats were recounted so often they acquired the legitimacy of legend.

During the 1920s in New York, Damon Runyon, who had met Ty on many occasions, must have heard those tales in one or another of their fanciful forms, since he based one of his most famous characters on him—Sky Masterson, the gambler in "The Idyll of Miss Sarah Brown." "Of all the high players this country ever sees," wrote Runyon, "there is no doubt that the guy they call The Sky is the highest. He will bet all he has, and nobody can bet more than this. The Sky is a great hand for propositions, such as are always coming up among citizens who follow games of chance for a living. And no one ever sees The Sky when he does not have some proposition of his own."

A proposition, it should be explained, is a neat and often preposterous ploy used to lure the innocent into parting with their cash. Thus the example given Sky Masterson by his father, prior to leaving home, that he should not bet a man who offers to make the jack of spades jump from a brand-new deck of cards and squirt cider in his ear is a proposition. Does the jack of spades have hydraulic talents or not? Therein lies the wager. In "The Idyll of Miss Sarah Brown," Runyon related several of Ty's cannier propositions. The reality, however, had a seductive and more complicated charm.

In the summer of 1917, for example, Ty was sitting on the porch of the Arlington Hotel in Hot Springs, Arkansas, eating a bag of Danish walnuts. He still had that fresh, uplifted look that often passes for innocence. A local merchant walked onto the porch, said hello, and the two men fell into conversation. Ty continued to eat the walnuts, occasionally offering the merchant one. The merchant seemed to like the walnuts, since he asked for another and referred in passing to their light, piquant qualities. Ty offered him the bag and then, almost absentmindedly, he said, "I'll tell you what. I've got an interesting proposition for you, since I know how much you like them. What odds will you give that I can't throw one of these Danish walnuts over that hotel cross the street?"

The merchant smiled, looking across the street at the hotel. It was five stories high. "Ty," he said, "you're some thrower, I know that, but not even Ty Cobb could throw a nut over that hotel. Not on a good day with the wind behind him."

"Maybe not," said Ty, "but I'm willin' to bet I can. Shucks, I'm willin' to bet a hundred dollars if you could see your way to givin' me odds of, uh, say, three-to-one."

"One of these walnuts, Ty?" said the merchant pointing to the bag.

"Yep. You can pick any walnut in this here bag." Ty cracked another, eating it noisily.

The merchant agreed to the odds and selected a walnut from the bottom of the bag. Balancing the walnut in the palm of his hand, Ty stepped off the porch and into the street. Cocking his arm and throwing effortlessly, he lofted the walnut over the hotel. He turned round and grinned. The merchant scratched his head, began to remonstrate, then reluctantly reached for his wallet. And he never discovered, as many others were not to do, that Ty had palmed the walnut for one of his own special nuts, which he carried with him everywhere—a Danish walnut filled with lead.

Another of Ty's propositions, which Runyon reworked in "Sarah Brown," occurred in Toledo, Ohio, in a club owned by Johnny ("Get Rich Quick") Ryan. The club was in an old building in the center of the city. To reach the men's room, one descended a broken flight of stairs and crossed a darkened storeroom. One night, returning from the men's room to the poker game, Ty nearly stepped on a large rat scuttling between the packing cases and he instinctively knocked one of the heavy cases over, pinning the creature to the floor. Assuring himself the rat was secure, Ty hurried upstairs to the card room.

A few minutes later, in the middle of a hand, Ty turned to the player at his left, a mobster from Cicero, and said: "Say, why are there so many rats in this place? There are so many rats runnin' loose in that room down there, a man could shoot one of 'em between the eyes inside a minute."

The mobster continued to look at his hand. "I saw 'em, mister," he said. "But get this. It'd take a sharpshooter to hit a rat in a cage. To hit a runnin' rat in the eyes in the dark, guy'd need a machine gun, at least."

"Hell," said Ty, "I used to pop rats when I was a kid. Ain't nothin' in that."

The mobster looked up at Ty. He took the cigar from his mouth. Turning, he looked around the table. "Boys," he said, "gotta kid here thinks he's Buffalo Bill. Kid, I'll lay you five hundred says there's more to it than you think."

"You got five hundred," said Ty. He put down his cards and picked up his gun from the floor. "But I want odds. This ain't no ordinary proposition."

"I'll give you two-to-one. Can't give a great ratkiller like you more'n that."

The game stopped and Ty covered an additional five hundred in side bets. Checking his gun, he walked to the door.

"Hey, kid, wait a minute," said the mobster. "Don't get cute with me. That rat better be warm. I ain't bettin' money on a rat you knocked off day 'fore yesterday. And I'm timin' you. You got sixty seconds, kid."

Down in the storeroom the rat was still struggling to get out from under the packing case. Ty shot it in the head, upended the case, took the rodent by the tail, walked back upstairs, and dropped it on the poker table. The mobsters, Ty recalled, treated him with a certain reverence thereafter.

Another of Ty's stratagems occurred in Joplin before the war. Ty had become friendly with two gamblers called Hickory and Beanie. They were local boys and when they were not gambling they took Ty around Joplin or to their fishing camp outside of town. Driving into town one day, Ty noticed some workmen putting up a signpost which said, JOPLIN—20 MILES. That night he returned to the site, dug up the signpost and planted it five miles nearer to Joplin, checking carefully on the way home that it was exactly fifteen miles to the city limits.

Next day, as the three men were driving back from the fishing camp, they passed the sign and Ty suggested they stop so that he could take a leak. Before getting back into the car he seemed to notice the sign for the first time and shook his head. "Hey, look at that sign," he said. "Those boys just don't know what they're talkin' about. That there sign is an outright lie. Couldn't be more than fifteen miles to Joplin from here."

"Oh, they're pretty careful about that sort of thing," said Beanie. "Check it real good. You better believe it."

"It ain't right, Beanie," said Ty. "I'd bet on it."

"How much?" said Hickory, nudging Beanie.

"Why, hell, I'd bet a hundred. That sign just couldn't be right. Only took me twenty minutes to drive into Joplin from about here yesterday. I remember that. I'd bet a hundred it's no more'n fifteen miles from here to Joplin."

"Well, I'll bet you five hundred it's at least sixteen," said Hickory.

"And I'll take five hundred on that too," said Beanie.

"Well, okay, boys," said Ty, "but I'm tellin' you. That sign is wrong."

The three men drove back to town and, of course, it was exactly fifteen miles. "Christ," said Beanie. "I'm gonna raise hell with the road department. They don't have no right foolin' the public that way."

In 1917 Ty married again—a seventeen-year-old girl called Alice, whom he had picked up in a Pittsburgh movie house. Alice was pretty and had a certain crafty charm. Hubert Cokes, who admired her, remembered her to be "a good driver, loyal as could be and one of the best shoplifters in the country."

In April of 1918 Ty was unexpectedly drafted into the Army and spent seven months and twenty days at Camp Taylor in Anniston, Alabama. The time, however, was not entirely wasted. The war was remote, too remote to interfere with Ty's more immediate concerns. He passed the time playing craps and cards and making propositions. He remembered earning about fifty thousand dollars in the Army. He had worked hard and was disappointed that the Armistice was signed so soon.

Discharged from the Army, Ty returned to Missouri—to St. Louis and the tenderloin. He had money now and in keeping with his station he hired an erstwhile hoodlum as a chauffeur-bodyguard. In those days it was customary for protection men to take ten percent of their employers' winnings and Ty believed, when gambling in dangerous neighborhoods, they more than justified the additional expense.

In St. Louis, Ty had taken to gambling in the back room of a tailor shop owned by a shakedown man. An intimate of bootleggers and bondsmen, he was a morose and truculent man, who drank too much and liked to play in his own game. He was a consistent loser. In three months of shooting craps, Ty won forty thousand dollars from him. He paid, reluctantly, but when he lost two thousand more he drunkenly refused payment. Ty shrugged and gave him twenty-four hours to change his mind. The next night, bringing his gun and his bodyguard, Ty returned. Now sober and repentant, the tailor paid up and as a show, perhaps, of further faith offered to steer Ty into a high-stake, payday crap game; in return, they agreed that he would cash the paychecks himself for twenty percent of Ty's winnings. That Friday Ty was taken to a warehouse on the Mississippi. Playing craps with river toughs and dockers he won twelve thousand dollars. He turned the checks over to the tailor, who promised payment the following night. At the appointed time Ty and his bodyguard drove round to the tailor's shop.

As usual the back room was crowded with players, with bondsmen and bootleggers, one or two reformed heisters and a few of the owner's chorus girls. Drinks were poured and he gave Ty his money. As Ty said good night and turned to leave, he noticed one of the tailor's flunkies at the back door flicking the light switch on and off. The switch, Ty knew, operated a light just outside the tailor shop. Talking loudly, Ty approached the door; he turned the handle, beginning to open it, then said to one of the chorus girls: "Darlin', I'll tell you one last story for the road." Closing the door, he began some old and favorite tale. As the girl began to giggle, Ty pulled out his .45. Yanking open the door, he looked down the stairs. There, motionless and waiting, were two men with handkerchiefs covering their faces. Surprised, they hurriedly raised their guns, but it was too late. Ty shot them both. They catapulted backward down the steep, dark stairs. Pushing the flunky aside, Ty turned on the back light. The men, like lovers, lay one upon the other. They were both dead.

Ty turned back into the room. "I oughta kill you for that," he said. The tailor cringed against the wall, but Ty's bodyguard persuaded Ty to leave. The two men decided to go to the police station, where Ty described the incident. He was detained. Later that night he was awakened by one of the chief detectives. "You're a lucky man," he said. "I'm going to let you go. Those two guys you killed were wanted for murder, kidnapping, and armed robbery. We've been after them for five years."

Not long afterwards, a similar incident took place in St. Joseph, Missouri. Ty and his bodyguard were playing five-card stud in a room above a closed saloon. It was a regular game and carefully guarded, since it had been hijacked before. The men who operated the game had wired the outside stairs with a bell-alarm—a crude, but effective early warning system. Late one night the alarm sounded. Ty ducked quickly under the table, pulling out his gun. Two hijackers rushed into the room, shooting. One of their shots missed Ty by inches. He and his bodyguard shot the two men down. The police were not involved on this occasion. Checking their wallets, Ty found the names and addresses of the gunmen. Before leaving town he sent telegrams to their wives, telling them their men were dead and where their bodies were.

It is difficult to know just what these deaths would have meant to Ty, even had he stopped to think of them. Presumably he would have told the usual tale that a man must protect himself, that the country was crammed with head-hunters, that he was only guarding what was rightfully his own. He would have felt no sense of wrong-doing or remorse, no complicated guilts. He had a simple give-take relationship with the world. "If a man comes at me with a gun," he had said, "he had better expect something. He ain't gettin' something for nothing. He's a fool to think otherwise. I ain't gonna lie down for no man. Now how can you call that murder? Heisters are enemies. You can't murder enemies. It's impossible." The idea of murder appalled him. He liked to imply that he had killed no one, that his victims had merely committed suicide.

In 1921 Ty went to Chicago. "Everybody was talkin' about a guy called Nick the Greek," he said, "and I decided it was time we met." At that time Nick the Greek Dandolos was considered the highest gambler in America. No gambler since the days of Richard Canfield had achieved his reputation. Nick claimed to have won and lost some $500 million in his lifetime. He once dropped $797,000 to Arnold Rothstein in the biggest stud-poker pot ever recorded, Nick's kings losing to Rothstein's diamond flush. "The exhilaration of this form of economic existence is beyond my power to describe," he liked to say. He died broke in 1966.

In 1921, however, Nick approached the zenith of his fame. Although he claimed to have been broke some seventy-three separate times in his life, he never seemed to want for money. "He used to go broke two or three times a year," said Ty, "and the next time you'd see him, he'd have a couple of hundred thousand in his pocket. Nobody ever knew where he got his money from."

The two gamblers met in Chicago and left almost immediately for San Francisco. They had heard rumors of high-stake poker games at the Kingston Club. Ty and the Greek were to spend more than a year playing poker there. It was a running game and big—three-hundred-twenty-dollar-limit poker. The players included many of the city's politicians, lawyers, bankers, bootleggers and a couple of local gamblers called Joe Bernstein and Nigger Nate Raymond, both cardsharps of talent.

Nick had the stamina to play for days at a time without sleep, whereas Ty, as he had always done, played for fifteen or sixteen con-secutive hours, then slept for twelve. They played as partners, or, as it was called, "did a little business together." They had practiced signals and by arranging their cards or nodding their heads in surreptitious ways they let one another know who had the best hand, when to raise or when to fold, and at the end of the day they split the take. Not that this chicanery was essential to their game: Ty was an excellent player and according to Hubert Cokes, "Anytime it got down to four or five in a poker hand, Nick was eight-to-five to win, he was that good." But it gave them the extra "advantage going in." With that advantage, at the end of eighteen months Ty had won two automobiles and just under a million dollars.

"Some folks," Ty recalled, "thought I bet too fast. They'd take me on because they reckoned I was bettin' without stoppin' to think. But I can't help thinkin' fast. These fellows who stroke their chins and say, 'Now, what was that proposition again?' are marks for me. I figured so far ahead of 'em that their money was gone before they knew they'd been bettin'.

"In poker," he said, "money is power. And I always made sure I had it. I not only played my own hand, I played everybody else's. I watched every card, every draw, every bet, every expression. I don't trust on luck. I am bettin' all around the table, on every card drawn by every player. I often have more on side bets than I have in the pot. I have to think fast and figure my percentages. I can't relax for a second. I treat everything like playin' roulette. And the only way to win at roulette is to own the wheel. I tell you, gambling is hard work."

During his San Francisco days Ty learned a new game—golf. He had just turned twenty-nine. Golf was to become his best game and his favorite, when he learned there were more ways to bet on golf than on cards or craps. It came naturally to him. The first time he ever hit a ball, he remembered, he drove it nearly three hundred yards. When the nightly poker sessions at the Kingston Club ended, Ty spent his mornings on a local course practicing golf. He told no one; he always practiced behind the bushes on the back nine, taking care to keep out of the sun. Since driving came easily to him, he concentrated on chipping and putting. In a matter of weeks he found he could almost always hole in two strokes and never in more than three from distances up to one hundred fifty yards. "It was the easiest thing you ever saw," he said. "I played golf almost as well as I breathed." However, he had never actually played a round.

One of those who came to watch the late-night poker games at the Kingston Club was a local golf professional called Buddy Brent. One night he and Ty fell into conversation and Ty, who liked to brag that he would bet on anything, told Brent that he could probably beat him at golf. "I hear golf is a child's game," said Ty, "pick it up in a morning." Brent knew that Ty had never played the game, but condescended to compete with him for ten dollars a hole.

The following day Brent beat Ty on every hole and collected ninety dollars for the nine-hole wager. Driving back into San Francisco, Ty sulked. He complained that nothing had gone right for him, that his luck had been atrocious, that his clubs were borrowed, that his back ached from all-night poker games, and that had he been fit he would have given a better account of himself. Brent smiled and sympathized; he could see, he said, that Ty was a natural golfer, that all he required was a little practice, but for the moment he should concentrate on playing poker. He said that Ty was a terrific poker player.

That night at the Kingston Club a few of the poker players, having heard the story, heckled Ty unmercifully. Ty glowered, insisting Brent had merely been lucky. Later that evening, when Brent dropped into the club, Ty challenged him to a match the next day; he would play, he said, for one thousand dollars a hole, but he had to have three shots a hole. Everyone laughed. The incredulous Brent agreed to the wager, but would only concede one shot a hole. Ty insisted the cash be put up front. As always happened, a group of enthusiastic gamblers wanted as much side action as possible and when the betting was concluded nearly sixty thousand dollars lay on the table. Ty covered the bets and went back to playing poker.

The next morning a little crowd of joyful gamblers gathered around the first tee. When Ty arrived there was much sympathetic applause. Ty, driving first, hit his ball about 275 yards down the middle of the fairway. Brent blanched. The gamblers looked uneasily at one another. Ty never remembered what he shot that day, only that it was a stroke or two better than Brent. He won $56,000. "I never, ever shot more than a stroke or two better'n the opposition," he said. "If a man shoots eighty-nine, I shoot eighty-eight. If a man shoots sixty-eight, I shoot sixty-seven. I never liked to add insult to injury."

It is inaccurate, of course, to give the impression that hustlers, even the best of them, never lose a bet. Ty himself lost dozens of wagers, but like most gamblers became wonderfully absentminded when one referred to them. One bet, however, which rankled him for years was made in San Francisco in 1922. He was playing golf with Nick the Greek and coming down to the last hole had beaten him for twenty thousand dollars. On the last green Nick was lying some twenty feet from the hole. Ty offered to bet him double-or-nothing on the twenty thousand if he could sink the putt and Nick agreed. "It was four-to-one Nick couldn't make that putt," Ty recalled. "Hell, it was two-to-one against me making it and I was a great putter. Nick had five hundred grand in his pocket that day and I could have got it all if he'd missed. But the son of a bitch put it in."

Toward the end of 1922 Ty and Nick the Greek set out for New York City. Nick wanted to gamble with Arnold Rothstein in one of that gambler's famous "floating crap games" and Ty assured the boys in the Kingston Club that he would take the Eastern tracks for millions. But Ty had never had much luck with the horses; he claimed to have lost over two million dollars at the track over the years. Even Nick, who gambled at anything, warned Ty that "only madmen and drunks bet seriously on the horses." Referring to the intensity with which such gamblers threw away their money, Nick claimed that "a woman could walk naked at Aqueduct ten minutes before post time and she'd be safer than riding in a Brink's truck with two eunuchs." But Ty was not so easily deterred.

Ty lost most of his Western winnings at the Eastern tracks. But he was never broke for long, nor long disheartened, and during the next few years, whenever he won at golf or cards or craps, he continued to hustle the horses.

*　*　*　*

During the mid-Twenties Ty lived mainly in California in a large home in Beverly Hills. Hubert Cokes was also in California at the time and the two friends saw a lot of one another. "We gambled night and day," said Cokes. "Gambled high at pool and golf and cards. Ty was a better golfer than me, but at pool he had no more chance than a Chow. Ty went to bed every night trying to figure out ways to fuck me and I did the same thing to him. Ty was extraordinary. He had a remarkable memory. You could give him a proposition he hadn't heard of in twenty years and he could give you the right odds on it. And great eyesight. He could see around corners."

On one occasion the two men were driving outside of Los Angeles when the car hit a rock on the side of the road. Hubert stopped the car and got out to see what had happened.

"My God," he said, "where did this enormous rock come from?"

"Don't rightly know," said Ty.

"Well, as long as we're here, I'll bet you five hundred I can guess the weight of this rock within two pounds."

Ty got out of the car to look at the rock. "Why hell, Hubert," he said, "that rock's not from this part of the country. Where'd you find it? That's a different class of rock altogether."

Hubert smiled. "You smart son of a bitch," he said. "They broke the mold when they made you."

Fabled Spots—Monte Carlo and Las Vegas

From a dubious career as a stock market manipulator in France (he served several months in jail), François Blanc went on to a highly lucrative one as a casino operator first in Homburg and then in Monaco. History was in the making, beginning with a deal with Prince Charles of Monaco: a cut of the profits for the impoverished prince, the maintenance of the prince's army of some one hundred warriors, a living wage for the local clergy to denounce and thereby publicize gambling from their pulpits. What was to become the world's most famous international casino opened over a hundred years ago, and, much expanded, still stands, an endlessly storied place. François Blanc died in 1877, leaving a fortune of 200 million francs and having married off his two daughters to royalty.

Scarcely less fabulous is our own Las Vegas, where gambling was legalized in 1931 under gangland auspices now less overt than they once were. When the late Lucius Beebe, author, editor, and columnist, became for a while a resident of Virginia City, he observed that his fellow Nevadans cultivated the delusion that "they are in no way different from other Americans in thought, habit or conduct and that the reputation their state has maintained since primeval times for unreconstructed ways and Western rowdy-dow is somehow not truly representative." Visitors, they try to insist, should see their schools and churches. "Fortunately or otherwise," Mr. Beebe noted, "a dim view of schools and churches is taken by the millions who visit Nevada." The figures bear him out, certainly in Las Vegas: a population of about 300,000 (up from 80,000 ten years ago) and a gross of $1 billion a year from hundreds of casinos operating twenty-four hours a day except for thirty seconds of silence at midnight on New Year's Eve. This touch of sentiment is said to be a matter of civic pride.

◇◇◇

Jaggers' System

Has anyone ever truly broken the bank at Monte Carlo? Writing in the mid-1920s (*The Romance of Monte Carlo*), Charles Kingston said that it had not happened as of then, and there is no available record that it has ever happened in the popular sense. Breaking the bank merely means that play at a given table is suspended until fresh funds arrive from the cashier's office. But here is the story of one who made a stout, ingenious try, and apparently had the good sense to quit while he was well ahead.

BY CHARLES KINGSTON

It is tantalizing to have to record that the only honest system which proved unbeatable during its brief career can be played no longer. This was Jaggers' system, which was based not on the law of averages—that illusory foundation of most systems—but on the fallibility of mankind and the imperfection of everything mankind produces. Jaggers, a clever mechanic who made a hobby of mathematics, evolved out of years of work on the most delicate of machinery the axiom that imperfect man cannot produce perfect machinery. He had previously experimented with a roulette wheel to test the law of averages, and when he made his discovery, which everybody afterwards declared was obvious, he saw the opportunity of making a fortune by proceeding to Monte Carlo and playing with his knowledge and his money against the imperfect portions of the numerous roulette wheels. He knew that it might take him weeks to discover these weaknesses, but he was certain that ultimate victory would be his, and although not a man of means he engaged six clerks to assist him. They did not know what his object was when he ordered them to record in their notebooks the numbers as they appeared at six tables. Every night they reported, and after the first day Jaggers was busy from morning until night analysing their figures. Five weeks after his arrival he had worked out his system, which was to play on the weak spot in each one of the roulette wheels which had been watched by his assistants. The law of averages enabled him to ascertain where these weaknesses were, for at each one of the six tables certain numbers appeared more frequently than the law of average permits. That indicated that the wheels were wrong, for the law of averages is infallible.

When he had compiled a list of the numbers which came up most frequently because of the defects in the cylinders, Jaggers and his staff gambled on them with steady and almost uninterrupted success. Although this capital was about the smallest any great gambler had attacked the casino with, he was a winner to the extent of fourteen thousand pounds on the first day, and four successive days' play brought him sixty thousand pounds. As the policy of the casino is to place an astute member of its staff at any table where the punter is winning sensationally, Jaggers was soon the object of special attention on the part of the administration. When the agent commanded to watch him reported that he was unable to follow the system played by the gentleman from England two other inspectors of vast experience were sent to reinforce him and they likewise admitted that although there was a certain similarity in the methods of the player and his assistants and that they favoured certain numbers, no system known to the administration was being played.

Then it suddenly occurred to one of the directors that it might have something to do with the working of the roulette wheel, a false balance or something of that sort. To test this solution of the riddle they interchanged the wheels between the various tables, and Jaggers fell into the trap to the extent of two-thirds of his winnings, which amounted by now to sixty thousand pounds. As for once the bank was playing against an infallible system and, therefore, ought not to have won, the inventor of the system perceived that he was playing it a wrong way. In other words he was applying the wrong figures to each roulette wheel, and therefore it behoved him to readjust matters by rediscovering the cylinders to which each set of his six tabulations belonged.

To a man with keen eyesight, a shrewd, quick thinking brain and steady nerve it was no difficult matter to track down the cylinders and identify them. Once he had done this he resumed his run of success, and three more weeks replenished his banking account to the extent of seventy thousand pounds. He was then ninety thousand pounds on the right side but this figure did not represent the total loss incurred by the casino in consequence of the exploitation of the Jaggers system. There is no place in the world so sensitive to rumour and so contagious to an epidemic of success as the casino at Monte Carlo, and hundreds crowded the tables where Jaggers and his clerks were playing and blindly followed their lead. It was not to be expected that the administration would tolerate the continuance of a system which would have ruined the casino in a year, but as by now the directors had rediscovered it for themselves they were able to take immediate steps to render it impotent.

The manufacturer of the roulette wheels was summoned from Paris to assist at a conference, which had been called for the purpose of extinguishing the Jaggers system, and this ingenious person quickly supplied a solution in the shape of movable partitions between the numbers in the wheel. The old immovable partitions were responsible for the success of the Jaggers system, because any irregularity in their construction gave to certain numbers an advantage which a shrewd observer must notice. By replacing them with movable partitions the numerous receptacles for the little white ball could be changed about at the will of the casino and need never be the same two days running. He therefore manufactured a completely new set of wheels with movable partitions and the moment they were installed the Jaggers system died. Jaggers did not discern this immediately, and when by sheer luck he won three coups out of five, he played with greater confidence than ever. One of the numbers he favoured at his table was seventeen, which according to his system was bound to come up four times in ten spins following the appearance of the number five. It would have done so had the immovable partition been there, but as the night before the receptacle which sheltered seventeen was exchanged with the partitions between which nine reposed, his maximums and those of his assistants at the other tables were lost. This was a surprise as well as a disappointment, but he was not deterred, and for two days he continued to search for his lost El Dorado and paid fifteen thousand pounds without finding it. Then he came to the conclusion that the casino had reasserted its supremacy, and that as he still retained nearly seventy thousand pounds of its money he had better retire and not court defeat.

That win of Jaggers—he left Monte Carlo with about sixty-five thousand pounds—must be a record in spite of the hundreds of dreary legends which are still in circulation about the alleged phenomenal luck of certain ex-convicts. Had Jaggers' system been a failure instead of a success the administration would have given him the hospitality of their subsidized press and his invention would have been hailed throughout the world as something marvellous. But, as it was, the only system which ever threatened the very existence of the casino was not utilized as the basis of another subtle appeal to the greedy, and the biggest win Monte Carlo has ever known was scarcely mentioned in the Blanc press simply because the directors were terrified by it.

Naturally, the amount of his gains has been grossly exaggerated. No writer on the subject ever puts Jaggers' final profit under eighty thousand pounds, and I have seen it stated that he returned to England with double that amount. I imagine that when he had paid all his expenses and rewarded his staff with a special bonus he had a clear profit of fifty thousand pounds, and whether he managed to retain it permanently depends on the number of visits he paid subsequently to Monte Carlo.

◇◇

"Monte"

Like many another neophyte at the gaming tables, Arnold Bennett on his first visit to Monte Carlo in 1904 overlooked an ancient axiom— i.e., the roulette ball, like its cousin the dice, has no memory. The eminent novelist-to-be had a memory, though, and a vivid one, as attested by this sketch from *Paris Nights and Other Impressions of Places and People.*

BY ARNOLD BENNETT

◇◇

MONTE CARLO—the initiated call it merely "Monte"—has often been described, in fiction and out of it, but the frank confession of a ruined gambler is a rare thing; partly because the ruined gambler can't often write well enough to express himself accurately, partly because he isn't in the mood for literary composition, and partly because he is sometimes dead. So, since I am not dead, and since it is only by means of literary composition that I can hope to restore my shattered fortunes, I will give you the frank confession of a ruined gambler. Before I went to Monte Carlo I had all the usual ideas of the average sensible man about gambling in general, and about Monte Carlo in particular. "Where does all the exterior brilliance of Monte Carlo come from?" I asked sagely. And I said further: "The Casino administration does not disguise the fact that it makes a profit of about 50,000 francs a day. Where does that profit come from?" And I answered my own question with wonderful wisdom: "Out of the pockets of the foolish gamblers." I specially despised the gambler who gambles "on a system"; I despised him as a creature of superstition. For the "system" gambler will argue that if I toss a penny up six times and it falls "tail" every time, there is a strong probability that it will fall "head" the seventh time. "Now," I said, "can any rational creature be so foolish as to suppose that the six previous and done-with spins can possibly effect the seventh spin? What connection is there between them?" And I replied: "No rational creature can be so foolish. And there is no connection." In this spirit, superior, omniscient, I went to Monte Carlo.

Of course I went to study human nature and find material. The sole advantage of being a novelist is that when you are discovered in a place where, as a serious person, you would prefer not to be discovered, you can always aver that you are studying human nature and seeking material. I was much impressed by the fact of my being in Monte Carlo. I said to myself: "I am actually in Monte Carlo!" I was proud. And when I got into the gorgeous gaming saloons, amid that throng at once glittering and shabby, I said: "I am actually in the gaming saloons!" And the thought at the back of my mind was: "Henceforth I shall be able to say that I have been in the gaming saloons at Monte Carlo." After studying human nature at large, I began to study it at a roulette table. I had gambled before—notably with impassive Arab chiefs in that singular oasis of the Sahara desert, Biskra—but only a little, and always at *petits chevaux*. But I understood roulette, and I knew several "systems." I found the human nature very interesting; also the roulette. The sight of real gold, silver, and notes flung about in heaps warmed my imagination. At this point I felt a solitary five-franc piece in my pocket. And then the red turned up three times running, and I remembered a simple "system" that began after a sequence of three.

I don't know how it was, but long before I had formally decided to gamble I knew by instinct that I should stake that five-franc piece. I fought against the idea, but I couldn't take my hand empty out of my pocket. Then at last (the whole experience occupying perhaps ten seconds) I drew forth the five-franc piece and bashfully put it on black. I thought that all the fifty or sixty persons crowded round the table were staring at me and thinking to themselves: "There's a beginner!" However, black won, and the croupier pushed another five-franc piece alongside of mine, and I picked them both up very smartly, remembering all the tales I had ever heard of thieves leaning over you at Monte Carlo and snatching your ill-gotten gains. I then thought: "This is a bit of all right. Just for fun I'll continue the system." I did so. In an hour I had made fifty francs, without breaking into gold. Once a croupier made a slip and was raking in red stakes when red had won, and people hesitated (because croupiers never make mistakes, you know, and you have to be careful how you quarrel with the table at Monte Carlo), and I was the first to give vent to a protest, and the croupier looked at me and smiled and apologized, and the winners looked at me gratefully, and I began to think myself the deuce and all of a Monte Carlo habitué.

Having made fifty francs, I decided that I would prove my self-control by ceasing to play. So I did prove it, and went to have tea in the Casino café. In those moments fifty francs seemed to me to be a really enormous sum. I was as happy as though I had shot a reviewer without being found out. I gradually began to perceive, too, that though no rational creature could suppose that a spin could be effected by previous spins, nevertheless, it undoubtedly was so effected. I began to scorn a little the average sensible man who scorned the gambler. "There is more in roulette than is dreamed of in your philosophy, my conceited friend," I murmured. I was like a woman—I couldn't argue, but I knew infallibly. Then it suddenly occurred to me that if I had gambled with louis instead of five-franc pieces I should have made 200 francs—200 francs in rather over an hour! Oh, luxury! Oh, being-in-the-swim! Oh, smartness! Oh, gilded and delicious sin!

Five days afterwards I went to Monte Carlo again, to lunch with some brother authors. In the meantime, though I had been chained to my desk by unalterable engagements, I had thought constantly upon the art and craft of gambling. One of these authors knew Monte Carlo, and all that therein is, as I know Fleet Street. And to my equal astonishment and pleasure he said, when I explained my system to him: "Couldn't have a better!" And he proceeded to remark positively that the man who had a decent system and the nerve to stick to it through all crises, would infallibly win from the tables—not a lot, but an average of several louis per sitting of two hours. "Gambling," he said, "is a matter of character. You have the right character," he added. You may guess whether I did not glow with joyous pride. "The tables make their money from the plunging fools," I said, privately, "and I am not a fool." A man was pointed out to me who extracted a regular income from the tables. "But why don't the authorities forbid him the rooms?" I demanded. "Because he's such a good advertisement. Can't you see?" I saw.

We went to the Casino late after lunch. I cut myself adrift from the rest of the party and began instantly to play. In forty-five minutes, with my "system," I had made forty-five francs. And then the rest of the party reappeared and talked about tea, and trains, and dinner. "Tea!" I murmured disgusted (yet I have a profound passion for tea), "when I am netting a franc a minute!" However, I yielded, and we went and had tea at the Restaurant de Paris across the way. And over the white-and-silver of the tea table, in the falling twilight, with the incomparable mountain landscape in front of us, and the most chic and decadent Parisianism around us, we talked roulette. Then the Russian Grand Duke, who had won several thousand pounds in a few minutes a week or two before, came veritably and ducally in, and sat at the next table. There was no mistaking his likeness to the Tsar. It is most extraordinary how the propinquity of a Grand Duke, experienced for the first time, affects even the proverbial phlegm of a British novelist. I seemed to be moving in a perfect atmosphere of Grand Dukes! And I, too, had won! The art of literature seemed a very little thing.

After I had made fifty and forty-five francs at two sittings, I developed suddenly, without visiting the tables again, into a complete and thorough gambler. I picked up all the technical terms like picking up marbles— the greater martingale, the lesser martingale, "en plein," "à cheval," "the horses of seventeen," "last square," and so on, and so on—and I had my own original theories about the alleged superiority of red-or-black to odd-or-even in betting on the even chances. In short, for many hours I lived roulette. I ate roulette for dinner, drank it in my Vichy, and smoked it in my cigar. At first I pretended that I was only pretending to be interested in gambling as a means of earning a livelihood (call it honest or dishonest, as you please). Then the average sensible man in me began to have rather a bad time, really. I frankly acknowledged to myself that I was veritably keen on the thing. I said: "Of course, ordinary people believe that the tables must win, but we who are initiated know better. All you want in order to win is a prudent system and great force of character." And I decided that it would be idle, that it would be falsely modest, that it would be inane, to deny that I had exceptional force of character. And beautiful schemes formed themselves in my mind: how I would gain a certain sum, and then increase my "units" from five-franc pieces to louis, and so quadruple the winnings, and how I would get a friend to practice the same system, and so double them again, and how generally we would have a quietly merry time at the expense of the tables during the next month.

And I was so calm, cool, collected, impassive. There was no hurry. I would not go to Monte Carlo the next day, but perhaps the day after. However, the next day proved to be very wet, and I was alone and idle, my friends being otherwise engaged, and hence I was simply obliged to go to Monte Carlo. I didn't wish to go, but what could one do? Before starting, I reflected: "Well, there's just a chance—such things have been known," and I took a substantial part of my financial resources out of my pocketbook, and locked that reserve up in a drawer. After this, who will dare to say that I was not cool and sagacious? The journey to Monte Carlo seemed very long. Just as I was entering the ornate portals I met some friends who had seen me there the previous day. The thought flashed through my mind: "These people will think I have got caught in the meshes of the vice just like ordinary idiots, whereas, of course my case is not ordinary at all." So I quickly explained to them that it was very wet (as if they couldn't see), and that my other friends had left me, and that I had come to Monte Carlo merely to kill time. They appeared to regard this explanation as unnecessary.

I had a fancy for the table where I had previously played and won. I went to it, and by extraordinary good fortune secured a chair—a difficult thing to get in the afternoons. Behold me seated next door to a croupier, side by side with regular frequenters, regular practicers of systems, and doubtless envied by the outer ring of players and spectators! I was annoyed to find that every other occupant of a chair had a little printed card in black and red on which he marked the winning numbers. I had neglected to provide myself with this contrivance, and I felt conspicuous; I felt that I was not correct. However, I changed some gold for silver with the croupier, and laid the noble pieces in little piles in front of me, and looked as knowing and as initiated as I could. And at the first opening offered by the play I began the operation of my system, backing red, after black had won three times. Black won the fourth time, and I had lost five francs.... Black won the sixth time and I had lost thirty-five francs. Black won the seventh time, and I had lost seventy-five francs. "Steady, cool customer!" I addressed myself. I put down four louis (and kindly remember that in these hard times four louis is four louis—three English pounds and four English shillings), and, incredible to relate, black won the eighth time, and I had lost a hundred and fifty-five francs. The time occupied was a mere nine minutes. It was at this point that the "nerve" and the "force of character" were required, for it was an essential part of my system to "cut the loss" at the eighth turn. I said: "Hadn't I better put down eight louis and win all back again, just this once? Red's absolutely certain to win next time." But my confounded force of character came in, and forced me to cut the loss, and stick strictly to the system. And at the ninth spin red did win. If I had only put down that eight louis I should have been all right. I was extremely annoyed, especially when I realized that, even with decent luck, it would take me the best part of three hours to regain that hundred and fifty-five francs.

I was shaken. I was like a pugilist who had been knocked down in a prize fight, and hasn't quite made up his mind whether, on the whole, he won't be more comfortable, in the long run, where he is. I was like a soldier under a heavy fire, arguing with himself rapidly whether he prefers to be a Balaclava hero with death or the workhouse, or just a plain, ordinary, prudent Tommy. I was struck amidships. Then an American person behind my chair, just a casual foolish plunger, of the class out of which the Casino makes its profits, put a thousand franc note on the odd numbers, and thirty-three turned up. "A thousand for a thousand," said the croupier mechanically and nonchalantly, and handed to the foolish plunger the equivalent of eighty pounds sterling. And about two minutes afterwards the same foolish plunger made a hundred and sixty pounds at another single stroke. It was odious; I tell you positively it was odious. I collected the shattered bits of my character out of my boots, and recommended my system; made a bit; felt better; and then zero turned up twice—most unsettling, even when zero means only that your stake is "held over." Then two old and fussy ladies came and gambled very seriously over my head, and deranged my hair with the end of the rake in raking up their miserable winnings.... At five o'clock I had lost a hundred and ninety-five francs. I don't mind working hard, at great nervous tension, in a vitiated atmosphere, if I can reckon on netting a franc a minute; but I have a sort of objection to three laborious sittings such as I endured that week when the grand result is a dead loss of four pounds: I somehow failed to see the point. I departed in disgust, and ordered tea at the Café de Paris, not the Restaurant de Paris (I was in no mood for Grand Dukes). And while I imbibed the tea, a heated altercation went on inside me between the average sensible man and the man who knew that money could be made out of the tables and that gambling was a question of nerves, etc. It was a pretty show, that altercation. In about ten rounds the average sensible man had knocked his opponent right out of the ring. I breathed a long breath, and seemed to wake up out of a nightmare. Did I regret the episode? I regretted the ruin, not the episode. For had I not all the time been studying human nature and getting material? Besides that, as I grow older I grow too wise. Says Montaigne: "Wisdome hath hir excesses, and no leise need of moderation, then follie." (The italics are Montaigne's) ... And there's a good deal in my system after all.

Rien Ne Va Plus

At one time or another Alexander Woollcott—drama critic, pioneer radio essayist, tireless traveler, and correspondent—managed to turn up almost anywhere and come away with a story. The story, of course, did not have to be certified under oath as true.

BY ALEXANDER WOOLLCOTT

WE WERE sitting under the midsummer stars at Monte Carlo, eating a soufflé and talking about suicide, when a passing newsmonger stopped at our table all aglow with the tidings that that young American with the white forelock had just been found crumpled on the beach, a bullet-hole in his heart. Earlier in the evening—it was shortly before we came out of the Casino in quest of dinner—we had all seen him wiped out by a final disastrous turn of the wheel. And now he lay dead on the shore.

I shall have to admit that the news gave a fillip to the occasion. It came towards the end of a long, luscious dinner on the terrace opposite the Casino. We were a casually assembled carful, who had driven over from Antibes in the late afternoon, planning to play a little roulette as an appetizer and then to dine interminably.

When we had arrived in the *Salles Privées* a few hours before, there was only standing room around our table at first. In this rapt fringe, I encountered Sam Fletcher, a dawdling journalist who lived on occasional assignments from the Paris offices of American newspapers. He pointed out the notables to me. There was Mary Garden, for instance, playing intently, losing and winning, losing and winning, with that economy of emotional expenditure which one usually reserves for setting-up exercises. Then there was an English dowager who looked as though she were held together by adhesive tape. She was betting parsimoniously, but Fletcher whispered to me that she lived in Monte Carlo on an ample allowance provided by her son-in-law, with the sole stipulation that she never embarrass the family by coming home. A moribund remittance woman. Next to her sat a pallid old gentleman whose hands, as they caressed his stack of counters, were conspicuously encased in braided gloves of gray silk. It seems that in his youth, he had been a wastrel, and, on her deathbed, his mother had squeezed from him a solemn promise never to touch card or chip again as long as he lived.

As for young White Lock, there was, until his final bet, nothing else noticeable about him except that he was the only man then at the table wearing a dinner coat. We heard later that at first he had lost heavily and had had to make several trips to the caisse to replenish his supply of plaques. By the time I came along he had settled to a more cautious play but finally, as if from boredom, he took all his plaques and counters and stacked them on the red. To this pile he added, just as the wheel began to turn, the contents of his wallet—emptying out a small cascade of thousand-franc notes, with a single hundred-franc note among them. But this one he retrieved at the last moment as if to be sure of carfare home. There was that breathless spinning moment, then the fateful "Rien ne va plus," issuing in the same dead voice with which the intoning of the mass falls on infidel ears. Then the decision. "Noir." Around that table you could hear the word for black being exhaled in every language the world has known since Babel.

The young man gave a little laugh as the croupier called the turn. He sat quite still as his last gauge was raked into the bank. With all eyes on him, he shoved his chair back from the table, reached for his wallet, took out the aforesaid hundred-franc note and pushed it, with white, fastidious fingers, toward the center of the patterned baize. "Pour le personnel," he said, with a kind of wry grandeur which hushed the usual twitter of thanks from the croupiers. "And that," he added, "is that." So saying, he got to his feet, yawned a little, and sauntered out of the room. I remember thinking, at the time, that he was behaving rather like any desperate young man in any Zoë Akins play. But it was a good performance. And now, it seems, he lay dead by the water's edge.

It was Fletcher himself who brought the news. It came, I say, just as we were eating soufflé and talking of suicide. This, of course, was no obliging coincidence. One always tells tall tales of self-slaughter at Monte Carlo. It is part of the legend of the principality—as strong in its force of suggestion, I suppose, as the legend of Lourdes is strong in its hint to hysterics that the time has come to cast away their crutches. Fletcher told us that the sound of the shot had brought a watchman running. The youth lay on his back, his chin tilted to the stars, one outstretched hand limply holding the revolver, a dark stain on the pleated whiteness of his breast. Before Fletcher could wire his report to Paris, he would have to await certain—well—formalities. In a conspiratorial whisper, he explained there had been so many such suicides of late that a new rule was but recently put into effect. Whenever any client of the

Casino was found self-slain with empty pockets, it was customary for the Casino to rush a bankroll to the spot before notifying the police, so that the victim would seem to have ended it all from *Weltschmerz*. Even now, Fletcher said, this trick must be in progress, and in the meantime he ought to be seeking such obituary data as might be gleaned in the registry office.

We were still lingering over our coffee when he came hurrying back to us, all bristling with the end of the story. Notified in due course, the *gendarmerie* had repaired to the beach in quest of the body. But there was none. Not at the indicated spot, nor anywhere else on the shore. After further search, the minor chieftain from the Casino, who had himself tucked ten thousand francs into the pocket of the now missing suicide and was still lurking, much puzzled, in the middle-distance, returned at last to the *Salles Privées*, only to find them humming with a new chapter. It seems that that young American with the white forelock—the one somebody or other had inaccurately reported as killed—had reappeared apparently restored in spirits, and certainly restored in funds. He had bet tremendously, lingered for only three turns of the wheel, and departed with a hundred thousand francs. The attendants assumed he had merely been out to dinner. At least the careless fellow had spilled some tomato sauce on his shirt front.

Las Vegas (What?) Las Vegas (Can't hear you! Too noisy) Las Vegas!!!!

Casino gambling has been approved by the voters of New Jersey, where
its debut in Atlantic City will be watched with interest by the citizens
of Nevada. The latter profess not to be concerned, however, about their
potential rival in the East. For one thing, they point out, how could
any place ever catch up with the Las Vegas portrayed here? The question may be regarded as rhetorical.

BY TOM WOLFE

HERNIA, HERNIA, hernia, hernia, hernia, hernia, hernia, hernia, hernia,
hernia, hernia, hernia, hernia, HERNia; hernia, HERNia, hernia, hernia,
hernia, hernia, HERNia, HERNia, HERNia; hernia, hernia, hernia,
hernia, hernia, hernia, hernia, eight is the point, the point is eight;
hernia, hernia, HERNia; hernia, hernia, hernia, hernia, all right, hernia,
hernia, hernia, hernia, hard eight, hernia, hernia, hernia, HERNia,
hernia, hernia, hernia, HERNia, hernia, hernia, hernia, HERNia, hernia,
hernia, hernia, hernia

"What is all this *hernia hernia* stuff?"

This was Raymond talking to the wavy-haired fellow with the stick,
the dealer, at the craps table about 3:45 Sunday morning. The stickman
had no idea what this big wiseacre was talking about, but he resented
the tone. He gave Raymond that patient arch of the eyebrows known as
a Red Hook brush-off, which is supposesd to convey some such thought
as, I am a very tough but cool guy, as you can tell by the way I carry my
eyeballs low in the pouches, and if this wasn't such a high-class joint
we would take wiseacres like you out back and beat you into jellied
madrilene.

At this point, however, Raymond was immune to subtle looks.

The stickman tried to get the game going again, but every time he
would start up his singsong, by easing the words out through the nose,
which seems to be the style among craps dealers in Las Vegas—"All
right, a new shooter . . . eight is the point, the point is eight" and so on

—Raymond would start droning along with him in exactly the same tone of voice, "Hernia, hernia, hernia; hernia, HERNia, HERNia, hernia; hernia, hernia, hernia."

Everybody at the craps table was staring in consternation to think that anybody would try to needle a tough, hip, elite *soldat* like a Las Vegas craps dealer. The gold-lamé odalisques of Los Angeles were staring. The Western sports, fifty-eight-year-old men who wear Texas string ties, were staring. The old babes at the slot machines, holding Dixie Cups full of nickles, were staring at the craps tables, but cranking away the whole time.

Raymond, who is thirty-four years old and works as an engineer in Phoenix, is big but not terrifying. He has the sort of thatchwork hair that grows so low all along the forehead there is no logical place to part it, but he tries anyway. He has a huge, prognathous jaw, but it is as smooth, soft and round as a melon, so that Raymond's total effect is that of an Episcopal divinity student.

The guards were wonderful. They were dressed in cowboy uniforms like Bruce Cabot in *Sundown* and they wore sheriff's stars.

"Mister, is there something we can do for you?"

"The expression is 'Sir,' " said Raymond. "You said 'Mister.' The expression is 'Sir.' How's your old Cosa Nostra?"

Amazingly, the casino guards were easing Raymond out peaceably, without putting a hand on him. I had never seen the fellow before, but possibly because I had been following his progress for the last five minutes, he turned to me and said, "Hey, do you have a car? This wild stuff is starting again."

The gist of it was that he had left his car somewhere and he wanted to ride up the Strip to the Stardust, one of the big hotel-casinos. I am describing this big goof Raymond not because he is a typical Las Vegas tourist, although he has some typical symptoms, but because he is a good example of the marvelous impact Las Vegas has on the senses. Raymond's senses were at a high pitch of excitation, the only trouble being that he was going off his nut. He had been up since Thursday afternoon, and it was now about 3:45 A.M. Sunday. He had an envelope full of pep pills—amphetamine—in his left coat pocket and an envelope full of Equanils—meprobamate—in his right pocket, or were the Equanils in the left and the pep pills in the right? He could tell by looking, but he wasn't going to look anymore. He didn't care to see how many were left.

He had been rolling up and down the incredible electric-sign gauntlet of Las Vegas' Strip, U.S. Route 91, where the neon and the par lamps—bubbling, spiraling, rocketing, and exploding in sunbursts ten stories high out in the middle of the desert—celebrate one-story casinos. He had been gambling and drinking and eating now and again at the buffet tables the casinos keep heaped with food day and night, but mostly hopping himself up with good old amphetamine, cooling himself down with meprobamate, then hooking down more alcohol, until now, after sixty hours, he was slipping into the symptoms of toxic schizophrenia.

He was also enjoying what the prophets of hallucinogen call "consciousness expansion." The man was psychedelic. He was beginning to isolate the components of Las Vegas' unique bombardment of the senses. He was quite right about this *hernia hernia* stuff. Every casino in Las Vegas is, among the other things, a room full of craps tables with dealers who keep up a running singsong that sounds as though they are saying "hernia, hernia, hernia, hernia, hernia" and so on. There they are day and night, easing a running commentary through their nostrils. What they have to say contains next to no useful instruction. Its underlying message is, We are the initiates, riding the crest of chance. That the accumulated sound comes out "hernia" is merely an unfortunate phonetic coincidence. Actually, it is part of something rare and rather grand: a combination of baroque stimuli that brings to mind the bronze gongs, no larger than a blue plate, that Louis XIV, his ruff collars larded with the lint of the foul Old City of Byzantium, personally hunted out in the bazaars of Asia Minor to provide exotic acoustics for his new palace outside Paris.

The sounds of the craps dealer will be in, let's say, the middle register. In the lower register will be the sound of the old babes at the slot machines. Men play the slots too, of course, but one of the indelible images of Las Vegas is that of the old babes at the row upon row of slot machines. There they are at six o'clock Sunday morning no less than at three o'clock Tuesday afternoon. Some of them pack their old hummocky shanks into Capri pants, but many of them just put on the old print dress, the same one day after day, and the old hob-heeled shoes, looking like they might be going out to buy eggs in Tupelo, Mississippi. They have a Dixie Cup full of nickles or dimes in the left hand and an Iron Boy work glove on the right hand to keep the callouses from getting sore. Every time they pull the handle, the machine makes a sound much like the sound a cash register makes before the bell rings, then the slot pictures start clattering up from left to right, the oranges, lemons, plums, cherries, bells, bars, buckaroos—the figure of a cowboy riding a bucking bronco. The whole sound keeps churning up over and over again in eccentric series all over the place, like one of those random-sound radio symphonies by John Cage. You can hear it at any hour of the day or night all over Las Vegas. You can walk down Fremont Street at dawn and hear it without even walking in a door, that and the spins of the wheels of fortune, a boring and not very popular sort of simplified roulette, as the tabs flap to a stop. As an overtone, or at times simply as a loud sound, comes the babble of the casino crowds, with an occasional shriek from the craps tables, or, anywhere from 4 P.M. to 6 A.M., the sound of brass instruments or electrified string instruments from the cocktail-lounge shows.

The crowd and band sounds are not very extraordinary, of course. But Las Vegas' Muzak is. Muzak pervades Las Vegas from the time you walk into the airport upon landing to the last time you leave the casinos. It is piped out to the swimming pool. It is in the drugstores. It is as if there were a communal fear that someone, somewhere in Las Vegas, was going to be left with a totally vacant minute on his hands.

Las Vegas has succeeded in wiring an entire city with this electronic stimulation, day and night, out in the middle of the desert. In the automobile I rented, the radio could not be turned off, no matter which dial you went after. I drove for days in a happy burble of Action Checkpoint News, "Monkey No. 9," "Donna, Donna, the Prima Donna," and picking-and-singing jingles for the Frontier Bank and the Fremont Hotel.

One can see the magnitude of the achievement. Las Vegas takes what in other American towns is but a quixotic inflammation of the senses for some poor salary mule in the brief interval between the flagstone rambler and the automatic elevator downtown and magnifies it, foliates it, embellishes it into an institution.

For example, Las Vegas is the only town in the world whose skyline is made up neither of buildings, like New York, nor of trees, like Wilbraham, Massachusetts, but signs. One can look at Las Vegas from a mile away on Route 91 and see no buildings, no trees, only signs. But such signs! They tower. They revolve, they oscillate, they soar in shapes before which the existing vocabulary of art history is helpless. I can only attempt to supply names—Boomerang Modern, Palette Curvilinear, Flash Gordon Ming-Alert Spiral, McDonald's Hamburger Parabola, Mint Casino Elliptical, Miami Beach Kidney. Las Vegas' sign makers work so far out beyond the frontiers of conventional studio art that they have no names themselves for the forms they create. Vaughan Cannon, one of those tall, blond Westerners, the builders of places like Las Vegas and Los Angeles, whose eyes seem to have been bleached by the sun, is in the back shop of the Young Electric Sign Company out on East Charleston Boulevard with Herman Boernge, one of his designers, looking at the model they have prepared for the Lucky Strike

Casino sign, and Cannon points to where the sign's two great curving faces meet to form a narrow vertical face and says:

"Well, here we are again—what do we call that?"

"I don't know," says Boernge. "It's sort of a nose effect. Call it a nose."

Okay, a nose, but it rises sixteen stories high above a two-story building. In Las Vegas no farseeing entrepreneur buys a sign to fit a building he owns. He rebuilds the building to support the biggest sign he can get up the money for and, if necessary, changes the name. The Lucky Strike Casino today is the Lucky Casino, which fits better when recorded in sixteen stories of flaming peach and incandescent yellow in the middle of the Mojave Desert. In the Young Electric Sign Co. era signs have become the architecture of Las Vegas, and the most whimsical, Yale-seminar-frenzied devices of the two late geniuses of Baroque Modern, Frank Lloyd Wright and Eero Saarinen, seem rather stuffy business, like a jest at a faculty meeting, compared to it. Men like Boernge, Kermit Wayne, Ben Mitchem and Jack Larsen, formerly an artist for Walt Disney, are the designer-sculptor geniuses of Las Vegas, but their motifs have been carried faithfully throughout the town by lesser men, for gasoline stations, motels, funeral parlors, churches, public buildings, flophouses and sauna baths.

Then there is a stimulus that is both visual and sexual—the Las Vegas buttocks décolletage. This is a form of sexually provocative dress seen more and more in the United States, but avoided like Broadway message-embroidered ("Kiss Me, I'm Cold") underwear in the fashion pages, so that the euphemisms have not been established and I have no choice but clinical terms. To achieve buttocks décolletage a woman wears bikini-style shorts that cut across the round fatty masses of the buttocks rather than cupping them from below, so that the outer-lower edges of these fatty masses, or "cheeks," are exposed. I am in the cocktail lounge of the Hacienda Hotel, talking to managing director Dick Taylor about the great success his place has had in attracting family and tour groups, and all around me the waitresses are bobbing on their high heels, bare legs and décolletage-bare backsides, set off by pelvis-length lingerie of an uncertain denomination. I stare, but I am new here. At the White Cross Rexall drugstore on the Strip a pregnant brunette walks in off the street wearing black shorts with buttocks décolletage aft and illusion-of-cloth nylon lingerie hanging fore, and not even the old mom's-pie pensioners up near the door are staring. They just crank away at the slot machines. On the streets of Las Vegas, not only the show girls, of which the town has about two hundred fifty, bona fide, in residence, but girls of every sort, including, especially, Las Vegas' little high-school buds, who adorn what locals seeking roots in the sand call "our city of churches and schools," have taken up the chic of wearing buttocks décolletage step-ins under flesh-tight slacks, with the outline of the undergarment showing through fashionably. Others go them one better. They achieve the effect of having been dipped once, briefly, in Helenca stretch nylon. More and more they look like those wonderful old girls out of Flash Gordon who were wrapped just once over in Baghdad pantaloons of clear polyethyleen with only Flash Gordon between them and the insane red-eyed assaults of the minions of Ming. It is as if all the hip young suburban gals of America named Lana, Deborah and Sandra, who gather wherever the arc lights shine and the studs steady their coiffures in the plate-glass reflection, have convened in Las Vegas with their bouffant hair above and anatomically stretch-pant-swathed little bottoms below, here on the new American frontier. But exactly!

None of it would have been possible, however, without one of those historic combinations of nature and art that creates all epoch. In this case, the Mojave Desert plus the father of Las Vegas, the late Benjamin "Bugsy" Siegel.

Bugsy was an inspired man. Back in 1944 the city fathers of Las Vegas, their Protestant rectitude alloyed only by the giddy prospect of gambling revenues, were considering the sort of ordinance that would have preserved the town with a kind of Colonial Williamsburg dinkiness in the motif of the Wild West. All new buildings would have to have at least the façade of the sort of place where piano players used to wear garters on their sleeves in Virginia City around 1880. In Las Vegas in 1944, it should be noted, there was nothing more stimulating in the entire town than a Fremont Street bar where the composer of "Deep in the Heart of Texas" held forth and the regulars downed fifteen-cent beer.

Bugsy pulled into Las Vegas in 1945 with several million dollars that, after his assassination, was traced back in the general direction of gangster-financiers. Siegel put up a hotel-casino such as Las Vegas had never seen and called it the Flamingo—all Miami Modern, and the hell with piano players with garters and whatever that was all about. Everybody drove out Route 91 just to gape. Such shapes! Boomerang Modern supports, Palette Curvilinear bars, Hot Shoppe Cantilever roofs and a scalloped swimming pool. Such colors! All the new electrochemical pastels of the Florida littoral: tangerine, broiling magenta, livid pink, incarnadine, fuchsia demure, Congo ruby, methyl green, viridine, acquamarine, phenosafranine, incandescent orange, scarlet-fever purple, cyanic blue, tessellated bronze, hospital-fruit-basket orange. And such signs! Two cylinders rose at either end of the Flamingo—eight stories high and covered from top to bottom with neon rings in the shape of bubbles that fizzed all eight stories up into the desert sky all night long like an illuminated whisky-soda tumbler filled to the brim with pink champagne.

The business history of the Flamingo, on the other hand, was not such a smashing success. For one thing, the gambling operation was losing money at a rate that rather gloriously refuted all the recorded odds of the gaming science. Siegel's backers apparently suspected that he was playing both ends against the middle in collusion with professional gamblers who hung out at the Flamingo as though they had liens on it. What with one thing and another, someone decided by the night of June 20, 1947, that Benny Siegel, lord of the Flamingo, had had it. He was shot to death in Los Angeles.

Yet Siegel's aesthetic, psychological and cultural insights, like Cézanne's, Freud's and Max Weber's, could not die. The Siegel vision and the Siegel aesthetic were already sweeping Las Vegas like gold fever. And there were builders of the West equal to the opportunity. All over Las Vegas the incredible electric pastels were repeated. Overnight the Baroque Modern forms made Las Vegas one of the few architecturally unified cities of the world—the style was Late American Rich—and without the bother and bad humor of a City Council ordinance. No enterprise was too small, too pedestrian or too solemn for The Look. The Supersonic Carwash, the Mercury Jetaway, Gas Vegas Village and Terrible Herbst gasoline stations, the Par-a-Dice Motel, the Palm Mortuary, the Orbit Inn, the Desert Moon, the Blue Onion Drive-In—on it went, like Wildwood, New Jersey, entering Heaven.

*　*　*　*

It is 7:30 A.M. and I am watching five men at a green-topped card table playing poker. They are sliding their Bee-brand cards into their hands and squinting at the pips with a set to the lips like Conrad Veidt in a tunic collar studying a code message from S.S. headquarters. Big Sid Wyman, the old Big-Time gambler from St. Louis, is there, with his eyes looking like two poached eggs engraved with a road map of West Virginia after all night at the poker table. Sixty-year-old Chicago Tommy Hargan is there with his topknot of white hair pulled back over his little pink skull and a mountain of chips in front of his old caved-in sternum. Sixty-two-year-old Dallas Maxie Welch is there, fat and phlegmatic as an Indian Ocean potentate. Two Los Angeles biggies are there exhaling smoke from candela-green cigars into the gloom. It looks like the perfect vignette of every Big Time back room, "athletic club," snooker house and floating poker game in the history of the guys-and-dolls lumpen-bourgeoisie. But what is all this? Off to the side, at a rostrum, sits a flawless little creature with bouffant hair and Stridex-pure skin who looks like she is polished each morning with a rotary buffer. Before her on the rostrum is a globe of coffee on a hot coil. Her sole job is to keep the poker players warmed up with coffee. Meantime, numberless uni-formed lackeys are cocked and aimed about the edges to bring the five Big Timers whatever else they might desire, cigarettes, drinks, napkins, eyeglass-cleaning tissues, plug-in telephones. All around the poker table, at a respectful distance of ten feet, is a fence with the most delicate golden pickets. Upon it, even at this narcolepic hour, lean men and women in their best clothes watching the combat of the titans. The scene is the charmed circle of the casino of the Dunes Hotel. As every-one there knows, or believes, these fabulous men are playing for table stakes of fifteen or twenty thousand dollars. One hundred dollars rides on a chip. Mandibles gape at the progress of the battle. And now Sid Wyman, who is also a vice-president of the Dunes, is at a small escri-toire just inside the golden fence signing a stack of vouchers for such sums as $4500, all printed in the heavy Mondrianesque digits of a Bur-roughs business check-making machine. It is as if America's guys-and-dolls gamblers have somehow been tapped upon the shoulders, knighted, initiated into a new aristocracy.

Las Vegas has become, just as Bugsy Siegel dreamed, the American Monte Carlo—without any of the inevitable upper-class baggage of the Riviera casinos. At Monte Carlo there is still the plush mustiness of the 19th century noble lions—of Baron Bleichroden, a big winner at roulette who always said, "My dear friends, it is so easy on Black." Of Lord Jersey, who won seventeen maximum bets in a row—on black, as a mat-ter of fact—nodded to the croupier, and said, "Much obliged, old sport," took his winnings to England, retired to the country and never gambled again in his life. Or of the old Duc de Dinc who said he could win only in the high-toned Club Privé, and who won very heavily one night, saw two Englishmen gaping at his good fortune, threw them every mille-franc note he had in his hands and said, "Here. Englishmen without money are altogether odious." Thousands of Europeans from the lower orders now have the money to go to the Riviera, but they re-main under the century-old status pall of the aristocracy. At Monte Carlo there are still Wrong Forks, Deficient Accents, Poor Tailoring, Gauche Displays, Nouveau Richness, Cultural Aridity—concepts un-known in Las Vegas. For the grand debut of Monte Carlo as a resort in 1879 the architect Charles Garnier designed an opera house for the

Place du Casino; and Sarah Bernhardt read a symbolic poem. For the debut of Las Vegas as a resort in 1946 Bugsy Siegel hired Abbott and Costello, and there, in a way, you have it all.

◇◇

The Pixie April

Old-timers who revere the memory of such frontier gambling ladies as Madame Moustache and Madame Vestal will rejoice that their tradition goes right on—even if the pixie presented here stops short of long black cheroots and six-guns.

BY IAN ANDERSEN

◇◇

NATURAL CAMOUFLAGE has provided women with the ability to become highly successful twenty-one players—femininity. Women automatically establish a complementary relationship with the exclusively male casino management. Male players must devote considerable attention to establishing warm, compatible relationships, while assiduously avoiding competitiveness and power struggles. Women, on the other hand, are well received from the outset. Casino representatives at all echelons lower their guard and begin to covet the affections of the fairer sex. They naturally fall into the role of wooing, rather than defending. The male wolf defends his territory against a male intruder. But a female intruder is actively sought after and, it is to be hoped, charmed into staying. These sexual roles aptly apply to a strange female entering the casino lair. The inhabitants of the gambling den will curiously sniff the alien female and, if finding her alluring, will actively pursue her in quest of her favors. A clever woman can fan these early sparks of desire and keep them smoldering. She is cautiously flirtatious and extremely feminine, accentuating her assets and minimizing her deficiencies. The courtship has begun and the astute female player is well on her way toward winning a fortune. She can have the dealer, pit boss, and executives all eating out of her hand, while carefully avoiding rivalries among her suitors. At every turn she remains sensual and provocative, soft, warm, and sensitive. She will find acceptance easy. Her entourage of casino personnel will actually go out of its way to facilitate her winning. Remember, Las Vegas is operating on the lower levels of human need— money, sex, and power. These needs are strong motivators for the locals. An attractive woman immediately strikes a sympathetic chord in the sex department. The door is wide open for the would-be female counter, and some are starting to take advantage of their built-in calling card.

April is one of this new breed of female player. At five-feet-one and ninety-eight pounds, she looks like a Kewpie doll. She radiates freshness, with rosy cheeks and bright blue eyes. She is vivacious, bubbly, and her petite nose wrinkles up like a rabbit when she laughs. Although pushing thirty, she still is frequently asked for her I.D. at bars, her girlish looks belying her age. This picture of innocence is a superb twenty-one player! And with the help she gets from dealers and pit bosses, she is a 10-to-1 favorite to win every time she plays!

I met April two years ago in Lake Tahoe. She used to deal black-jack, but had given it up to become a player. She bet $5 to $25, averaging $100 per day. One day she slid into the chair next to me while I was playing. The dealer directed her attention to the $100-minimum sign at the table. She turned to me, eyes pleading, her mouth pursed in a slight pout, and asked me if I would really mind if she played with me. Like many others, I fell into her trap. She looked so hurt and so cute that I had to laugh, my frustration at the interruption rapidly melting. Her nose wrinkled as she giggled, and I had company. But before long my amusement changed to bewilderment. She played perfectly, and within minutes had the pit boss peeking at the dealer's hole card, advising her when to hit and stand. She won $150 while I lost $1,000, and, patting me affectionately on the hand, thanked me for allowing her to play and rose to go. I left too, inviting her to have a drink. "Sure," she said, "you were nice enough to let me play. I'm buying. After all, I'm the big winner," she said with a wink. She was quite guarded about her expertise, but when I opened up first, she responded with alacrity. With the ebullience of a child she explained how she had learned to play blackjack from her old boyfriend, a computer wizard. Together they worked on the blackjack program that she packaged into her pixie style. She practiced counting when she was dealing, and when she had it down pat, quit her job and started playing. She proudly told me that she had made nearly $10,000 in six months and had taken a lot of time off to enjoy life. She lauded the merits of being her own boss and making her own hours. She found this new freedom exhilarating.

I asked April if she had ever been to Las Vegas. She said she hadn't but was just about ready to make a trip. I told her I was on my way there and asked if she would accompany me. I also volunteered to stake her play. We struck a bargain and off we went.

April was just perfect for Vegas. Her cheerleader appearance caught them off guard and in no time she had the old-time casino hands laughing with her. Once again the dealers and pit bosses bent over backward to help her, despite her $100 and $200 bets. During her ten-day stay, she averaged $500 per hour! April had hit the big time! In ten days, her share of the winnings came to nearly $10,000. In a scant ten days she had equaled her earnings of the past six months. Now, adequately financed, she ventured off on her own. Since her Las Vegas debut, I have run into April several times. Each time, she had stacks of green $25 chips in front of her, her face alive with that impish grin, charming her willing hosts.

And Elsewhere

There have been all kinds of them, from the suave clubs and casinos (White's, Brooks's, Monte Carlo), through mammoth, cafeteria-like places such as Harrah's at Lake Tahoe and Reno catering to the great middle class (come and bring the children), to the dismal, nameless honky-tonks in the back streets of cities, and the mining camp joints where a quick gun responded with finality to an ace falling out of an opponent's sleeve. Wherever new territory opened, the gambler was there. In pre-Civil War Chicago—sometimes called the toughest gambling city America ever knew—the gambler was lucky if he was a client of John Sears, the totally decent gambling proprietor noted for his love of Shakespeare. In modern times the gambler may also consider himself on safe ground at the large establishments in Nevada. Allowing for the fact that a gambling house must have a percentage edge to stay in business, there have always been establishments where an investor had a reasonable run for his money. Not, to be sure, at Morrissey's, but at least at those of two others whose enterprises are described herewith.

◇◇

John Morrissey

They don't make them like John Morrissey anymore. and doubtless it's a good thing: the pioneer sharper-thug who could throw a lethal left hook with one hand and a pair of dubious dice with the other. Here he is, at a safe distance.

BY CLYDE BRION DAVIS

THE MOST colorful figure in the history of gambling in America, not even excepting Richard Canfield, was John Morrissey, and John Morrissey was not cut from the same bolt of goods as John Davis and Edward Pendleton. Morrissey was no cultured gentleman and, although in his later years he made a valiant attempt to crash society for his wife's sake, he couldn't make the grade.

Morrissey was a ruffian, a brawling gang leader, a furious rough-and-tumble fighter who didn't learn to read and write until he was grown, a professional pugilist who gained recognition as heavyweight champion of America, a member of Congress and of the New York State Senate, a co-boss of Tammany Hall, a multimillionaire from gambling operations, and an associate of Commodore Cornelius Vanderbilt.

John Morrissey was born in Ireland in 1831 and came to America with his parents in 1834. In Troy, New York, the father devoted himself to raising game cocks and the boy grew up in the streets, becoming the leader of a gang of juvenile delinquents at an early age. He attended school only a few months. Before he was eighteen he had a police record with numerous arrests on charges of burglary, assault and assault with intent to kill. But a sixty-day jail term was his only sentence.

At eighteen Morrissey decided Troy was too small for him and went to New York to become a prize fighter. Slightly under six feet in height, he weighed about 185, with heavy shoulders, deep chest and powerful arms. He swaggered into a downtown saloon frequented by a pugilist called Dutch Charley Duane looking for a fight. Dutch Charley was out but half a dozen other thugs gave the bumptious boy immediate action, beating him to a bloody pulp. However, the young roughneck's fortitude and ferocity impressed the saloonkeeper, and the saloonkeeper was an important Tammany leader named Captain Isaiah Rynders, a refugee from the wrath of vigilantes who had cleaned up Vicksburg. When

Morrissey recovered from his beating, Rynders, who maintained a goon squad, hired him for general thug work and as a runner for a disreputable boardinghouse.

Morrissey acquired the nickname of "Old Smoke" through a battle with another hoodlum named Tom McCann over a Duane Street prostitute named Kate Ridgley. The battlers knocked over a stove and McCann rolled Morrissey into the live coals, setting his clothing afire. That, however, wasn't enough to stop the flaming, smoking Morrissey who went on to whip McCann—and presumably win the favors of the presumably charming Kate.

Old Smoke made his debut both as a professional gambler and prize fighter in San Francisco. Somehow the twenty-year-old hoodlum with the shock of bushy black hair managed to raise enough money in 1851 to answer the call of California gold, although it is not likely he had any thought of pick and shovel work. Some of his New York associates had acquainted him with the method of operating a gaffed faro box, and it was as a faro dealer that Morrissey sought and found his California gold.

Just to keep his hand in, young Morrissey also engaged in free and easy brawling with rough miners and sailors who sometimes questioned inadvisedly the honesty of his faro dealing. He had a local reputation when a blustering giant named George Thompson, known in the professional ring as Pete Crawley's Big One, appeared on the scene. Thompson was calling himself heavyweight champion of California or the Pacific Coast or something, so Morrissey challenged the big fellow for a side bet of $1,000. It was accepted and a purse of $4,000 on a winner-take-all basis was raised.

The fight was held on Mare Island, loosely under the London Prize Ring rules with bare knuckles, of course, and Morrissey won by a knockout in nineteen minutes.

Back in New York in 1853 with plenty of money in his pockets, the twenty-two-year-old Morrissey opened a faro bank and saloon and proclaimed himself heavyweight champion of America on the basis of the one professional fight in California. That claim was not taken too seriously by the sporting gentry, however, because of the presence of a professional called Yankee Sullivan who generally was recognized as titleholder. Yankee Sullivan was a comparatively small man—actually a middleweight weighing 155 pounds—whose real name was James Ambrose and who may or may not have been an escaped convict from Australia.

Ambrose, or Sullivan, had been terribly beaten in 1849 in a championship fight with Tom Hyer. But Hyer retired from the ring in 1850 and

Yankee Sullivan, proprietor of a saloon called the Sawdust House on Walker Street, New York, was accepted as heavyweight champion.

So Old Smoke Morrissey issued a challenge which was accepted, and the old champion Tom Hyer took over as promoter only to run into difficulties. Prize fighting was illegal in most eastern states. A great deal of publicity had been given the proposed match and Hyer was promised immediate arrest for himself and all principals if he attempted to hold the fight at any apparently available spot.

Then Abraham Vosburgh, post master and hotelkeeper at the village of Boston Corners, communicated with Hyer. There were reasons why Boston Corners, about one hundred miles north of New York, would be ideal for the event. Because of faulty surveys, a narrow strip in the Boston Corners area was a no man's land, claimed by Massachusetts, Connecticut and New York State. While the claims were pending, no state would allow another jurisdiction and, consequently, there was no law in the land. It was a place where horse thieves and other outlaws found sanctuary. There would be no interference with the fight at Boston Corners.

* * * *

Sullivan was a scientific boxer, for the day, but he looked very small and inadequate compared with the powerfully built Morrissey. According to the New York *Clipper*, a sports publication of that time, the fight lasted fifty-five minutes and went thirty-seven rounds with Morrissey the winner.

Old Smoke's last professional fight was in October of 1858 at Long Point, Ontario, with John C. Heenan, who later gained international fame from his forty-two-round draw with Tom Sayers in England. Morrissey beat Heenan in twenty-one minutes for a side bet of $5,000, after which he wrote a letter to the New York *Tribune* announcing his retirement from the prize ring. Morrissey (or his ghost writer) declared, "My duties to my family require me to devote my time and efforts to purposes more laudable and advantageous."

So he expanded his gambling business and took a more active part in Tammany politics.

Early in Civil War times (a conflict which Morrissey and his breed took lightly) Old Smoke acquired a famous resort at 8 Barclay Street, which, incidentally, had an uninterrupted run as a gambling house from 1859 to 1902. He had learned from observation of Joe Hall's place how a gambling hall could be operated as a luxurious resort, and Hall, of course, had learned that lesson in Washington from Edward Pendleton. Morrissey's reputation as former heavyweight champion and his growing influence in politics attracted chumps and politicians with fat bank rolls. Old Smoke graduated to a frock coat and diamonds, and in the five years he ran the Barclay place he became a millionaire. Then he sold the house to a former associate named Matt Danser, who also made a fortune fleecing the uptown chumps at faro. Morrissey achieved an ambition by acquiring Joe Hall's palatial resort at 818 Broadway and an interest in another elegant gambling hell at 5 West Twenty-fourth Street.

Hall's extravagance and dissolute living had led the one-time gambling king of New York near the end of the road. He ended his career as a street beggar.

But John Morrissey, the Troy juvenile delinquent, the black-browed brawler, the faro sharper, the ex-champion pugilist, was on the march. He was an efficient ward heeler. No less a person than William M. Tweed, indubitably the most successful and crooked boss in the sometimes odorous history of Tammany Hall, honored Morrissey with an accolade, declaring Old Smoke without a superior as an organizer of repeaters at the polls.

Then Morrissey achieved another ambition. Thirty miles or so above Morrissey's boyhood home was a gathering place of swells called Saratoga Springs. Saratoga represented something special to John Morrissey and he invaded the spa about the same time he acquired the Barclay Street place.

Gambling had been established for some years at Saratoga, but Morrissey was successful with his relatively modest casino on what is now Woodlawn Avenue. Not only did his reputation as former heavyweight champion help him, but Morrissey was growing smart. When reformers started periodical campaigns against him and other crooked gamblers, Old Smoke countered with lavish gifts to various churches, to the town itself and charities—to say nothing of icing politicians and officeholders. So he prospered in Saratoga as well as in New York and built the Saratoga Club House which was declared to be one of the most magnificent casinos in the world and which still enjoyed that status years later when operated by Richard Canfield.

In New York Morrissey permitted no women to enter his gambling houses. At Saratoga they were barred from the gambling rooms but thousands were welcomed and entertained in the Saratoga Club drawing rooms while their menfolk were being sheared inside. He also followed the system of Monte Carlo in allowing no residents of the village to gamble.

There was a small track at Saratoga when Morrissey opened his first casino, but horse racing there was unimportant until he built the track which still is one of the nation's leaders. That did all right, too.

By 1866 John Morrissey was the biggest entrepreneur of gambling in America. In recognition of this distinction as well as his fame as former champion and as a reward for his skillful work in organizing thugs to intimidate voters and carry on crooked balloting, Tammany nominated and elected Old Smoke to Congress. At that time he was thirty-five years old, still an extraordinarily powerful and vigorous man and almost as hot-tempered as in his brawling youth. Always an advocate of direct action, he was somewhat baffled by the wordy battles on the floor of the lower house. To his mind the most telling argument in any debate was a large and hard fist against the jaw and at one point he bellowed a furious challenge to the opposition—he, Old Smoke Morrissey, could and would thrash any ten of the lily-livered so-and-so's on the Republican side who would dare step outside with him. There may have been some thought then that Morrissey was taking in too much territory, that perhaps he could whip five selected Republicans at once, and possibly even seven. But not ten. However, the challenge was not accepted, although they used to elect some pretty lusty boys to the House of Representatives in those days.

By the end of his first term in Congress Morrissey had grown so arrogant that he grumbled over taking instructions even from Boss Tweed, but he was re-elected for a second term. The breach widened, however, and finally Tammany expelled him for insubordination. Then Old Smoke became a leader in the fight to oust Tweed and when this objective was attained, "Honest John" Morrissey was right-hand man to "Honest John" Kelly who succeeded Tweed. That is, he was until he quarreled with Kelly and was once more expelled from Tammany.

From then on Morrissey was a bitter enemy of Tammany Hall and was elected twice to the State Senate on an anti-Tammany ticket. In Albany all Old Smoke needed to know about a bill was Tammany's position. If Tammany was for it he was against it. And violently so.

Of the millions Morrissey took in from his various gambling houses, only $75,000 was left when he died at age forty-seven of pneumonia.

At Saratoga he had become acquainted with Commodore Cornelius Vanderbilt and was immensely flattered by Vanderbilt's advice on financial affairs. As Morrissey took the chumps at faro, so he was taken by the stock market. He lost half a million in one day alone—the Black Friday of 1869.

Morrissey had little trouble with the police. Mostly, he owned them. But apparently he believed in being prepared for raids. The place at 818 Broadway was raided several times after Morrissey sold it to a syndicate of sharpers. The officers found a number of well-dressed gentlemen sitting around the club chatting or perhaps playing chess or whist, but no gambling paraphernalia or evidence of gambling. The mystery wasn't solved until 1900 when workmen discovered a between-the-walls vault and a trick door that opened from a seemingly solid brick wall. On a tip that a raid was coming, the gambling layouts were simply shoved into the vault to remain until after the baffled raiders departed.

On Old Smoke's death, two of his New York associates, Albert Spencer and Charles Reed, took over operation of the Saratoga Club House and race track. Reed returned to New York after a few years and in 1893 Spencer took in as partner in the Club House a man whose name was to become practically a synonym for gambling—Richard Albert Canfield.

◇◇◇

Canfield's Creation

All through the literature of American gambling late in the last century and early in this one you find him called The Prince of Gamblers, and by most accounts the title was a just one—unless you accept Nick the Greek's dictum that a casino proprietor is not a gambler in the real sense, because in the long run he cannot lose. Richard Canfield himself said as much. Still, he typifies the golden day of chance as our forebears knew it: the unquestionably honest man who never welshed, whose establishments were elegant and serene, who was a connoisseur of art and a student of the classics.

BY L. J. LUDOVICI

◇◇◇

IT IS a relief to leave aside gangsters with their killings and sluggings and revert to earlier times in New York, to perhaps the last of the grand-scale promoters of gambling. His name was Richard A. Canfield. He again was in the tradition of Davis and Pendleton. His houses were said to have surpassed all others in luxury and magnificence. Play at his tables was 'higher than anywhere else in the world.' Canfield did not use his position to become involved in politics or to try to pull strings. He was quite content to pass over the protection-money necessary to buy off both politicians and police in order to assure for himself an undisturbed life. Canfield was emphatic that he never stooped to crooked methods. 'The percentage in favour of a gambling-house is sufficient to guarantee the house all the profit it wants,' he said. The only thing needed to make sure the house would win was time. Let the gambler keep on playing and the house had to keep on winning. There is absolutely no doubt that the good gaming-house proprietor runs the one kind of business in the world which need not sustain loss. Losses occur through defects in the character of the promoter. John Scarne, the renowned American card-manipulator, who, at the request of the War Department, helped to protect soldiers from crooked gambling-promoters and gamblers during World War II, echoes Canfield's view. There need not be any occasion for cheating, he maintains, since professional establishments operate on a percentage basis which makes it impossible for a patron to win in the long run. In some houses the percentage basis is such that any hope whatsoever of the patron winning is shut out.

Canfield was the son of a printer of New Bedford, Massachusetts, and like many gamblers got a taste for his calling when he was still only a boy. By the time he was eighteen he owned a small Poker-room in Providence, Rhode Island. He made enough money to visit Europe and to see for himself how Europeans managed their gambling. He spent some time at Monte Carlo, but did not win much. However, he insisted that he learned while abroad the single lesson that matters so far as the promoter of gambling is concerned: in the long run the only winner in any so-called game of chance is the man who holds the bank. Canfield had little formal education, but took the trouble to instruct himself by ceaseless reading. Meanwhile, he ran another Poker-room, serving coffee and sandwiches to the players. It is highly characteristic that he bought only the best coffee and the best available bread and filling for the sandwiches. Good food and refined living were his passions. To these he added, as he grew richer, a love of art. He had an absolute horror of flashiness and dressed expensively but discreetly. He was doing very nicely as a gambling-promoter in Providence, Rhode Island, when the police moved in and he served a short jail sentence.

Canfield left for New York in 1886, convinced that only in a big city could he build for himself a really great reputation according to a policy he had long ago decided upon. He started small by running a Poker-room on borrowed capital, but saw it would lead him nowhere. He borrowed once more and opened up in the more exclusive neighborhood of the Delmonico and Madison Square. The site was within easy reach of some of the leading hotels, from where he hoped for customers.

His gaming-house may justifiably be called his 'creation'; rarely had anything like it been seen before, and it was a long march from the garish establishments to which most gamblers usually resorted. In 1890 Canfield bought out his partner and embarked on his amazing career. By 1899 he had several houses, the most famous of them the Saratoga in East Forty-Fourth Street. On this luxurious establishment he is said to have lavished over 1,000,000 dollars. It was full of wonderful Chippendale chairs, peach-blow vases, Chinese porcelain, pictures, etchings and bronzes. The walls were hung with tapestries. One private gaming-room had teak flooring and its walls were lined with Spanish leather, hand-tooled in gold. His own private office contained white mahogany furniture, inlaid with mother-of-pearl. For security he had two entrance doors fitted which opened by electricity. Every evening, sharp at eleven, suppers of the finest quality were served, prepared by chefs on the premises. Cigars at a dollar apiece, and wines and liqueurs from a cellar full of the rarest vintages, were provided with the food—at no cost to his clients.

In 1902 Canfield took over the Club House at Saratago and built an Italian garden which cost several hundred thousand dollars. It was regarded in its day as both charming and beautiful. He also installed a dining-room in which, for the first time in America, indirect lighting was used. The restaurant was one of the truly great eating-places of the world, comparable with the finest in France. Food and service were unequalled anywhere. He paid his French chef 5,000 dollars for the season and during the off-season sent him to Europe to discover new dishes and new ideas for improving upon perfection. These expeditions Canfield himself financed.

Roulette was the chief source of his income. The fixed percentage of 5–6 per cent in favour of the house disposed of the big overheads. In two years Canfield made 1,500,000 dollars. Yet he had to pay protection money to policemen and politicians. In those days policemen owned yachts and country estates, and politicians retired to lives of luxury. One particular policeman, for example, controlled all the gambling in the Tenderloin district. He was an extraordinary man with an extraordinary philosophy: 'There's more law at the end of a policeman's nightstick,' he believed firmly, 'than in any decision of the Supreme Court.' At any rate he made a fortune.

In his best days Canfield baffled strangers who tried to guess what he was. Critic? Man of letters? Financier? He was a friend of Whistler and bought a number of his pictures. Whistler painted his portrait. Canfield rose every day between six and seven in the morning and had a light breakfast. He next studied his post and went for a regular stroll. He often dined at Delmonico's, where he tended to over-eat rich foods and over-drink splendid wines. By the time he retired to bed at midnight he was often in a jumbled state of mind. Day after day he read through Gibbon's *Decline and Fall of the Roman Empire*, which was a book he adored. He had forty suits in his wardrobe and fifteen pairs of shoes. He never gambled (except on the stock market), and his employees were under the strictest orders never to gamble. He did not hesitate to inform gamblers that they could not possibly win against the bank. He advised those who could not afford it on no account to play.

Canfield attracted to his gaming-house a group of the most reckless gamblers in the history of America. Many of them were millionaires and multi-millionaires who were ready to plunge in with sums of the kind few people earned in their whole lives. The group included Reggie Vanderbilt, Phil Dwyer, the 'racetrack king', and John W. [Bet a Million] Gates, who had made a gigantic fortune through his operations with the American Steel and Wire Company and the U.S. Steel Corporation.

◇◆◇

Tex Rickard

To Americans of the 1920s Tex Rickard was the supreme sports promoter of the time, the man responsible for the first million-dollar gate in prizefight history (the Dempsey-Carpentier heavyweight title bout in 1921). However, nothing about him surprised those who knew him in gold-rush Alaska in the 1890s, where life itself was a gamble. He won and lost there, but above all he learned—not only about gambling but the virtues of honesty.... With a hometown friend from Henrietta, Texas, he arrived in Juneau in 1895, two years before the Klondike strike. We first see him here when after crossing the perilous Chilkoot Pass, he comes to Circle City, a charming town boasting twenty-eight saloons and dance halls.

BY **CHARLES SAMUELS**

◇◆◇

TEX WAS stone-broke when he finally stumbled into this strange town. He lost no time getting himself a job in Sam Bonnifield's gambling shack. Rickard told Bonnifield that he intended to go out prospecting for gold as soon as he got together a decent-sized stake for himself.

And that was the day that Tex—in that fairy-tale sort of town, fittingly enough—walked through the invisible door into that all-male, never-never land in which he spent the rest of his life. For no one is more of a fantasist than the professional gambler, a man forever lost if he once admits there is a tomorrow.

Sam Bonnifield, the Yukon gold rush's most famous gambler, was then thirty, a tall, slim, handsome, quiet-spoken man. He was originally from West Viriginia, but had worked for a few years at his trade in the Kansas cowtowns before going on to the North. Westbrook Pegler, who met him thirty-one years later in Chicago at the second Dempsey-Tunney fight, described him as a "quiet, almost deferential old man whose eyes were fascinating . . . so blue and clear and unfaded . . ."

For better or for worse, Rickard accepted Bonnifield as his model. And the West Virginian was that incongruity in the profession, an honest man, the fact being that honest professional gamblers are rare enough to be regarded as freaks.

To be this sort of gambler requires other qualities besides the gift for sensing ahead of others the ever-changing tides of luck, sometimes rhythmical, sometimes not. The gambler must have the oxlike sort of patience to wait for the rumble inside his head that calls the turn. He has to peel off emotion from his thinking, to concentrate as though there was nothing on earth but these cards or dice or spinning roulette wheel, and the men around him.

All that, and whatever else an honest gambler requires to win like a man and lose like a champion, Tex Rickard had.

As a crooked blackjack dealer in a southern California beach town said recently, "Good Christ! It is hard enough to make a living at this racket cheating. I'd starve to death if I ever started playing on the level."

Tex also got the curious idea in Circle City that all business should and could be run in much the same way as Jack McQuesten ran his trading post there. McQuesten, a huge and hearty man with a large blond mustache, had been trading with Indian fur trappers up and down the Yukon for a quarter-century when Tex first met him. Before coming to the valley, the middle-aged McQuesten had survived enough adventures to fill a half-dozen action-crammed novels, first as a boy sailing before the mast, then as a young frontiersman fighting in Oregon's Indian wars.

His partner, Al Mayo, who began life as a circus acrobat, had charge of the steamboat end of their business. Between them, they established most of the fur-trading posts on the river—Fort Reliance, Forty Mile, and Fort Yukon. As commission agents for the Alaska Commercial Company, McQuesten and Mayo held what amounted to a monopoly on all the pre-gold-rush business done in the valley with Indians and early mining prospectors.

McQuesten worked on the theory that every man was honest, and gave credit to all comers. Occasionally a prospector he had grubstaked a year before would come to his trading post to explain that though he had enough gold dust to pay off he had not been on a spree for months. Jack always understood that. "Go have your spree," he'd say, "and pay me whatever you have left."

Sometimes the miner, with head hung low, would return a few days later to say he had been having such a great binge he'd used up all his gold dust. McQuesten's answer to that was, "All right, now let's get together the stuff you need for next year. But when you come back I'll have to have *something* on your bill."

It is unusual to find a book about the Klondike that fails to describe both the love of the Indians for McQuesten, and his famous thermometer. The thermometer consisted of four vials, standing side by side in a rack. The first held quicksilver, the second whiskey, the third kerosene, the fourth "Perry Davis Pain Killer."

They froze in that order.

When the patent medicine named for Mr. Davis started turning solid, everybody ran to his cabin, leaped into his bunk with all his clothes on, and piled everything but the door and his Yukon stove on top of him.

Working in Sam Bonnifield's Circle City shack, Tex began getting his basic training in high-powered gambling almost immediately. During his first week there, he did everything from running the craps table to sweeping up. He also watched the West Virginian deal a card in a faro game on which $10,000 was riding. Louis (Goldie) Golden, another no-limit gambler, had bet $5,000 bucking the tiger, on the queen.

Faro, long the most popular gambling game in America, is almost as simple to play as Old Maid. This, however, is not the reason it has vanished from gambling houses from coast to coast. It is also the game which gives the customer the closest to a fifty-fifty chance of winning. In betting $5,000 in gold dust on the queen, Goldie Golden was wagering that whenever that pasteboard lady appeared in a turn, it would be the second of the pair of cards Bonnifield, the dealer, would draw from the box. If the queen came out first, the house would win.

The queen, when one was finally dealt, turned up second, winning $5,000 in gold dust for Goldie. Bonnifield did not even look up. "Tex," he called over to Rickard at the table, "if Goldie is quitting, pay him off. Five thousand dollars comes to a little over nineteen pounds and a half in dust. Oh, hell, give him an even twenty pounds!"

"Who's quittin'?" demanded Goldie in a hurt voice, and took the pay-off in yellow, hundred-dollar chips. Before he left, at four o'clock the next morning, he had lost the $5,000, and $17,000 more.

Three nights later Tex saw Bonnifield lose $72,000 in gold dust, and the gambling shack as well, in a poker game. Sam was about to turn over the premises to the winner when a friend came in with a couple of heavy gold pokes which he put at Bonnifield's disposal. In six hours Bonnifield had his fortune and shack back, and also had cleaned out the customer.

If Rickard did not bring Sam Bonnifield good luck, the West Virginian thought he did. Within a month after Tex started to work for him, Bonnifield had enough gold dust on hand to buy the biggest, flashiest-looking place in town. In a typical gambler's gesture he turned over to Tex his old shack, its craps and roulette tables, chips, cards, and stock of liquor.

When the astonished Rickard asked why Bonnifield was doing that for him, Sam said, "You're a born gambler, Tex, and I think you'll stay an honest one." And he held out his smooth-as-silk hands, adding, "Look at these hands, my young friend. They are my tools. When you first came to work for me you said something about going prospecting after a while. After you got a stake, I think was the way you put it.

"I got only one thing to say about that: Either be a gold miner or a gambler. You can't be both. No man's hands can do rough work and handle cards or dice as a gambler has to every day. With hands like mine a man can concentrate on the game because his hands work almost by themselves."

For the rest of his life Tex Rickard gambled as though Sam Bonnifield were looking over his shoulder. But he didn't yet know his percentages as well as he thought he did.

In less than two weeks he lost the gambling house Bonnifield had given him. Tex shook hands with the customer who had won it, wished him luck. Then he put on his fur parka, walked down the street to Sam's fancy new joint, and asked Bonnifield for his old job back. Sam put him behind the bar.

The old sourdoughs agree that Tex was a good man behind the bar, but a better man in front of it. "Great talker," they say. "Sure had the gift of gab, that feller." Of course, no greater tribute could be paid to Rickard's genius for listening. Whenever you run into survivors of the gold rush who knew Tex, you will hear that same thing. Nothing can persuade them that this was merely because he had hung on their every word with such utterly intense absorption in the joints of Circle City, Dawson, Rampart, and Nome.

(ED. NOTE: *In the company of Harry Ash, a fellow bartender, his next stop was Dawson City. There, Tex, having sold his share in two Klon-*

dike claims, teamed up with a Juneau friend, Tom Turner, to operate the first of his Northern saloons.)

When they got to Dawson, at the junction of the Klondike and the Yukon rivers, they found a booming tent town that was already bigger than Circle City. In a few days they had their place up, furnished with gambling equipment and supplied with liquor. Tex named it "The Northern."

From the day The Northern opened, the partners did a land-office business. After four months they had $155,000 in the till.

But one night a half-dozen prospectors from Circle came in and started playing roulette. They concentrated on Nos. 17 and 23, and also played the middle twelve numbers, 13 to 24. The newcomers couldn't seem to do anything wrong. It was just one of those nights.

"Whenever they lost they just piled on more dust and told us to roll the ball," Rickard said. "We rolled ourselves right out of house and home that night. At the same time other customers were taking us good at faro. I'd put the fifty-seven thousand dollars I had left over from my Bonanza-strike money into that place, along with plenty of Turner's dough. That night we lost the whole joint, and every nickel we had in the world."

When Tex walked out of his Dawson gambling house that night he didn't have a place to sleep. And, as he said, it was getting colder.

Tex spent the next fifteen months working as a twenty-dollar-a-day bartender, faro dealer, and front man in various Dawson pleasure palaces. During most of that time he was a fixture at the Monte Carlo. This was a combined saloon, gambling house, and theater which "Swiftwater Bill" Gates had started. Whenever asked what the limit was at his gambling tables, Swiftwater Bill, the Klondike's most celebrated spendthrift, would cry gleefully, "The sky's the limit, boys. Tear the roof off."

Harry Ash and a partner named Manning had taken over the place by the time Tex got his job there. Under Ash and Manning there was a limit on bets. Unless coaxed and pleaded with, they held players down to $1,000 per throw at their craps table. They also discouraged poker pots that ran over the $5,000 mark.

As far as Tex's worldly education was concerned those fifteen months were the most important of his career. Though he was drawing down $20 a day, Tex often went to bed hungry. Even in a red-hot boom town like Dawson this is not easy for anyone except a professional gambler to do so frequently. But Tex stubbornly kept betting every grain of gold dust he was paid—there was no other currency in circulation in Dawson —on faro, and the cards kept refusing to be good to him.

Rickard's year and a quarter of uninterrupted insolvency included the summer when crooked gamblers in force swept into Dawson with the successive waves of gold rushers. And they all seemed to be making money hand over fist. The Royal Canadian Northwest Mounted Police did their best to stop the use of loaded dice, shaved or pricked cards, and fixed faro boxes. But a crooked gambler can operate quite efficiently without these gimmicks when he has to. He can shuffle a deck ten times, have it cut by the sucker ten times, and still throw the fifty-two cards out in the precise order he wishes to. Being what he was, Tex Rickard, even while surrounded by larceny in Dawson, remained both honest and also true to his Westerner's code of live and let live. If he was shocked or even disturbed by the constant swindling that went on nightly in the various places where he worked, he never betrayed it.

(ED. NOTE: *But a born gambler never quits, and when a place called Nome began to boom, Tex and Jim White, an old customer of his ill-fated Dawson resort, established the second and legendary Northern.*)

Sports historians agree that Tex Rickard's promotion of the 1921 fandango called the Dempsey-Carpentier fight was his most brilliant operation.

Viewed in retrospect, however, it seems no more remarkable than his pyramiding of a $21 bankroll—it had shrunk to that before he got to Nome—into a half-ownership in The Northern there that brought him $100,000 during its first year, and $500,000 altogether in the four years he retained a big piece of the place.

Few famous men ever hit their stride under more confusing circumstances. A conflict which at times verged on massed combat had erupted there even before Tex, his partner, and his partner's indispensable tent arrived. During the previous fall three miners from Golovin Bay, sixty miles away, had investigated reports of gold deposits along the creeks there.

When the reports turned out to be true, forty men staked out, against all existing territorial laws, a mineral empire for themselves, covering twenty-five square miles in the peninsula's southeast corner. They named this the Cape Nome Mining District.

But all winter long miners, hearing rumors of the strike, streamed in from all parts of the valley, mostly in teams of two driving dog sleds. By May, the month before Tex's arrival, there were 250 of these seasoned old sourdoughs, angrily disputing the ownership rights of the original forty pioneers to the entire gold-loaded area.

They had held miners' meetings to declare the rights vacated, but these were broken up by a detachment of soldiers sent over from the fort at Saint Michael. The miners resented the military interference, but there were no civil authorities they could appeal to. They had taken to guarding their claims back in the hills with their Winchesters.

Civil strife, as one observer put it, was threatening to break out at any moment. If it did, it would be armed conflict under weather conditions that would make Valley Forge seem a June picnic on the Vassar campus.

Mother Nature really outdid herself in the matter of disagreeableness at Nome, which was without a harbor and unprotected from the sea in any other way. Its beach was battered most of the year with everything from driftwood and ice floes 30 feet high, blood-chilling blasts that came bowling in from the Bering Sea and Siberia, and an occasional tidal wave.

The driftwood on the beach—tangled up with every sort of debris the frozen sea had cast up—was the only wood in sight. Back of the beach lay endless soggy tundras, treeless as any desert.

And even during the ice-free months, Nome was no beauty spot. Torrential summer rains drenched it almost daily, converting the sponge-like tundra into quagmire as treacherous as Dawson's Front Street in mid-July.

But it was in this most inhospitable corner of God's good earth that Rickard made his first great parlay of luck and opportunity. Tex's first bit of luck lay in getting to Nome while there were only a few dozen tents up. These were strung along the sand spit lying between the open sea and the narrow Snake River.

If Tex and his partner had arrived a few weeks later they would have been unable to get a good lot for their tent. As it was, they were able to buy one for $100 on Front Street, Nome's pleasure-house and business street, with a few dollars' option money.

Then, the day after getting to Nome, Rickard went down to the beach to find wood for the tent's floor. Everything there was hopelessly messed up with other debris.

But at the beach he saw a man unloading planks from a raft, and asked if he could spare enough for the tent floor. The man looked him over, rubbed his chin, and said, "Well, I am going to leave this wood here. Suppose you just pick out what you want and use it?"

Tex said that he and his partner were a little short of cash at the moment. "Why, you can take what you need and pay for it later," the man told him.

Tex thanked him and got Jim White down there in a hurry. In two days they had hammered together a good solid floor. Tex told Jim White, "I reckon I'll go visiting down at the beach again. Might find another friendly feller who has his helping hand out."

That day he saw a boat unloading whisky, wine, and brandy. As Tex explained to his partner later, "When I told the feller we had a tent with enough room to store them he seemed mighty grateful."

"All right," the man had replied, "you store the stuff for me. And if you want to use any of it, just keep tab on it, and we can settle next time I come back to Nome."

The next man Tex met was George Murphy, a cigar salesman. He was taken in as a partner on the strength of his panatelas and a modest bankroll.

Five days later, on July 4, Rickard staged his grand opening of The Northern in Nome. "We sold whisky at fifty cents a drink," said Tex, "and the roulette wheel and the faro bank opened under proper auspices. Miners came in from miles around. That was a gala day in my life and also a big day in the social life of Nome. Our gross receipts, at the bar alone, were $935 on opening day.

"I was working behind the bar and one of my first customers that day was an old fellow with long whiskers. He came up to me and said, 'Fill 'em up, boy!' and he waved to the crowd, meanin' he wanted to buy drinks for the house.

"All drinks were fifty cents a throw, and you could have whisky, gin, brandy, or wine. The old man slapped a small poke on the bar and untied the string. 'Weigh her up,' he said, 'and let's have another one.' The tab for them two rounds came to about fifty dollars. I weighed his poke for him. He had more than five pounds of gold dust in that little poke, which come to nearly twelve hundred dollars. When that prospector went out, he said, 'Put the rest of it away for me, boy.' Now he had never seed me before, remember. That was the way we did business up there then in Alaska.

"Business kept on being so strong during that week or two that White sold out his piece of the business for ten thousand dollars ten days after we opened.

"But that old man, the first to leave his poke with me in my Nome place, never come back. He went into the mountains, or up some creek. We never heard of him again. Very few prospectors ever left an address. Sometimes they didn't even leave their names on their pokes."

One night Tex watched a bearded old sourdough go up to his bartender and after a short conversation walk away. The old man retired to a bench and sat there, holding his head between his hands.

"What did he want?" Tex asked the bartender.

"He's broke, and he asked for another free drink. I gave him two already."

"And you turned him down, did you?" asked Tex. Giving the bartender a disgusted look, Rickard walked over to the prospector. "What's the matter, old-timer, haven't you got any money?"

"Nope—flat broke. Lost it all last night, I reckon."

"No, you're not broke," Rickard told him. "I've got your gold. You gave it to me last night to put in the safe."

Tex found the poke and handed it to him. The prospector had three or four thousand dollars worth of gold dust in it but had forgotten all about it.

"He was a very grateful old man," explained Tex. "It would have been all the same if it hadn't been there. He didn't know and never would have kicked. In a few minutes he was buying for the house again. Finally he wandered out into the cold.

"Six months later the old man came in and he was worth two hundred thousand dollars. He had made one of the strikes. Yes, and he left a lot of *that* with me, too."

Tex seemed to take as much pride in the trust the miners placed in him as in his gambling saloon's success. Incidentally, The Northern was the only saloon never held up in that lawless town.

As the cynical [Wilson] Mizner remarked, "You can't write off the fact that there were many desperate and vicious men in Nome that winter. Yet, in these surroundings Rickard was a man who could be trusted under all conditions. His back bar was always piled with miners' pokes. No other place parked so many pokes filled with gold, but Rickard's place never was raided though the others were held up right along. Gold on Rickard's back bar was like gold in the bank. In fact, Rickard was Nome's banker."

Those Were the Days

Of the company to be found here, as writers and characters, Bret Harte and Mark Twain knew each other well—all too well, as Mark Twain was to recall bitterly long after their first meeting in San Francisco. But you find yourself believing that Elijah Skaggs and Madame Moustache would have understood each other at once, and that Madame Moustache and Madame Vestal would have recognized each other's skills immediately and respected them accordingly.

In a San Francisco
Gambling Saloon

The young Bret Harte was scarcely the bohemian indicated by the title
of his paper "Bohemian Days in San Francisco" from which this account
of his gambling debut is excerpted. Nevertheless, it remains among
the most delightful of his writings, together with others in *Under the
Redwoods*, published in 1901, the year before his death.

BY **BRET HARTE**

PERHAPS FROM my Puritan training I experienced a more fearful joy
in the gambling saloons. They were the largest and most comfortable,
even as they were the most expensively decorated rooms in San Francisco. Here again the gravity and decorum which I have already alluded
to were present at that earlier period—though perhaps from concentration of another kind. People staked and lost their last dollar with
a calm solemnity and a resignation that was almost Christian. The
oaths, exclamations, and feverish interruptions which often character-
ized more dignified assemblies were absent here. There was no room
for the lesser vices; there was little or no drunkenness; the gaudily
dressed and painted women who presided over the wheels of fortune or
performed on the harp and piano attracted no attention from those
ascetic players. The man who had won ten thousand dollars and the
man who had lost everything rose from the table with equal silence
and imperturbability. *I* never witnessed any tragic sequel to those
losses; *I* never heard of any suicide on account of them. Neither can I
recall any quarrel or murder directly attributable to this kind of gambling. It must be remembered that these public games were chiefly
rouge et noir, monté, faro, or *roulette,* in which the antagonist was
Fate, Chance, Method, or the impersonal "bank," which was supposed
to represent them all; there was no individual opposition or rivalry;
nobody challenged the decision of the "croupier," or dealer.

I remember a conversation at the door of one saloon which was as
characteristic for its brevity as it was a type of the prevailing stoicism.
"Hello!" said a departing miner, as he recognized a brother miner
coming in, "when did you come down?" "This morning," was the
reply. "Made a strike on the bar?" suggested the first speaker. "You
bet!" said the other, and passed in. I chanced an hour later to be at the

same place as they met again—their relative positions changed. "Hello! What now?" said the incomer. "Back to the bar." "Cleaned out?" "You bet!" Not a word more explained a common situation.

My first youthful experience at those tables was an accidental one. I was watching roulette one evening, intensely absorbed in the mere movement of the players. Either they were so preoccupied with the game, or I was really older looking than my actual years, but a by-stander laid his hand familiarly on my shoulder, and said, as to an ordinary *habitué*, "Ef you're not chippin' in yourself, pardner, s'pose you give *me* a show." Now I honestly believe that up to that moment I had no intention, nor even a desire, to try my own fortune. But in the embarrassment of the sudden address I put my hand in my pocket, drew out a coin, and laid it, with an attempt at carelessness, but a vivid consciousness that I was blushing, upon a vacant number. To my horror I saw that I had put down a large coin—the bulk of my possessions! I did not flinch, however; I think any boy who reads this will understand my feeling; it was not only my coin but my manhood at stake. I gazed with a miserable show of indifference at the players, at the chandelier —anywhere but at the dreadful ball spinning round the wheel. There was a pause; the game was declared, the rake rattled up and down, but still I did not look at the table. Indeed, in my inexperience of the game and my embarrassment, I doubt if I should have known if I had won or not. I had made up my mind that I should lose, but I must do so like a man, and, above all, without giving the least suspicion that I was a greenhorn. I even affected to be listening to the music. The wheel spun again; the game was declared, the rake was busy, but I did not move. At last the man I had displaced touched me on the arm and whispered, "Better make a straddle and divide your stake this time." I did not understand him, but as I saw he was looking at the board, I was obliged to look, too. I drew back dazed and bewildered! Where my coin had lain a moment before was a glittering heap of gold.

My stake had doubled, quadrupled, and doubled again. I did not know how much then—I do not know now—it may have been not more than three or four hundred dollars—but it dazzled and frightened me. "Make your game, gentlemen," said the croupier monotonously. I thought he looked at me—indeed, everybody seemed to be looking at me—and my companion repeated his warning. But here I must again appeal to the boyish reader in defense of my idiotic obstinacy. To have taken advice would have shown my youth. I shook my head—I could not trust my voice. I smiled, but with a sinking heart, and let my stake remain. The ball again sped round the wheel, and stopped. There was a pause. The croupier indolently advanced his rake and swept my whole pile with others into the bank! I had lost it all. Perhaps it may be difficult for me to explain why I actually felt relieved, and even to some extent triumphant, but I seemed to have asserted my grown-up independence—possibly at the cost of reducing the number of my meals for days; but what of that! I was a man! I wish I could say that it was a lesson to me. I am afraid it was not. It was true that I did not gamble again, but then I had no especial desire to—and there was no temptation. I am afraid it was an incident without a moral. Yet it had one touch characteristic of the period which I like to remember. The man who had spoken to me, I think, suddenly realized, at the moment of my disastrous coup, the fact of my extreme youth. He moved toward the banker, and leaning over him whispered a few words. The banker looked up, half impatiently, half kindly—his hand straying tentatively toward the pile of coin. I instinctively knew what he meant, and, summoning my determination, met his eyes with all the indifference I could assume, and walked away.

◇◇

Madame Vestal

The moral here? Obviously, as the charming Madame Vestal learned, it is simply that romance and the roulette wheel are uneasy companions. An eminent, sometime Confederate spy really should have known better.

BY FORBES PARKHILL

◇◇

DENVER WAS a lusty, wide-open, free-spending young frontier city in 1876. Born of the Pikes Peak gold rush, nurtured on the wealth pouring from the mines of the richest square mile on earth at Central City, it had been transformed from a boom town to a boom city by the coming of the Kansas Pacific Railroad six years earlier. The resultant real estate and building boom yielded a golden harvest equal to anything produced up to that time by the nearby gold diggings.

This brave, new, Western world boasted some of America's most extraordinary characters, bad and not so bad. Of the most colorful many were denizens of the frontier's bold and brash new underworld.

Bad and better alike, they had plenty of money and no lack of ways to spend it. If one tired of spending it for real estate or mining stocks, there was always whisky. Or one could go down amid the red lights of Holladay Street, the wickedest street in the West's most sinful city, and spend his money on women.

And then, of course, there was Madame Vestal.

Soft-spoken Ed Chase, steely of eye and prematurely gray, was king of the gamblers, and Madame Vestal, dainty, dark of eye, and black of hair, was the Goddess of Chance. She held forth in a huge tent on Blake Street and it was a positive delight to lose one's money to her, for she was accounted the most adept twenty-one dealer west of the Mississippi.

"Cards, gentlemen?" she would inquire gently in a cultivated voice sweetened by a soft Southern accent that seemed to breathe of the atmosphere of a plantation drawing room.

And when a bearded player would examine his hand and call, "Hit me, ma'am," she'd flip him another card with skill born of long practice—and smile. Smile faintly, a Mona Lisa wisp of a smile, a smile hinting of intriguing mystery.

It was this enigmatic smile that set her apart from all other professional gamblers, whose stock-in-trade is the frozen face. It set her apart from her own permanent employees, the impassive Fancy Dans who kept case at the faro bank, dealt stud, threw monte, spun the wheel, or tipped the keno goose. They were her trusted aides, the ones she had brought with her from yon side of the River. Her cappers and shills and ropers-in were local folk.

The young madame's flashing brown eyes were as unreadable as her wisp of a smile. Many an uncouth miner, fresh from the diggings, would have given all the dust in his poke to fathom their mystery.

None tried. In pioneer Denver one never questioned another about his —or her—past. Those who violated this quaint Western custom sometimes died abruptly, for many boomers, male and female, had had compelling reasons to leave their real names on the east bank of the Missouri. There, in her early thirties, Madame Vestal had left her real name, a famous name, a name every player in the gambling hell would have recognized. In fact, the good madame was in habit of changing her name every time she changed towns.

Madame Vestal's establishment included, as a matter of course, a bar, a temporary affair of rough planking; for to follow the booms she was prepared to fold her tent and move her equipment on a moment's notice. But in one respect her place was unlike any of the Blake Street gambling hells; it was a place for men without women.

She employed no feminine ropers-in, with their sweet talk, low necks, short skirts, and spangles. She was not like Katie Fulton and Minnie Clifford and Lizzie Preston and other madames of Holladay Street for, as perhaps her name was intended to indicate, Madame Vestal had nothing to sell but the chance to win something for nothing, plus the customary refreshments. Moreover, her games were reputed to be on the square.

All manner of men thronged through the madame's gaming establishment, so it is remotely possible that someone might have recognized her—someone from Jefferson City, Missouri, who had been a guest at the society debut, shortly after her graduation from the Female University at Lexington, of the charming young kinswoman of Missouri's last governor before the Civil War. Or one of the dashing young junior officers attached to the headquarters of Union generals H. W. Halleck and Newton M. Curtis; the young men who had escorted her to box parties at De Bar's Opera House at St. Louis and had lost their hearts and some of the Union's most vital military secrets.

For the name that Madame Vestal had left behind her on the eastern bank of the Missouri was the name of the celebrated Confederate spy, Belle Siddons.

In December, 1862, General Curtis ordered her arrest as a spy. She fled on horseback but was captured near Ste. Genevieve. Documentary evidence of her activities was found on her person, and she was taken back to St. Louis. The petite prisoner confessed her guilt to General John M. Schofield, boasting that she had kept Confederate generals Nathan B. Forrest and Sterling Price informed of every movement planned at Union headquarters.

"I was the one," she proclaimed defiantly, "who provided the information enabling Forrest to cut off Grant's troops by his raid on the Memphis & Mobile railroad."

Sentenced to the Grant Street rebel prison, she speedily exerted her charms on the provost marshal. After keeping her prisoner for four months, he released her on condition she leave the state.

After the war she returned to Jefferson City, where she made use of her charms by becoming a lobbyist. There she met and married Dr. Newt Hallett of Kansas City, an army surgeon. The couple went to Texas, where he instructed her in the study of medicine and taught her dissection. When he died of yellow fever, she became for a time a tutor at the Red Cloud Indian Agency, and subsequently a skilled twenty-one dealer in a gambling house at Wichita. Later she operated her own gambling establishments at Ellsworth, Fort Hays, and Cheyenne. The winter of '75–76 found her in Denver, operating her tented gambling hell under the name of Madame Vestal.

Meanwhile, in 1874, gold had been discovered in the Black Hills of South Dakota. The Indians objected to the appropriation of their lands by gold-seekers but, as usual, they finally were ejected, and their lands were thrown open to the whites.

By the winter of '75–76, Denver was almost depopulated of its boomers. The click of the roulette wheel in Madame Vestal's canvas Palace of Chance became more and more infrequent, and the twenty-one table no longer resounded to the sucker's cry of "Hit me again, ma'am." One by one her cappers and shills deserted her, victims of the gold fever.

The enterprising madame was prepared for just such an emergency. She bought a freight wagon to transport her tent, her gambling paraphernalia, her spindlemen, her dealers, and her case keepers. For herself she acquired—of all things—an omnibus, which she furnished like a boudoir, with dainty lace curtains and satin cushions.

Ensconced in this strange vehicle which resembled, as much as anything, a modern automobile trailer, she set out in regal seclusion and splendor for the new boom town of Deadwood, followed by her entourage in the freight wagon. Somewhere along the line she changed her name again. When her fancied-up omnibus rolled down the muddy main street of Deadwood, she called herself Lurline Monte Verde.

The lovely newcomer set up a gambling establishment in her tent on Main Street near Wall, in the heart of what was known as Deadwood's "Bad Lands" district. Among her patrons were outlaws, gunmen, prospectors, businessmen, law officers, soldiers; all the boomers and riffraff and adventurers and legitimate fortune-seekers who had been lured to the latest boomtown by the hope of gaining quick and easy riches.

Among them was the famed marshal and gunman, Wild Bill Hickok, who was shot from behind in another gaming house by Jack McCall on August 2, 1876, while holding what came to be known as the "dead man's hand."

Always, until this time, the petite lady gambler had kept her admirers strictly at arm's length, for she was convinced that romance and the cold business of gambling would not mix. And then, late one night, into her place strolled a burly young ruffian who walked with a swagger, stared at her long and boldly, and lost his last cent because he was unable to keep his mind on his cards.

Perhaps it was because he lost with a laugh instead of an oath, but something about him touched the sensibilities of the lady.

"Can I stake you to breakfast money?" she asked him, her feelings masked by her ever-present Mona Lisa smile.

"Thank you, ma'am, but no woman pays for Archie Cummings' grub," he replied, with a good-natured grin that revealed the absence of a front tooth. "But, if you don't mind, I'm coming back when my luck turns, and take you out to breakfast. Is it a go?"

A week later he was back, with a pocket full of gold. Perhaps she was unaware that he had acquired it by holding up a stagecoach, or perhaps she knew and just didn't care.

Everyone else knew that the young ruffian's real name was Archie McLaughlin and that he had fought as one of Quantrill's guerrilla raiders on the Kansas border during the last year of the Civil War. Now, as an enterprising road agent, he was accumulating sufficient wealth to make quite a splurge in Deadwood's various gambling hells.

She learned about his record soon enough, but by this time she was desperately in love with Archie. Whether he returned her affection is uncertain, but it is quite certain that he took advantage of her facilities for acquiring important information.

Heavy winners often were robbed of their take within a few minutes of leaving a gambling establishment. Some of these robberies were engineered by the gambling house proprietors themselves as a means of recouping their losses. Others resulted from tips provided by dealers and croupiers, who came in for a cut of the proceeds.

But Archie was shooting for bigger game. He was no penny-ante back-alley holdup. His specialty was the treasure chests containing gold shipped by stagecoach from the Deadwood mines. Drivers and guards and company employees with a drink too many under their belts were inclined to talk too much if wheedled a bit by a charming young lady with a Mona Lisa smile. Most of Archie's tips came through his sweetheart.

But criminals were not the only ones who made use of underworld clearinghouses of information. Boone May, a former stagecoach driver who became a famous peace officer, became acquainted with Belle Siddons-Vestal-Monte Verde and from her learned of plans for a stagecoach holdup in Whoop-up Canon between Deadwood and Rapid City.

On the night of July 2, 1878, the stagecoach carrying the treasure box was filled with special deputies armed with an arsenal of rifles and revolvers.

Archie, along with young Billy Mansfield and other members of his band of road agents, expected to turn an easy trick. When the coach was forced to halt by a cottonwood tree felled across the road, the highwaymen closed in. Alexander Casswell yelled "Up with 'em!" and grabbed for the bits of the coach horses. Archie and the others surrounded the vehicle.

As soon as they were all in the open, the deputies cut loose with a volley. Casswell dropped dead, a slug through his head. Bandit John H. Brown was shot through the abdomen, the bullet lodging near his spine. Archie was slightly wounded. Billy Mansfield and Jack Smith were unhurt. The surviving road agents fled, with the wounded Brown clinging desperately to the horn of his saddle. They holed up in a shanty in the timber near Deadwood.

For ten days Brown suffered as his wound festered, for his friends feared to call a doctor. It was Archie who finally solved the problem, for Belle had told him she had studied dissection under her army surgeon former husband. He sent Billy Mansfield to arrange a meeting with her in a Deadwood opium den.

"Can you dig a lead slug out of a man's carcass?" he asked her.

"I can try," was her response. "But why should I?"

"Because Archie wants you to," said Billy. That settled it so far as she was concerned. She followed the highwayman to the shanty where Brown lay, gritting his teeth in agony. With no other equipment than a short length of wire she probed the wound and succeeded in extracting the bullet.

According to one version of the story, one of the road agents wanted to kill her to make certain their secret was safe, and Archie was forced to draw a gun on him while she left the cabin and returned safely to Deadwood.

Could she have foreseen the consequences of her act of mercy, in all likelihood she would have let Brown die. For shortly after he recovered he was arrested and confessed, implicating Smith, Mansfield, and her sweetheart Archie.

Traveling by night, the three fled from the Black Hills country but a few months later were arrested and jailed at Cheyenne. Belle had planned to join him at San Francisco. On the night of November 3, 1878, on their way back to Deadwood in irons to stand trial for grand larceny, their stagecoach was halted by five masked Vigilantes at Little Cottonwood Creek, a mile north of Fort Laramie. The guards were overpowered and the prisoners were taken to a cottonwood grove near Watson's saloon, where ropes were looped about their necks. Billy Mansfield, the youngest, wept and begged for mercy. But Archie remained defiant to the last.

"Go ahead and hang me and to the hell with you," he challenged as he cursed his captors. "But you'll never find the $8,000 in loot that I stashed away in the hills."

They lynched him, along with his pals, and they never found the loot.

According to another version, the Vigilantes promised to spare his life and permit him to stand trial on the robbery charge if he would reveal the hiding place of the loot. He agreed to the proposal and led them to the spot where the gold was buried, but after they had recovered the money they broke their pledge and hanged him.

Brokenhearted at the death of her sweetheart, Belle swallowed poison. Failing to kill herself, she set about drinking herself to death and became addicted to the use of opium. She could bear the associations of Deadwood no longer. She dismissed her employees, sold her paraphernalia, and went to Cheyenne, but stayed only a short time.

She drifted to Leadville in 1879, and for a few months operated a dance hall on State Street. Then, her interest in life gone, she went to Las Vegas, New Mexico, to Tombstone, Arizona, and finally to San Francisco.

As one of the most skillful twenty-one dealers in the West, she never lacked for money, but spent most of it attempting to assuage her sorrow with whisky.

In October, 1881, she was arrested and jailed at San Francisco. The newspaper account of her arrest reported that she was far from destitute but was at the point of death from dissipation. She was transferred from her cell to the hospital ward where, after the chaplain had urged her to confess her sins, she revealed the story of her life substantially as here set forth.

There the record of Belle Siddons–Mrs. Hallet–Madame Vestal–Lurline Monte Verde ends. Perhaps she died in jail, dreaming of the days of her youth when she was daring death as one of the nation's leading spies—or, more likely, dreaming of the sweetheart who died at the end of a hempen rope under a cottonwood limb.

Elijah Skaggs

The right man met the right game when a speciously clerical-looking
Kentucky frontiersman became acquainted with faro—the fairest of
gambling games, unless the player finds himself up against a dealer like
Elijah Skaggs, a pioneer in the company of Price McGrath of Versailles,
Kansas, thimble-rigger par excellence, and Canada Bill Jones, three-card
monte expert.

BY HERBERT ASBURY

A GREAT many of the gamblers who prowled the American hinterland
during the thirty years which preceded the Civil War operated under
the patronage and direction of an extraordinarily astute and far-seeing
gambler who introduced nepotism into gambling and performed the
remarkable feat of putting Faro and *Monte* on a sort of chain-store
basis. His name was Elijah Skaggs, but he was better known as "Brother
Skaggs, the preaching Faro dealer," because of his costume, which
never varied throughout his professional life regardless of climate or
weather—frock-coat and trousers of black broadcloth, black silk vest,
white shirt with high standing collar, white cravat of the choker type
wound several times around his scrawny neck, black stove-pipe hat, and
black patent-leather gaiters. These somber garments covered a long,
gaunt and awkward frame and emphasized a sour and saturnine phys-
iognomy. And Brother Skaggs' private life appears to have been as austere
as his appearance—he neither smoked nor drank, women meant nothing
to him, and he was never known to laugh, or even smile. He so closely
resembled the traveling parson so common in early America that even
among people who knew him he evoked surprise when he opened a
Faro snap instead of a prayer meeting. But he was an amazingly successful gambler, and one of the cleverest tricksters that the United
States has yet produced. Also, he probably had more to do with the
spread of gambling in this country than any other one man.

Brother Skaggs was a Kentuckian, born in the back country near
the Tennessee border, and reared with numerous brothers, sisters and

---

* John O'Connor, novelist, who under the pseudonym John Morris, wrote *Wander-
ings of a Vagabond.* —ED.

cousins on a small farm from which, as O'Connor* says, "they extracted sufficient hog and hominy to keep them from starvation." But Elijah had visions of greater things; he craved wealth and luxury, and as a youngster decided that the easiest and quickest way to get them was by gambling. He obtained a pack of cards, and while less ambitious Skaggses grubbed in the cotton patch young Elijah sat on a stump and practiced dealing, stacking, and otherwise manipulating the cards. At sixteen he began his career by trimming his cousins and brothers, and with the family cash for a bank roll began making trips to the Kentucky settlements, playing principally Brag, All-Fours, and Twenty-Card Poker, at none of which did he deal honestly. He even ventured as far north as Lexington, which an English traveler in 1812 had described as "a flourishing town," where "the prevailing amusements are drinking and gambling." By the time he was twenty years old Brother Skaggs had accumulated $2,000, a considerable sum in those days, and the ease with which he had acquired the money convinced him that he was ready to set upon his travels and enlarge his knowledge. So he crossed the state line into Tennessee and went to Nashville, a lively town at the junction of the Natchez Trace and the Wilderness Road, and one of the resorts of the bandits and cutthroats who prowled those lonesome trails.

In Nashville Brother Skaggs adopted the costume by which he became known throughout the South, and employed an itinerant school-master to teach him to read and write—he could already count the pips on a playing card. More important, however, he learned about Faro, which had lately been introduced into Nashville by a band of sharpers from New Orleans. Skaggs was too shrewd to play a game with which he was not familiar, but he was greatly impressed by the popularity of Faro, by the opportunities it offered for chicanery, by the fact that the deal remained always in the hands of the man who ran the game, and by the expedition with which the artists emptied the pockets of the local sports. He promptly settled upon Faro as his life work, and abandoned the short games, to master which he had devoted so much time and effort. For the next few years, accompanied by his private tutor, Brother Skaggs traveled about the country, gambling occasionally, but most of the time watching Faro dealers at work in such gambling centers as New Orleans, Mobile, the Pinch Gut district of Memphis, and those twin hell holes of the Mississippi, Natchez and Vicksburg. Whenever he saw a Faro dealer display a new bit of skullduggery, he compelled the sharper to divulge the trick under threat of exposure, or, if necessary, bought the knowledge—he is said to have paid $1,800 for the secret of manipulating tie-ups, with which he afterward made thousands.* Once he knew how a trick was done, he went into seclusion and practiced until he could perform it to his own satisfaction, so expertly that detection was unlikely.

By 1830 Brother Skaggs unquestionably knew as much about dealing Faro dishonestly as any gambler in the country. Also he had, as he considered, completed his secular education. So he dismissed his school-teacher and embarked upon a gambling tour of the South, returning to New Orleans about 1832 with $50,000. Then he began to put into effect one of the most extraordinary schemes in the annals of American gambling. On his tour he had bespoken the services of a large number of pleasant, personable young men whom he met in various gambling houses, and as they arrived in New Orleans he put them through an intensive course of instruction in cheating at Faro. When they had become proficient he sent them out in pairs, one to deal and the other to keep cases. Each team was under the supervision of one of Skaggs' brothers, cousins or nephews of whom he seems to have had a great store. They acted as cappers and ropers-in and looked after the finances, and the dealers and case-keepers did the rest. Brother Skaggs paid all expenses, furnished money for the bank, and gave each team twenty-five per cent of its profits. One of these bright young men was the brother of John A. Murrel, who joined Brother Skaggs' forces after the famous bandit had been sent to prison for ten years in 1834. Murrel attempted to deal Faro in various Tennessee and Arkansas towns, and although there was a great deal of sentiment against him because he was supposed to have been concerned in his brother's schemes, he succeeded in avoiding trouble until he reached the little town of Columbia, Arkansas, late in 1835. He "was one night playing as usual," wrote Jonathan H. Green [in An Exposure of the Arts and Miseries of Gambling] "when suddenly the lights were put out by someone in the room, and he was then literally cut up; one of his hands was cut entirely off, and he was most horribly mangled. Several stabs penetrated the region of the heart. He, however, escaped out of the house, and ran a short distance and fell dead. Several persons were arrested but no convictions ensued. The citizens generally approved the act, and thought it a good thing for the community that they were rid of such a man, even by such means. . . . There was no doubt of his being a very desperate man."

---

* Tie-ups were cards, sometimes as many as nine, stacked to make the last four cases in a deal lose. Each card was pierced with a fine needle, and the lot tied together with a horse hair. After the shuffle the dealer cut the deck above the tie-ups, thus placing them at the bottom of the pack. "While placing the cards in the dealing box," said O'Connor, "he cut the hair on the sharp edge of the plate inside the box, which was sharpened for that purpose. He now had four case cards to lose on the last four turns of the deal, and it is upon these turns that gamblers generally play their heaviest bets during a deal."

At one time Brother Skaggs had no fewer than a hundred of these chain-store gamblers scattered about the country. Among other professionals they were known as "Skaggs' Patent-Dealers," and their names were synonymous with "all sorts of fraud and dishonesty at the gaming table." For almost twenty years Skaggs' patent-dealers prospered exceedingly, and the money rolled like an avalanche into the pockets of the Master in New Orleans, for strangely enough most of the traveling teams seem to have rendered an honest account of their labors. Meanwhile Brother Skaggs had invaded other fields—he speculated successfully in mules, cotton, and bank-stocks, financed gambling houses in New Orleans, and, in the middle eighteen-forties, bought two hundred slaves and a cotton plantation in Louisiana. He also turned a receptive ear to anyone with an idea for increasing the chances of the bank at Faro, and advanced money for experiments, the inventor agreeing to give him the exclusive use of the device or trick for one year before putting it on the market. Skaggs thus assisted in the development of many of the crooked dealing boxes which appeared during the 1830's and the 1840's. Brother Skaggs seldom gambled in New Orleans, but occasionally went on brief trips to make certain that he had not lost his dexterity. He added *Monte* to his repertoire during the War with Mexico, and led a band of his patent-dealers into Texas and the border towns along the Rio Grande. He also spent a prosperous year in the mining camps of California, and for several months operated a Faro game in San Francisco.

During the late 1850's Brother Skaggs reached his goal—he was worth a million dollars. In 1858 or 1859 he liquidated his chain-store business, discharged his patent-dealers, and left gambling to its fate—never again did he turn a card or enter a gambling house. He also abandoned his distinctive dress, and outfitted himself with gaudy raiment made by one of New Orleans' fashionable tailors. Surrounded by his favorite relatives he settled down to enjoy the life of a gentleman on his cotton plantation. When the Civil War began, however, he lost his slaves, and his real estate depreciated in value to such an extent that he was again a very poor man. He made another fortune running the Federal blockade and speculating in sugar and cotton, but was ruined by an abiding faith in the future of the Confederacy. All of his resources went into Confederate money and bonds, and when the War ended he is said to have had about $3,000,000 tied up in this worthless paper. He sought relief from his disappointment in the whisky bottle, and died a drunkard in Texas in 1870, penniless except for a few acres of prairie land.

◇◇

Science vs. Luck

In 1870 a new magazine called *Galaxy* had the good fortune to sign
the up-and-coming Mark Twain to write a column, "Memoranda," in
the broad humorous vein he had created a few years earlier as a Western
newspaperman and lecturer. He later collected his columns, of which
this is one, in *Mark Twain's Sketches, New and Old* (1875).

BY MARK TWAIN

◇◇

AT THAT time, in Kentucky (said the Hon. Mr. K——), the law was
very strict against what it termed "games of chance." About a dozen
of the boys were detected playing "seven up" or "old sledge" for money,
and the grand jury found a true bill against them. Jim Sturgis was
retained to defend them when the case came up, of course. The more
he studied over the matter, and looked into the evidence, the plainer
it was that he must lose a case at last—there was no getting around
that painful fact. Those boys had certainly been betting money on a
game of chance. Even public sympathy was roused in behalf of Sturgis.
People said it was a pity to see him mar his successful career with a
big prominent case like this, which must go against him.

But after several restless nights an inspired idea flashed upon Sturgis,
and he sprang out of bed delighted. He thought he saw his way
through. The next day he whispered around a little among his clients
and a few friends, and then when the case came up in court he acknowledged the seven-up and the betting, and, as his sole defense, had the
astounding effrontery to put in the plea that old sledge was not a
game of chance! There was the broadest sort of a smile all over the
faces of that sophisticated audience. The judge smiled with the rest.
But Sturgis maintained a countenance whose earnestness was even
severe. The opposite counsel tried to ridicule him out of his position,
and did not succeed. The judge jested in a ponderous judicial way
about the thing, but did not move him. The matter was becoming
grave. The judge lost a little of his patience, and said the joke had gone
far enough. Jim Sturgis said he knew of no joke in the matter—his
clients could not be punished for indulging in what some people chose

to consider a game of chance until it was *proven* that it was a game of chance. Judge and counsel said that would be an easy matter, and forthwith called Deacons Job, Peters, Burke, and Johnson, and Dominies Wirt and Miggies, to testify, and they unanimously and with strong feeling put down the legal quibble of Sturgis by pronouncing that old sledge *was* a game of chance.

"What do you call it *now?"*said the judge.

"I call it a game of science!" retorted Sturgis; "and I'll prove it, too!"

They saw his little game.

He brought in a cloud of witnesses, and produced an overwhelming mass of testimony, to show that old sledge was *not* a game of chance but a game of science.

Instead of being the simplest case in the world, it had somehow turned out to be an excessively knotty one. The judge scratched his head over it awhile, and said there was no way of coming to a determination, because just as many men could be brought into court who would testify on one side as could be found to testify on the other. But he said he was willing to do the fair thing by all parties, and would act upon any suggestion Mr. Sturgis would make for the solution of the difficulty.

Mr. Sturgis was on his feet in a second.

"Impanel a jury of six of each, Luck *versus* Science. Give them candles and a couple of decks of cards. Send them into the jury-room, and just abide by the result!"

There was no disputing the fairness of the proposition. The four deacons and the two dominies were sworn in as the "chance" jurymen, and six inveterate old seven-up professors were chosen to represent the "science" side of the issue. They retired to the jury-room.

In about two hours Deacon Peters sent into court to borrow three dollars from a friend. [Sensation.] In about two hours more Dominie Miggles sent into court to borrow a "stake" from a friend. [Sensation.] During the next three or four hours the other dominie and the other deacons sent into court for small loans. And still the packed audience waited, for it was a prodigious occasion in Bull's Corners, and one in which every father of a family was necessarily interested.

The rest of the story can be told briefly. About daylight the jury came in, and Deacon Job, the foreman, read the following:

We, the jury in the case of the Commonwealth of Kentucky *vs.* John Wheeler *et al.*, have carefully considered the points of the case, and tested the merits of the several theories advanced, and do hereby unanimously decide that the game commonly known as old sledge or seven-up is eminently a game of science and not of chance. In demonstration whereof it is hereby and herein stated, iterated, reiterated, set forth, and made manifest that, during the entire night, the "chance" men never won a game or turned a jack, although both feats were common and frequent to the opposition; and furthermore, in support of this our verdict, we call attention to the significant fact that the "chance" men are all busted, and the "science" men have got the money. It is the deliberate opinion of this jury, that the "chance" theory concerning seven-up is a pernicious doctrine, and calculated to inflict untold suffering and pecuniary loss upon any community that takes stock in it.

"That is the way that seven-up came to be set apart and particularized in the statute-books of Kentucky as being a game not of chance but of science, and therefore not punishable under the law," said Mr. K——. "That verdict is of record, and holds good to this day."

◇◇◇

Alias Madame Moustache

There were those in her time who called her the greatest of American women gamblers and, moreover, one so honest that her customers were known to emerge with profit even when playing the game at which she specialized, vingt-et-un. She was also one of the most widely traveled, her favorite hunting grounds the mining camps from Montana to California. Her finale was sad, as you will see, but the road to it was consistently lively.

BY HARRY SINCLAIR DRAGO

◇◇◇

WHEN ONE of Jim Birch's northbound Sacramento-Marysville stages pulled up at the Shasta House in Nevada City to discharge passengers, among the three or four who got down that April afternoon in 1854 was an exceedingly attractive, smartly attired young woman. The way she carried herself and the smiling dignity with which she met the stares of the male onlookers bespoke a cultured background. At the hotel desk, she signed the register: Madame Emma (Eleanora) Dumont, of New Orleans—which may or may not have been her true name. But she was undeniably French and very likely from New Orleans, from where the great majority of California's growing French population had come.

Identifying herself as Madame Dumont, rather than as Mademoiselle, raised some piquant questions, but Nevada City, with its ore mills, two newspapers and growing prosperity, beginning to regard itself as a sophisticated town rather than the brawling mining camp it had so recently been, put aside its questions and welcomed the new and charming arrival. It was to have good reason to congratulate itself on its wisdom. Madame Emma Dumont was to become a legend in the gold and silver camps in her lifetime and she still retains a prominent place in the galaxy of notorious women of the mining West, for she was the tragic and unforgettable Madame Moustache.

A tremendous amount of sensational nonsense has been written about her. Actually no one has produced any evidence to throw any light on who she was and what her background was before she arrived in Nevada City in 1854. She was an experienced and expert gambler was evident when she opened what she called a vingt-et-un (popularly known as twenty-one or blackjack) parlor. That was her only game, and throughout her career she played no other.

The novelty of playing against a "lady" dealer, and a pretty one at that, appealed to the miners who put their dust on the table. One declared that he "would rather lose to the Madame than win from someone else." She lost with a smile and won with a deprecating movement of her beautiful shoulders. The odds of the game being with the dealer, she won oftener than she lost.

She had been in Nevada City only a few weeks when she rented a place across the street from the hotel and proceeded to make it over to her taste, furnishing it with rugs on the plank floor and installing candle chandeliers. Over the front she had a modest blue-and-white sign placed, naming it the Vingt-et-Un. The establishment had an air of elegance about it. No women were allowed, nor was any rowdyism permitted. To those of her patrons who cared to indulge, she offered champagne—and it was "on the house."

Nevada City approved of the way she ran her establishment and conducted herself. She continued to live quietly at the Shasta House, her virtue questioned only by the cynics who refused to believe that a young woman as attractive as Emma Dumont did not have a man in her life. But that unknown stranger failed to put in an appearance.

It is generally agreed among old-time mining camp commentators, such as Thompson and West, that the sobriquet "Madame Moustache" did not come into use much before 1871, when Emma Dumont's face had coarsened and she had become a tragic figure, drifting from one camp to another. As a young woman, she had what was described as "blonde peach fuzz" on her upper lip which was not regarded as a disfigurement.

In 1855, Nevada City's gold production fell off drastically for the first time since the founding of the camp. It gave rise to the rumor that the diggings were worked out. That was not true, but it gave the town a warning that resulted in a tightening of the belt. The Vingt-et-Un felt it. Madame Dumont was considering closing up and moving on when Lucky Dan Tobin, a card sharp and professional gambler, temporarily footloose and looking for a spot in which to light, rolled into town. He looked the Vingt-et-Un over and liked what he saw, including the proprietor.

Tobin must have been a persuasive talker. The fair Emma was in trouble and needed help, so she listened. The following day the town learned that she and Tobin had joined forces. Tobin brought in poker tables, a keno outfit, chuck-a-luck and a faro-bank. Madame Dumont had made some stipulations, which he ignored. But there was one on which she was adamant: women were to be barred from the premises.

Over their liquor the cynics said that Tobin and the Madame were more than partners; that he was her long-awaited lover. They were mistaken; Tobin found his pleasure elsewhere and his partner remained aloof from the entanglements of sex.

With diversified entertainment to offer, the Vingt-et-Un became prosperous again. Nevada City experienced another boom, but this time it was the feast before the famine. In 1856, the partners closed up shop and went their separate ways. Tobin headed east—some say as far as New York—while Madame Dumont, a bird of passage, moved from one camp to another and finally established herself in Columbia, which after the great fire of 1857 that leveled it, became the most prosperous and hell-roaring town on the Mother Lode. The new town of brick and stone that replaced the one that had gone up in flames was so stoutly built that some of its storied buildings are occupied today. The builders had good reason for their optimism, for gold was close to the surface all around Columbia. In the late fifties and early sixties $87,000,000 worth of the yellow metal was mined within its corporate limits.

From what is still visible today, one can believe that Columbia was the most beautiful as well as the wealthiest of all California hill towns. A multitude of stately trees, Lombardy poplars, locusts and weeping willows, recovering from the damage the fire had inflicted, gave the town a false air of tranquillity. On Broadway, its principal thoroughfare, there were two solid blocks of saloons, some of them extending all the way through to Main Street, which paralleled it in the rear. In every one there was a faro-bank or other games for separating the customer from his money.

Madame Dumont set up her *vingt-et-un* table in George Foster's City Hotel, where the food and the stock of wines and liquors were the best in town. Columbia could take anything in stride, even a lady gambler, but it went wild when John Strain dug up a nugget on Kennebec Hill on the outskirts of town that broke all known records. The group of exuberant miners who accompanied Strain to the Wells Fargo office gaped in silent amazement when Will Daegner, the express company agent, placed the nugget on his gold scales and announced that it weighed thirty pounds and was valued at $7,438.50.

In any town where men outnumbered women ten to one, prostitution was considered a necessary adjunct. Columbia was no exception to the rule. It was tolerant of its whores, but no one paid much attention to them as they came and went. Its twin diversions were whisky and gambling. With money so abundant, it followed that Madame Dumont prospered. In fact, it would appear that the year and a half she spent in Columbia was the most prosperous period in her life—or in that part of it of which there is any record. But it was a hard, aging life, an endless matching of wits with rough men, none of them saints, that had no compensations other than the money it produced. She sought to soften it by being generous to the unfortunate. How many miners she staked to a second chance in their quest for gold is unknown, but it occurred often enough to give rise to the comment in the saloons along Broadway that "the Madame is an easy touch."

Why she left Columbia and the prosperity she was enjoying there to join the great "rush to Washoe" in 1859–60 can be explained only as a reflection of the mass hysteria that sent thousands of men and women over the Sierra Nevada when the cry of "bonanza" was raised. It happened time after time whenever word of a rich new strike came winging over the mountains, whether in Nevada, Montana or elsewhere. People dropped whatever they were doing and on foot, horseback or wagon headed over the trails to the scene of the excitement. It was a phenomenon that continued into the twentieth century when—in the saline reaches of southern Nevada—Tonopah, Goldfield, Rhyolite and a dozen more ephemeral towns blossomed into the headlines. By then the rushing hordes were stampeding across the barren wastes in their Fords and Stanley Steamers.

The lurid, allegedly "true tales of the West," centering on the woman they identify as Madame Moustache, have very little to say about her in the year she was in Virginia City. Actually, nothing is known about her activities in the brief time she was on the Comstock. Presumably she was gambling, but while it was the custom for gambling establishments to insert a card (a small paid advertisement) in the columns of the *Enterprise*, her name does not appear. If she was a stranger in Virginia City, so was everyone else. Certainly she was not unknown to the hundreds of miners from Columbia, Nevada City and other California camps, who had preceded her across the Sierra, and with whom she had been popular. Why she seemingly made no impression on the town and left it unnoticed for greener fields in eastern Nevada remains a mystery.

The Comstock so overshadowed the less important mining districts of Nevada in the 1860's and 1870's that they have been largely ignored. They were strung out from west to east like pods on a pea vine— Austin, Eureka, Hamilton, Ely, Pioche, the wildest of them all, and half a dozen other camps that faded almost as quickly as they flowered. Some of them have survived. Hamilton, the gaudiest, perched so high on Treasure Hill that it was often lost in the clouds when viewed from below, is gone, leaving nothing to remind the visitor that its population once numbered a boasted fifteen thousand and that it was the site of the greatest find of surface silver chloride the world has ever known.

But it was Pioche, a hundred miles across the wastelands to the southeast, that outdid them in the amount of wealth it produced and in the violence of its citizenry. Pioche was the center of a surrounding mining district. Disputes that began anywhere in the Ely Mountains were brought to town to be settled, and without benefit of law. There was constant strife, most of it due to accusations of claim jumping. Destroying another man's monuments and taking possession of the claim he had staked was not a common occurrence in other Nevada camps, nor is there any evidence that it was actually widespread at Pioche. But the suspicion that the big owners had banded together to drive the little fellows out by one means or another was there, and it was enough to keep the partisan feud burning. The situation was not helped when the Pioche Consolidated, the district's biggest producer, imported cheap Mexican labor to work its ore.

The *Pioche Record* noted Madame Emma Dumont's arrival in September, 1861, adding the information that "the noted lady gambler has engaged space in Handsome Jack McKnight's popular emporium and will be found there nightly from now on. If you enjoy a fast game of twenty-one, pay the little lady a visit."

Pioche was destined to become the turning point in Emma Dumont's life. Not since Columbia had she been so well received. The town was tougher than any she had known, but the men liked her, and in her presence they seemed to forget temporarily the violence that swirled about them. She had not been there long when the *Pioche Record* had occasion to mention her again. It related how she had run out into the street one night and confronted a mob of jobless miners who were on their way to wreak vengeance on the Mexicans who had replaced them. With her laughter and good sense she made them realize that their quarrel was with the owners of the Pioche Con, not with the Mexicans who had been brought in to replace them.

For years she had lived almost exclusively among men, and it might have been expected that she had learned how to judge them. She now proved that she had not, for she fell in love with Jack McKnight and married him. He was handsome, debonair, popular—and worthless. That she hoped to find peace and quiet and divorce herself from the life she had led for the past ten or more years is indicated in her purchase of a ranch "in eastern Nevada," according to that compendium of grass-roots history *Pioneer Nevada,* published in Reno in 1951. Unfortunately no further information is given regarding its exact location. The best ranching country in that part of the state was in White Pine County, particularly in the valley of the Shell Creek Range, so it may be presumed that it was there that she and McKnight settled down.

It was not to be for long. The isolation and pleasant monotony of ranch life that his wife found so satisfying did not appeal to Mc-Knight. He had married her for her money, after convincing himself that she possessed a tidy fortune. Biding his time for some months, he got his hands on it in some manner and promptly deserted her. All she had left was the unimproved ranch, which was a liability rather than an asset.

Apparently she sold the ranch and, using the money as her grub-stake, returned to her old trade of dealing *vingt-et-un,* moving on from one camp to the next as fortune dictated. Speaking of McKnight's desertion and treachery and the effect it had on her, Thomas Wilson, the editor of *Pioneer Nevada,* says:

"From the profound emotional shock, a change took place in the fortunes and appearance of Madame Moustache. Until then the records indicate she had a fresh, girl-like beauty and vivacity. Now her features coarsened, and a growth of dark hair, previously absent or virtually invisible, appeared on her upper lip, from which she derived the name of Madame Moustache.

"Her old light touch, and her skill as a gambler, seemed to desert her and she failed to rise from a grinding poverty that followed her from mining camp to camp. Hairy-faced, her features coarsened, and now in her late forties, she became an outstanding object of pity."

In summing up in this fashion, Mr. Wilson is covering a period of sixteen years. But Emma Dumont's slide downhill into obscurity was gradual. She was in Fort Benton, Montana, in 1866, three years after Jack McKnight robbed and deserted her, and she was far from being an object of pity during her stay there. Fort Benton, the head of navigation on the Missouri River, was booming. Gold had been discovered in quantity in Alder Gulch in June, 1863. Virginia City (Montana) had grown mushroomlike into a city of fifteen thousand. Fort Benton was the easiest and quickest way of reaching the Montana diggings. Once only a fur-trading post, it was now thinking of itself as the great inland seaport of America.

Some of this optimism was warranted. In 1863, after several years of trying, seven steamboats succeeded in making it all the way up the Missouri to Fort Benton; by 1865, the arrivals numbered forty. They arrived in the late spring in the season of high water and left on the return voyage to St. Louis several weeks later, or before the run-off from the melting snow in the mountains had passed and the river was dropping, a seasonal occurrence that annually made the upper reaches of the Missouri unnavigable.

In that year of 1865, 1,000 passengers, 6,000 tons of merchandise, and 20 quartz mills were received at Fort Benton. The ultimate destination of the newcomers and the mountains of freight piled up on the riverbank (the raw town had no levee or man-made landing as yet) was Virginia City and the Alder Gulch diggings. Freight was forwarded by bull teams; human beings got where they were going by being bounced around in one of Oliver and Company's stages (not Concords; they came later) for twenty-four hours, when the mud was not too deep. Anyone who wanted to eat on the journey brought his own food, for not so much as a cup of coffee could be purchased between Fort Benton and Virginia City. The fare was a modest $30.

As it was only a way station or port of entry for the hordes of men and women the steamboats were bringing up the Missouri, Fort Benton was shaped to suit the needs of transients. They had no money to spend on reaching Montana, and when they left several years later—the lucky ones, that is—they were too busy arranging passage down-river and putting their gold in the steamboat's strong room to have any time for whoring. As a consequence, although every other building on Front Street housed a combination saloon and gambling parlor, prostitution never flourished in Fort Benton.

The fanciful story is told that Emma Dumont did so poorly in Fort Benton that she turned from gambling to operating a bordello, offering herself to the trade along with her "girls." Although she was now fat and fortyish, drinking heavily and unquestionably going downhill, she retained the respect of the town, for when word was received that the steamboat W. B. *Dance* was coming up the Missouri with smallpox aboard, she led a group of men to the riverbank and at pistol point forbade the captain of the boat to land. Fort Benton had been scourged by smallpox on several occasions in its past. In the great epidemic of 1837, in fur-trading days, an estimated 6,000 Indians had died.

After a few tense minutes the captain of the W. B. *Dance* swung the wheel and the steamer retreated downriver to Cow Island, one hundred and thirty miles below, where it remained for four weeks, by which time the epidemic had disappeared.

For five years after she left Fort Benton, Madame Moustache— the name was beginning to have some publicity value—wandered from one Montana mining camp to another. In 1870, she was in Virginia City (Montana), dealing twenty-one in a Jackson Street gambling house. Later she was in Helena, the booming camp in Last Chance Gulch, far to the north. Of course by now she was merely chasing rainbows, satisfied to be earning enough to keep her supplied with brandy and to have a roof over her head. Whenever a new gold strike was rumored, she was ready to hit the trail.

She was in Bannack when word came over the mountains that a bonanza had been uncovered at Salmon, Idaho, on the other side of the Bitter Root Range, no more than twenty-five miles away as the crow flies but close to two hundred miles by way of Monida Pass, which was the only way of getting there. Although it was late spring, there was so much snow on the ground in the high places that coach travel was impossible. But Oliver and Company, always ready for such emergencies, provided the travelers with horse-drawn sleds and guaranteed to get its patrons through to Salmon. They did, despite frequent upsets that pitched the travelers into the snow and froze the marrow in their bones in the make-shift stations where they were forced to spend the night. But the pioneers from Bannack reached Salmon in time to stake claims along the Salmon River.

The Salmon River Mining District soon petered out. It was on to Lewiston for Emma Dumont, and from there to the Coeur d'Alenes. On and on—Murray, Eagle City, Idaho City—a dozen places. She had not been looking for gold or even modest riches for a long time. What kept her going was the hope that somewhere, sooner or later, she would cut Jack McKnight's trail. She was prepared for that moment, her pistol never being far from her hand. But as she went on, almost a penniless wanderer, it began to seem that the West was too big, too wide, for her.

In 1878 she was back in Nevada. Gamblers and bartenders who

had known her in happier days befriended her. Some of them had known McKnight, but they couldn't tell her where she would find him. In Reno, an old-time barroom "professor" (piano player) whom she had known in her flush days in Columbia gave her a dollar and told her to get a "reading" from the Washoe Seeress. Eilley [Orum] gazed into her peep-stones at length, but the best she could tell her caller was that her quest would end somewhere in California—which was taking in a generous amount of territory. Miraculously, it was to be fulfilled, but scarcely in the manner implied or in the way Emma Dumont interpreted it.

Bridgeport, the seat of Mono County, lies in a pleasant green valley crossed by sparkling creeks. With its Gothic courthouse and steepled church it is more typical of New England than California. Four miles to the south a weed-grown road takes off to the east. Fifteen miles on that now unused road brings you hard up against the Nevada line. There you will find what is left of "bold, bad Bodie of the 1860's and '70's," which, but for Wells Fargo's ancient vault and cellars filled with broken bottles and rusted iron doors, is nothing at all. Today Bodie is the ghostliest of all ghost towns.

No cowtown or mining camp was ever tougher than Bodie or more boastful of its wickedness and horrendous number of homicides. Not to be outdone by the Comstock, the Esmeralda Mining District, which included Bodie and adjacent Aurora, claimed to have a population of 20,000. But mining statistics are always suspect, and there is no reason to believe that the true figure ever exceeded 12,000. By way of Sonora Pass, which was kept open most of the year, it was only a hundred and thirty miles to Sacramento. It gave the state capital such a vested interest in Bodie that the Sacramento Union stationed a permanent correspondent there and printed the latest tidings in every issue.

Wells Fargo records disclose that the express company suffered more from the depredations of road agents on the Bodie run than elsewhere. This was due to the fact that the Esmeralda District was shipping bullion rather than ore. Flowing over Sonora Pass, a stream of bottled luxuries and crated comestibles passed unmolested. With thirty saloons, ranging from such posh caravansaries as the Occidental and the Bodie House down to the groggeries where miners off duty congregated, with three breweries going full blast, Bodie was a bibulous town. With honest pride it could say that there was no delicacy a man could find in Virginia City that couldn't be found in Bodie. It couldn't brag about the quality of its whores, who were the overage castoffs of other camps, but with two newspapers and a railroad of its own, the little narrow-gauge Bodie and Benton which brought up timber for the mines from the low country to the east, it was self-sufficient.

How she got there does not appear on the record, but in September, 1879, Madame Moustache appeared in Bodie. From some unknown source she had garnered a little money. In the Grand Central she stepped up to the bar and sipped her brandy. Only a few of the old-timers remembered her. No one could tell her anything about Jack McKnight.

After a few days she disappeared from Bodie. On the morning of September 8, her dead body was found beside the road, two miles from town, an empty vial of poison clutched in her hand. She had taken the only escape left to her.

In its self-righteous hypocrisy Bodie buried its prostitutes in what was called the "outcasts cemetery." When it appeared that Madame Moustache would have to be buried at the county's expense and interred in the "outcasts cemetery," money was raised in the saloons and she was buried in consecrated ground farther up the hill.

Those pioneer Nevada historians, Thompson and West, append a fitting epitaph to her passing: "Let her many good qualities invoke leniency in criticising her failings."

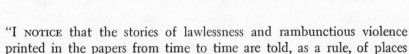

A Gambler's Pistol Play

The turn-of-the-century *New York Sun*, continuing the tradition of readability fostered by its great editor, Charles A. Dana, liked to treat its devoted followers to this kind of offbeat story. In fact, it ran a series of poker tales like this one later collected under the title *Queer Luck*.

BY DAVID A. CURTIS

"I NOTICE that the stories of lawlessness and rambunctious violence printed in the papers from time to time are told, as a rule, of places far West or out of the usual run of travel," said the gray-haired young-looking man who sat in the card-room of an up-town club the other night after the game had broken up. "I don't mean by that," he continued, "to question the truth of any of these stories. It only occurs to me that the writers take unnecessary pains in going so far away for their material. I have seen, right along the banks of the Mississippi River—and we call that pretty well East now—some things as exciting as any of the mining-camp yarns. And everything was wide open in some of the towns, too. I haven't been out there since '82, but that's not so long ago, and then it was not uncommon to find a gambling saloon on the main floor of the principal hotel in a flourishing town. You could walk in as freely as you could into the barroom and play faro, keno, or poker at any hour of the day or night.

"The great flood of '82 rather accentuated the devil-may-care condition of things; partly, I suppose, because there was not so much traveling on the river as usual and none at all by rail. Strangers were scarce in the river towns, and the inhabitants were reduced to the necessity of gambling among themselves. No, there wasn't what you might call very much shooting, but every man carried a pistol, and occasionally there would be some. There was enough, at all events, to make the citizens of Memphis enforce pretty strictly a city ordinance against carrying concealed weapons."

"That's right," said a drummer who was of the party. "I was in Memphis then, and I remember the Mayor of a Kentucky city being sent to jail for ten days for carrying a pistol. He had plenty of money and plenty of influence, too, but neither could save him from jail."

"Well, Memphis was the only city I struck on the river," said the first speaker, "where such a law was observed. I got caught in Arkansas City, I remember, when I was trying to get to Little Rock. I arrived there just after the train had gone, so I had to stay over for forty-eight hours. It's only about a hundred miles, but there was only one train, and that took all day going up and all next day coming down. It was an accommodation train, and I saw it stop fifteen minutes for a darky who signaled from a distance, with a basket of eggs on his arm which he wanted to ship as freight. The conductor told me, when I asked about it, that that was quite usual, and a little while afterward he stopped the train to let a passenger get off and get a quail that he shot from the car.

"But the stop in Arkansas City was lively enough, if it was only two days. A darky was drowned trying to get across the street, the first day I was there, for the town was so far under water that the railroad track on top of the levee had been washed away. Only the houses on the highest ground were habitable, and there wasn't such a thing as a sidewalk visible. A few timbers were strung along here and there, and people jumped from one to another of these when they went from house to house, unless they were going far enough to take a skiff. This poor fellow jumped and missed his footing, and was drowned in sight of a dozen people. I asked the man who told me about it whether any effort had been made to save him, and he said no, that there was no boat handy. And when I expressed some horror he seemed surprised and said:

"'Why, 'twas only a nigger. You couldn't expect a white man to take chances to save him.' Niggers were not so valuable then as they were before the war."

"I don't know that the color line was so strictly drawn, though," interrupted the drummer again. "I saw a roustabout fall into the river one night at New Madrid, and he was a white man, too, but no effort was made to save him. The mate stepped to the side of the boat and looked over, but he did no more, and not one of the other rousters stopped work even for a moment. They were unloading freight in a great hurry, and I think they were afraid of the mate. It was dark, to be sure, and the current was swift enough to carry off the strongest swimmer, but still I was surprised to see no effort made to save the poor devil. Before I recovered from my surprise it was too late to do anything, and it didn't seem to be wise to say anything, either."

"Good policy, sometimes, not to," resumed the young-looking gray-haired man. "I learned to keep my mouth shut at a card table a long time ago, and that is why I had no part in a little disturbance that occurred the second day I was in Arkansas City. I don't think there was more than one other stranger in town when I was. He had come there the day before me, on the train, and was waiting for a boat up the river. I struck up an acquaintance with him, and he told me he was on his way home, after a business trip. I congratulated him and we took a drink on it, next door to the hotel.

"We were both tired waiting, and there was nothing better to do in the place, so we both sauntered to the room just back of the bar. The door was wide open, and we saw card-playing inside. Three men were playing poker, and we stood for a few moments looking on. One of the three was a comical-looking old fellow, evidently a superannuated gambler. He must have been seventy years old, and his hands were very shaky, but I could not make up my mind whether he was palsied or had been drinking, or whether he was assuming decrepitude in order to watch the cards more carefully as he dealt them. The latter seemed likely enough, and I suspected marked cards, so I pleaded ignorance of the game when one of the other players—the proprietor of the place, as I learned later—looked up with a pleasant smile and suggested that perhaps my friend and I would like to join in.

"My 'friend,' as he called him—I didn't even know his name—was willing enough, and he sat in. I stood by, smoking and looking on for a few minutes, though I pretended not to be watching the game very closely. You can't be too careful about observing the etiquette of the place you're in, as I have always noticed, no matter what place it is, and the people around a card table are always liable to resent an outsider's interest if it even borders on inquisitiveness. Where the resentment is liable to be expressed with a knife or a pistol, a wise man avoids showing his interest if he has any.

"In this case I hadn't a great deal. I saw the game was crooked, but it made no difference to me whether the other stranger knew it or not. If he did it was dog eat dog, and if he didn't he deserved to lose for playing with strangers in such a place. However, I noticed pretty soon that the old fellow, whom the others called Major, and the proprietor, whom they all addressed as Pete, were looking uneasily at me and at each other from time to time, and that the third player, whose back was turned toward me, was making an ostentatious show of hiding his cards from me, as if he suspected or feared me and wanted me to know it. Accordingly I thought the wisest thing for me was to stroll back to the front room and treat the bartender.

"While we were drinking, another man came in. He wore no coat, vest, or hat. He was, I think, the handsomest man I ever saw, though he was slightly flushed with liquor; not drunk, by any means, but he had evidently been drinking. He was a little above the medium height, with a symmetrical form, magnificent chest and shoulders, and the easy motion and graceful carriage of a skilled athlete. He passed directly to the card-room, nodding to the barkeeper and merely glancing at me, and I heard him say:

" 'Do you want another in the game?'

"The response was pleasant, and he took a seat. Up to this time I had not been greatly interested, as I said, and I continued talking to the man behind the bar, simply because I had nothing else to do. The newcomer, however, was talkative, and, as I noticed in a few moments, inclined to be surly. He seemed to be trying to pick a quarrel with the stranger, and I lingered, with some natural curiosity, to see if he would succeed. Presently the explosion came. He lost a jack-pot which the stranger won on three tens.

" 'You opened that pot on a pair of tens,' he exclaimed with an oath, 'and when we catch any cross-roads gambler playing that kind of a game in this town we commonly hang 'em, do you understand?'

"It was said noisily and furiously, and I looked in expecting to see a fight, but the stranger spoke as coolly as though the other had been calling for his draw.

" 'I did nothing of the sort, sir. I came in on a pair of tens, as I had a perfect right to do, after the Major opened it, and I caught the third ten in the draw.'

" 'I say you opened it,' shouted the newcomer with another oath.

"The stranger looked at him with the most perfect composure and said:

" 'I appeal to the table. Gentlemen, did I open it?'

" 'No, sir,' said the old Major, promptly enough. 'I opened it myself, and dropped out after I was raised twice. Jack, shut up! The gentleman is playing all right.'

"But Jack wouldn't shut up. On the contrary, he became more furious.

" 'This is a hell of a game!' he shouted, and leaped to his feet like a panther, totally oblivious of the few chips in front of him. He had lost nearly all he had bought on coming in.

"The stranger never moved, though I expected to see weapons drawn. He looked Jack full in the face with a sort of bewilderment on his own face, and said nothing. Jack stood for a moment, and while I was wondering whether the stranger was showing nerve, or was really bewildered, he turned suddenly and dashed out of the room.

"The stranger looked around at the other players, and there was a distinct drawl in his words as he said:

" 'What is the matter with that man?'

" 'Oh, nothing,' said Pete, carelessly. 'You mustn't mind him. He killed a man yesterday, and he's been drinking a good deal to-day. He's a little excited, but it doesn't mean anything.'

" 'But why did he rush out so curiously?' persisted the stranger.

" 'Well, I suppose he went out to get heeled,' said Pete; 'but you needn't be disturbed. The boys won't let him come back.'

" 'Well, perhaps they won't,' said the stranger, still drawling his words, 'but it's just as well to be on the safe side. If you will excuse me for a few minutes I'll step over to the hotel and get my gun. I left it in my satchel.'

" 'Why, certainly,' said the others, and he arose, leaving his chips on the table, and went out of the place. He said nothing when he passed me, and I thought it best to say nothing, too, but you couldn't have dragged me away just then. I suppose every man likes to see a fight, and I thought there was a good chance for one. I don't drink fast as a rule, but it seemed to be a good time to treat again, and when the glasses were emptied I said:

" 'Did he really kill a man yesterday?'

" 'Yes,' said the bartender indifferently. 'There was a fellow tried to get funny with him in his saloon next door, and when Jack ordered him out and he wouldn't go Jack shot him.'

" 'No, he wasn't exactly arrested, but he appeared before the Coroner and told how it was, and the Coroner said he'd have to lay the matter before the Grand Jury.'

" 'He wasn't locked up, then?' I persisted.

" 'Oh, no. You see, Jack's very popular around here, and he's got quite some property, too. I don't think the boys would have liked it much if he'd been locked up.'

"While I was meditating on this the stranger came back, and, resuming his seat at the table, laid his pistol alongside his chips, which the others had not disturbed. They dealt him a hand, and the game, which had not been interrupted by his absence, went on as before. No one made any remark about the pistol or about the man who had gone out to get heeled, but the old Major pulled out a double-barreled derringer and laid it on the table, and I looked to see the others do the same thing, but they did not. I had no doubt, however, that they were armed, and they were all looking for trouble.

"They had not long to wait. There was a sound of voices outside, presently, and looking out I saw Jack, still furious with anger, apparently, breaking away from two or three men who were evidently trying to detain him, but who had a wholesome respect for the revolver he had in his hand. I looked around. The Major was dealing, and the other players were watching him, apparently, but I was satisfied that they had heard the talk outside, and were all alert. The bartender was safe to drop behind the bar when the shooting began, and I looked for some place where I should be able to see and yet not be in range. There was a window in the partition between the rooms, about twelve feet to one side of the door, and I stepped over there as Jack came in toward the door.

"Through this window I saw the most magnificent display of cool nerve that ever came under my notice. The stranger never changed color, nor moved in his chair, but I could see his eyelids contract and his lips tighten as he quickly and quietly put his hand on his revolver and looked toward the door, at which Jack was just appearing, pistol in hand.

"On the instant Pete drew a bowie knife, with a motion so quick that I could not tell where the knife came from, and drove it square through the stranger's hand into the table underneath, nailing it fast to the wood.

"If the stranger had even flinched, he would have been dead in another moment, for Jack's pistol was leveled at him, but with a motion as quick as Pete's he reached over with his left hand, seized his revolver, and shot Jack through the pistol arm, shattering his elbow, just as he was pulling his trigger. And the next instant he had shot Pete through the heart, and turning to the Major, he shouted, 'Drop that gun!'

"The old fellow dropped it, and threw up his hands. The other man had gone under the table like a flash, being only anxious to get out of the trouble. And Jack, with a howl of pain and terror, had turned and run. The fight was over before it was fairly begun, and the stranger had not moved from his chair.

"With his left hand he pulled out the knife and wrapped up his right in a handkerchief, and, stepping to the bar, said to the bartender:

" 'You want to have a doctor here damned quick to dress my hand. And while you are about it, you'd better notify the Coroner, if there's one around. I propose to have this inquest held before the witnesses get away.

"The Coroner was around; in fact, he was playing cards only four or five doors away, and in half an hour he was holding his inquest. The stranger had shown his good sense in demanding immediate action, for though he was a stranger, the facts were too plain for a dispute, and even one or two of Pete's friends on the jury were forced to admit that the stranger had killed his man in self-defense.

"He was accordingly informed by the Coroner that he could go on his own recognizance to appear before the Grand Jury, and after treating the crowd at the dead man's bar, and paying for the treat with the chips he had on the card table, he went over to the levee and boarded a boat that had stopped on her way up river.

"He had given his name to the Coroner as Dick Davis of Tuscumbia, Ala., and I afterward heard that he was really a crossroads gambler, as traveling card sharps used to be called, and was a famous pistol shot. Why he did not kill Jack as well as Pete I never really understood, for if the stories of his marksmanship were one-half true, he could have done it easily enough. I never knew what the Grand Jury did about it."

◇◇◇

The Heathen Chinee

Perhaps no poem in American literary history has known the instantaneous popularity of Bret Harte's "Plain Language from Truthful James," persistently called "The Heathen Chinee" since its first appearance in 1870. Harte, then editor of *Overland Monthly*, had apparently forgotten these sixty humorous lines until he took them from a drawer to fill an empty space in an issue of his magazine. Then, according to his biographer, Richard O'Connor: "Its impact was as great a surprise to the author as anyone else. Cheap reprints were sold in the streets of most cities. It was set to music. It was collected in anthologies published as far away as London and Australia. Every parlor in the country echoed to the recitation of its stanzas."

BY **BRET HARTE**

◇◇◇

Which I wish to remark—
　And my language is plain—
That for ways that are dark,
　And for tricks that are vain,
The heathen Chinee is peculiar,
　Which the same I would rise to explain.

Ah Sin was his name;
　And I will not deny
In regard to the same
　What that name might imply;
But his smile it was pensive and childlike,
　As I frequent remarked to Bill Nye.

It was August the third;
　And quite soft was the skies:
Which it might be inferred
　That Ah Sin was likewise;
Yet he played it that day upon William
　And me in a way I despise.

Which we had a small game,
　And Ah Sin took a hand.

It was Euchre. The same
 He did not understand;
But he smiled as he sat by the table,
 With a smile that was childlike and bland.

Yet the cards they were stocked
 In a way that I grieve,
And my feelings were shocked
 At the state of Nye's sleeve:
Which was stuffed full of aces and bowers,
 And the same with intent to deceive.

But the hands that were played
 By that heathen Chinee,
And the points that he made,
 Were quite frightful to see—
Till at last he put down a right bower,
 Which the same Nye had dealt unto me.

Then I looked up at Nye,
 And he gazed upon me;
And he rose with a sigh,
 And said, "Can this be?
We are ruined by Chinese cheap labor—"
 And he went for that heathen Chinee.

In the scene that ensued
 I did not take a hand;
But the floor it was strewed
 Like the leaves on the strand
With the cards that Ah Sin had been hiding,
 In the game "he did not understand."

In his sleeves, which were long,
 He had twenty-four packs—
Which was coming it strong,
 Yet I state but the facts;
And we found on his nails, which were taper,
 What is frequent in tapers—that's wax.

Which is why I remark,
 And my language is plain,
That for ways that are dark,
 And for tricks that are vain,
The heathen Chinee is peculiar—
 Which the same I am free to maintain.

One Thing
and Another

If these assorted anecdotes and incidents prove anything, it would seem to be that a gambler with money burning holes in his or her pocket—or hoping to acquire some to burn there—will bet on just about anything at all, anywhere, anytime.

Phileas Fogg and the Jumping Frog

No one has to believe absolutely everything in this roundup of weird wagers, but who would want to bet that one or another of them did not actually take place? In any case, you would do well not to overlook the one that opens J. Bryan III's singular compilation, and is resolved at the conclusion of it.

BY J. BRYAN III

"ALL RIGHT," Bobby said. "You're so dam' smart, how would you pick *this* one? A chum of mine at Meadow Brook bet he could run the length of the polo field and back, on foot, before this other guy could run it on a pony, pro-*vi*-ded the other guy dismounted and drank a glass of water at the far end. They ran it, and who won?"

Nothing tricky about the glass?—an ordinary tumbler, easily accessible? The water itself: not "heavy water," by any chance, and not adulterated? And the pony: not lame or hobbled or doctored or ungovernable? He wasn't assigned a back-breaking weight? Normal tack? No interference with the run?

No, said Bobby, nothing like that.

I sifted the conditions once more. If there was a gimmick, I couldn't find it. I said, "The rider won."

"Wrong," Bobby said. "The runner. But I won't tell you how he did it until you've stewed awhile."

I started to stew right then, but presently I strayed from the bet at issue to bets in general. I began to jot down all the great bets I could remember: historic bets and fictional bets; bets on strength and skill and endurance; bets won by quick wits; bets on eating and drinking; foolish bets and gallant bets. I excluded sheer gambling, no matter how high the stakes; the bets I wanted had to have something picturesque about them. I also excluded mathematical bets and smart-aleck bets; some of them may be picturesque, but they taste of tin. What was left, I winnowed, and here they are.

I'll skip the classics (the bets there are dullish) and begin at modern fiction, with two men who made bets of worldwide fame. One, Jim Smiley, of Calaveras County, California, lost forty dollars in very little more time than it took to tell the two frogs, "One—two—three—git!"

The other, Phileas Fogg, of Savile Row, London, won £20,000 in very little less time than precisely eighty days.

The scene of Mr. Fogg's bet was, of course, the Reform Club. There is something in the climate of clubs, particularly of club *bars*— a tropical warmth (of argument) and moisture (of glass)—that makes betting flourish, whether in the Reform or the Meadow Brook or the Billiards, where (Lord Dunsany's readers will remember) Jorkens taunted Terbut into betting that it was no farther from Westminster Bridge to Blackfriars Bridge than from Blackfriars Bridge to Westminster Bridge.

One of the greatest bets in a London club was "made over port"— you see?—"just before Christmas, 1748, while a distinguished group were discussing the incurable gullibility of the man in the street." The Duke of Montague submitted that even if someone promised to perform a feat that was utterly preposterous, enough fools would pay to fill a playhouse, in the naïf expectation of watching him attempt it.

Lord Chesterfield had doubts. "If a man promised to jump into a quart bottle, surely no one would believe *that?*"

The climate was benign, and a bet bloomed.

Two weeks later, "a celebrated conjurer" advertised that in the Little Theatre, Haymarket, on January 12th, he would take "a common walking cane from any of the spectators and thereon play the music of every instrument now in use," and secondly, take "a common wine bottle, which one of the spectators may first examine; this bottle is placed on a table in the middle of the stage and he goes into it, in the sight of all and sings in it."

Even though the price of the tickets had been raised, every seat was sold. The "conjurer" failed to appear, and the audience wrecked the theater, but Montague had won his bet. (Here may have begun a losing streak for Lord Chesterfield, because we find a record of his betting his brother that after September 1751, he would never again bet more than a guinea.)

*   *   *   *

The betting at White's was as high as a cat's back, and so wild that when, one evening in 1750, a slight tremor shook the house, and the members promptly began betting whether it was an earthquake or an explosion, an outraged parson damned them for "such an impious set of people that if the Last Trumpet were to sound, they'd bet Puppet-Show against Judgment!" Never mind what the parson was doing at White's. The point is, his outrage makes him almost unique in the century. Time and again we will see his brothers of the cloth not only taking sides in bets, but backing their own performances. It was written of one such brother, the Rev. Lord Henry Fitzroy,

> Behold the reverend Lord, good Fitzroy, stand
> With Holy Bible in his precious hand;
> Or so it seems, I doubt it as I look;
> Is it his Bible or his betting book?

The motto of White's might have been a line of Terence's: "Make way for your betters!" All bets laid at the club, impious or not, were entered in the Betting-Book. It is still in use today, though the stakes are rather smaller. Where, 200 years ago, Lord Alington bet £3,000 on which of two raindrops would first reach the bottom of a pane in the front window, now Mr. Ralph Milbanke bets £5 and a set of golf clubs that Mr. Richard Sutton "will not propel a golf ball with a golf club from 69 St. Thomas' Str., City, to the steps of White's in less than 2,000 Strokes." (Mr. Sutton won, in 193 strokes.) Nor do today's members seem quite so rascally as the one in the 1860's who bet that he would "have" a lady in a balloon.

But the heyday of betting in England was the 18th Century. Annals of the period are spiced with fantastic bets. Horace Walpole wrote Horace Mann on October 17, 1756: "My Lord Rockingham and my nephew, Lord Orford, have made a match for five hundred pounds between five turkeys and five geese to run from Norwich to London." Rockingham won. His gaggle of geese kept waddling, whereas Orford's turkeys insisted on roosting at night. Orford appeared at Newmarket driving a team of four stags. Even so, as coachman, he falls far short of Postmaster Huddy, of Lismore, Ireland, who in 1821 bet he could drive the twelve miles to Fermoy in "a Dungarvon oyster tub drawn by a pig, a badger, two cats, a goose and a hedgehog." The rollicking old scamp (he was then ninety-seven) put on a large red nightcap, whipped up his team, "blew on a common cow's horn to encourage them" and —I am delighted to report—flashed over the finish line "going away."

*   *   *   *

Currency was again a stage prop when a gentleman "laid a wager to a considerable amount" that he would stand on London Bridge for a whole day, offering a trayful of fresh-minted gold sovereigns at a penny apiece, and not find a single buyer. He took his post and made his pitch. Londoners had readily paid to see a man climb into a bottle, but pay a penny for a sovereign? Be damned if they were *that* gullible!'*

The 18th century always seemed to be betting against time. A Miss Pond bet 200 guineas that she could ride 1,000 miles in 1,000 hours without changing mounts, and did it easily. A few years later, a clergyman from Essex (still another of those sporting parsons!) bet twenty pounds that he could ride 100 miles in fourteen hours; he, too, won easily.

* * * *

From riding they turned to walking. In 1788, a twenty-two-year-old Dubliner named Thomas Whalley bet £20,000 that he would walk to Jerusalem, play ball against its walls, and walk back within a year; he did it in nine months. (Whalley also bet that he'd jump from his drawing-room window into the first barouche that passed and kiss its occupant; he won that bet too.)

* * * *

Some walkers preferred handicap races. In 1764, a man from Lincolnshire took a two-to-one bet against his walking three and a quarter miles in three hours, with a fifty-pound weight in each hand; he made it in an hour. That same year, a drunken baker bet two guineas that he could carry a 168-pound sack of flour for a mile without stopping; he did it in twenty-five minutes.

* * * *

A number of races against time took place in the barroom or the dining room, since guzzling and gormandizing offer especially attractive opportunities for a flutter. If the Wheel Tavern survives in East Anglia, I am confident that its clients still discuss that night in 1787 when a local farmer bet he could eat two dozen small mutton pies and drink a gallon of ale within half an hour. When he had won, he complained that he was still hungry, so he tamped down a loaf of bread and a pound of cheese. Even this left a few crannies, but a leg of cold pork—a gift from the bug-eyed landlord—filled him up nicely. That the Bottomless Farmer then told the landlord, "I hate to go to bed on an empty stomach," I reject as an improbable gloze.

---

* The following news story appeared in the London *Observer* for May 28, 1961: "For a bet an art-gallery in Villefranche-sur-Mer offered a Modigliani landscape for sale for a fortnight at a price of 120 N.F. [about $24]. It's worth five million [about $1,000,000]. There were no offers."

* * * *

Hugh Troy once bet that a horrid little poem he had composed as a joke would be printed in *The New York Times*. Hugh, who later became famous as a muralist and illustrator ... [began] by borrowing an old lady's name. As a notional "Miss Julia Annsbury, of Auburn, N.Y.," he wrote to inquire of the *Time*'s Sunday book section if anyone could help her identify a poem that had "haunted her since long-gone childhood"—a poem about a gypsy lass struck ill on the trail and left behind, alone. Two weeks passed. Then, "Why, yes!" replied "Poetry Lover, Rahway, N.J." (Troy again, of course.) "I happen to remember the poem Miss Annsbury seeks. It is by Hugh Troy, and if memory does not fail me, its last lines run like this:

> *So we leave her,*
> *So we leave her,*
> *Far from where her swarthy*
> *kindred roam,*
> *In the scarlet fever,*
> *In the scarlet fever,*
> *Convalescent home.*"

* * * *

Would you like to know now how the man on foot at Meadow Brook beat the man on the polo pony? Remember, the rider had to dismount at the far end of the field and drink a glass of water. Well, the water was boiling hot.

A Veteran Looks Back

A longtime gambler, a sometime convict, John Philip Quinn reformed in time to write an enduring work of scholarship and reminiscence, *Fools of Fortune*, of which the two sketches below are characteristic. He rued the day when, only a few years after his birth in Missouri in 1846, he became a gambler. Still, like others before and after him, he seems to have enjoyed the recollection of certain entertaining moments.

BY JOHN PHILIP QUINN

IN VARIOUS chapters throughout this work, I have related experiences of my own in which I have exhibited myself in the light of being naturally rather timid. I do not think that my inborn proclivities were towards physical cowardice, however much they may have inclined me towards vice. The truth is, that "conscience doth make cowards of us all." A few incidents in my own career may serve to illustrate the truth of this principle.

I was once playing poker with a partner and a stranger. My confederate and myself had succeeded in winning a large amount of money from the greenhorn who had been rash enough to try his luck against us. Success had so far emboldened me that I lost all regard for ordinary prudence. I dealt the greenhorn four kings and gave myself four aces. He was irritated in no small degree by his losses and determined to bring matters to a focus. When he looked at his cards and saw that he had four kings, he drew a Remington six shooter from his pocket, and laying it upon the table announced his intention of shooting any man at the board who had a hand to beat his. My partner was struck with terror and signalled me to allow the man to win. I felt rather uneasy myself, but determined that if I must die I would at least pass out of this life with the best grace possible under the circumstances. Looking at my adversary with a bland expression I said, in dulcet tones, "You don't mean before the draw, do you, sir? I would rather look for a free lunch than for a fight any day." This remark appeared to mollify him somewhat, and I asked him how many cards he wanted. He looked at me grimly and said, "None." "Well," said

I, "I believe that I shall have to take two." Having said this, I discarded two aces, drawing in exchange the first two chance cards which happened to lie upon the top of the pack. Of course, this ruined my hand, but I am inclined even to this day, to believe that it saved my life.

*   *   *   *

There exists a class of people—and its members are far too numerous—who, while condemning gambling in the abstract, are particularly outspoken in their denunciation of the vice when practiced by members of their own family, nevertheless they have such a respect for money, that "lucre," even when won at the gaming table, is not too filthy to command respect for its owner. The motto of such people seems to be: "Get money—honestly if you can, but get it." An old acquaintance of mine once told me the following story, which is an illustration of the foregoing reflection, for the truth of which he vouched:

The young man, whom we will call James, once lived in a small Western city. His fondness for amusement led him into bad company, and he plunged into all sorts of dissipation, soon becoming a devotee of the green cloth. His parents deplored his lapse from morality, and frequently consulted altogether as to the best means of effecting his reformation. To deny him admission to the house might be to send him to ruin; persuasion they had found to be utterly without avail; example he derided and threats were a subject for mockery. Accordingly they decided to adopt an attitude of what might be called, for want of a better name, "armed neutrality." They determined to allow him to occupy his room and take his meals at home, but never to speak to him. The wayward son used to return to the paternal roof at all hours of the early morning, and after a few hours of sleep would make his appearance at the breakfast table. His father filled his plate and his mother poured his coffee. The rest of the family carried on a conversation, but no one spoke to James. One night the youth had been "playing in great luck" and had returned home a winner to the amount of several hundred dollars. The following morning at the breakfast table his little sister asked her mother for half-a-dollar, with which to buy a school book. The old lady referred her to her father, who looked sour and querulously said that he saw no reason why he should buy it. The prodigal had heard what had been said, and drawing a roll of bills from his pocket handed the little one a five dollar bank note, saying: "Here, sis, get your book and keep the change." His mother looked at the old man, and the latter stared at his son. Raising her spectacles and looking at her erring boy with a glance of mingled affection and pride, she asked in honied tones: "James, son, dear, is your coffee sweet enough?"

◇◇◇

The Whang-doodle

And this one is merely to suggest that, in the old days at least, the wise poker player who was a stranger in town did well to look around and read the signs before raising a bet.

FROM ESQUIRE'S BOOK OF GAMBLING

◇◇◇

AT LEAST these days everybody is playing the game the same way. There was a time when the game varied according to geography. If Hoyle had the rules down, there was some agreement, but a game like poker was open to the widest interpretation. If you learned in Omaha you played Omaha-style. When Omaha-style sat down with New York-style, they weren't even playing the same game.

The classic of the stories that illustrate this point is the one about the stranger who sat down to a game of poker in a cattle town. After a run of so-so hands he picked up the ace, king, queen, jack, ten of hearts—a royal flush. Primed for the kill, he kept upping the ante until there was only one player left in the betting against him. This fellow, with the assurance of a man who knows he is holding the best hand in the deck, matched him raise for raise. Finally the stranger out of sheer compassion called his foolhardy opponent, and unveiled his dreamboat.

"Royal flush," he said and without bothering to look at the other's cards began raking in the pot.

A brown paw shot out to detain him. "Hold your horses, stranger. . . . I got a hand here that's a mite better. . . . A Whang-doodle."

The stranger stared down at the cards the other had laid down: a seven, five, four, trey and deuce—and not even in the same suit. He was moving for his gun when one of the players caught his eye and nodded at a sign on the wall behind him.

It read: "Nothing in this house beats a Whang-doodle."

Mindful of the fact that poker customs vary with localities, the stranger eased his shooting iron back into the holster and continued with the game. Sure enough, some hands later he picked up a hand containing a seven, five, four, trey and deuce—and not in the same suit. Accordingly he bet the limit and again found himself in a show-down with one other hand.

"This time," he announced triumphantly, "this time no son of a such and such can have a hand to beat this one." He spread his hand. "Read 'em and weep. . . . A Whang-doodle."

The opponent, laying down a full house, shook his head commiserat-ingly and pointed to another sign on the wall behind the stranger. It read: "Only one Whang-doodle a night per table."

We don't recommend trying that on your visiting cousin from out-of-town, especially if cousin is bigger than you are.

A Poker Game

Out of a random miscellany of writings of Stephen Crane's post-humously published as *Last Words* (1902) comes this sketch with a characteristic Crane touch—i.e., one in which the winner is also a sort of loser.

BY STEPHEN CRANE

USUALLY A poker game is a picture of peace. There is no drama so low-voiced and serene and monotonous. If an amateur loser does not softly curse, there is no orchestral support. Here is one of the most exciting and absorbing occupations known to intelligent American manhood; here a year's reflection is compressed into a moment of thought; here the nerves may stand on end and scream to themselves, but a tranquillity as from heaven is only interrupted by the click of chips. The higher the stakes the more quiet the scene; this is a law that applies everywhere save on the stage.

And yet sometimes in a poker game things happen. Everybody remembers the celebrated corner on bay rum that was triumphantly consummated by Robert F. Cinch, of Chicago, assisted by the United States courts and whatever federal power he needed. Robert F. Cinch enjoyed his victory four months. Then he died, and young Bobbie Cinch came to New York in order to more clearly demonstrate that there was a good deal of fun in twenty-two million dollars.

Old Henry Spuytendyvil owns all the real estate in New York save that previously appropriated by the hospitals and Central Park. He had been a friend of Bob's father. When Bob appeared in New York, Spuytendyvil entertained him correctly. It came to pass that they just naturally played poker.

One night they were having a small game in an uptown hotel. There were five of them, including two lawyers and a politician. The stakes depended on the ability of the individual fortune.

Bobbie Cinch had won rather heavily. He was as generous as sunshine, and when luck chases a generous man it chases him hard, even though he cannot bet with all the skill of his opponents.

Old Spuytendyvil had lost a considerable amount. One of the lawyers from time to time smiled quietly, because he knew Spuytendyvil well, and he knew that anything with the name of loss attached to it sliced the old man's heart into sections.

At midnight Archie Bracketts, the actor, came into the room. "How you holding 'em, Bob?" said he.

"Pretty well," said Bob.

"Having any luck, Mr. Spuytendyvil?"

"Blooming bad," grunted the old man.

Bracketts laughed and put his foot on the round of Spuytendyvil's chair. "There," said he, "I'll queer your luck for you." Spuytendyvil sat at the end of the table. "Bobbie," said the actor, presently, as young Cinch won another pot, "I guess I better knock your luck." So he took his foot from the old man's chair and placed it on Bob's chair. The lad grinned good-naturedly and said he didn't care.

Bracketts was in a position to scan both of the hands. It was Bob's ante, and old Spuytendyvil threw in a red chip. Everybody passed out up to Bobbie. He filled in the pot and drew a card.

Spuytendyvil drew a card. Bracketts, looking over his shoulder, saw him holding the ten, nine, eight, and seven of diamonds. Theatrically speaking, straight flushes are as frequent as berries on a juniper tree, but as a matter of truth the reason that straight flushes are so admired is that they are not as common as berries on a juniper tree. Bracketts stared, drew a cigar slowly from his pocket, and, placing it between his teeth, forgot its existence.

Bobbie was the only other stayer. Bracketts flashed an eye for the lad's hand and saw the nine, eight, six, and five of hearts. Now, there are but six hundred and forty-five emotions possible to the human mind, and Bracketts immediately had them all. Under the impression that he had finished his cigar, he took it from his mouth and tossed it toward the grate without turning his eyes to follow its flight.

There happened to be a complete silence around the green-clothed table. Spuytendyvil was studying his hand with a kind of contemptuous smile, but in his eyes there perhaps was to be seen a cold, stern light expressing something sinister and relentless.

Young Bob sat as he had sat. As the pause grew longer, he looked up once inquiringly at Spuytendyvil.

The old man reached for a white chip. "Well, mine are worth about that much," said he, tossing it into the pot. Thereupon he leaned back comfortably in his chair and renewed his stare at the five straight diamonds. Young Bob extended his hand leisurely toward his stack. It occurred to Bracketts that he was smoking, but he found no cigar in his mouth.

The lad fingered his chips and looked pensively at his hand. The silence of those moments oppressed Bracketts like the smoke from a conflagration.

Bobbie Cinch continued for some moments to coolly observe his cards. At last he breathed a little sigh and said, "Well, Mr. Spuytendyvil, I can't play a sure thing against you." He threw in a white chip. "I'll just call you. I've got a straight flush." He faced down his cards.

Old Spuytendyvil's fear, horror, and rage could only be equaled in volume to a small explosion of gasoline. He dashed his cards upon the table. "There!" he shouted, glaring frightfully at Bobbie. "I've got a straight flush, too! And mine is Jack high!"

Bobbie was at first paralyzed with amazement, but in a moment he recovered, and, apparently observing something amusing in the situation, he grinned.

Archie Bracketts, having burst his bond of silence, yelled for joy and relief. He smote Bobbie on the shoulder. "Bob, my boy," he cried exuberantly, "you're no gambler, but you're a mighty good fellow, and if you hadn't been you would be losing a good many dollars this minute."

Old Spuytendyvil glowered at Brackett, "Stop making such an infernal din, will you, Archie?" he said morosely. His throat seemed filled with pounded glass. "Pass the whisky."

How to Do It

Working professionals of Las Vegas and elsewhere argue strenuously that only idiots play systems. But even they might grant that there is such a thing as good advice in general from an old master. There is at least one blackjack method that appears to be demonstrably effective when given the benefit of a distinctly fast mathematical mind and a highly retentive memory. And for the superstitious there are what might be a valuable tip or two (who knows?) involving rusty horseshoe nails and the like.

◇◇

Advice from Nick the Greek

Nicholas Andreas Dandolos (1883, probably, to 1966), was generally regarded as the most famous gambler of his era. He reputedly won or lost over $500 million, beginning in 1919 when he hit the bank at Monte Carlo three times for $20,000. The range of his friendships included Albert Einstein, the Prince of Wales (later Edward VIII), and Jack Dempsey. In the judgment of Ted Thackrey, Jr., from whose *The Gambling Secrets of Nick the Greek* the following meditations are taken, he was a cultivated and honorable man. To his quasi-namesake, Jimmy the Greek, the Las Vegas oddsmaker, he was of "mean, suspicious mind," of doubtful skills as a gambler, and a cheat when opportunity offered. Anyhow, here is Nick the Greek speaking for himself.

BY TED THACKREY, JR.

"THE ONLY difference between a winner and a loser," said Nick The Greek, "is character.

"Of course, that's just about the only difference you can really find between people anyway. But what a man really is, and what he really thinks of himself, seems to come out more swiftly at the gaming table than anywhere else.

"Even when he's got a big stack of chips in front of him, you can spot a loser from the moment you can see and hear him. And you can just about predict everything he'll do until the moment he walks out the door with empty pockets."

It was a cool evening in the middle of a week.

Summer had come to Nevada. Along the Las Vegas Strip the casino action was slow—tourists confined themselves to weekends; and to the nights, at that, despite the omnipresent air-conditioning of the casinos.

Nick had spent an hour at the Craps table, lost about $500 and switched to Blackjack, where he won back about $300 in a dull game. When the cards seemed to turn against him, he moved away and sat down to wait for the Faro game to open at the Stardust.

"In a way," he said, "it is a pity that we have to play for money to make these games interesting. It's really just a way of keeping score. It's not real. Not something of intrinsic value.

"Money is not a good in itself.

"Too often—much too often, believe me—money is used as a crutch. A balm for wounded egos. A weapon for men of vicious nature. A substitute for character in the individual.

"That is a pity, as I said before. And all the more so because it leads to an entirely fallacious line of thought concerning money. Worst of all, it encourages the stupid and the ignorant to look upon money as an end in itself, which in turn causes them to allow money to control them.

"Such a course of action, followed to its inevitable end, can only result in the total destruction of the individual and the impoverishment of an entire society...." He paused, seeing that his listeners were, in the main, not following his thought to any marked degree.

"Such philosophical conclusions aside," Nick continued, "the consideration of money as an end in itself is also likely to lead to the poorhouse.

"Every time I enter a casino," he mourned, "I know that at some point in the evening I will hear some player state that he doesn't 'want to win a lot—just a couple of hundred to cover expenses.'

"Isn't that terrifying?

"With such an attitude, how can a man have any hope at all of winning so much as a five-dollar bill?

"And then, again, you hear the false humor of the player who proclaims, 'I'm just in it for the fun. All I want is to break even... that's all.'

"A peculiar cast of thought, you must agree. After all, the poor fellow was even when he walked in the door. If that's all he wants, what was his point in gambling in the first place?

"Still, I understand well enough what these people are doing.

"It's a common failing, and by no means confined to those who come to the tables of chance. You'll find people doing just the same things—and using almost the same words—in almost every line of endeavor.

"The player who laughs uproariously when he loses his last dollar, and then stays around to laugh just as loudly when anyone else loses. (Of course, a person like that is going to get hurt anyway!)

"The player who disturbs everyone at his table by actually praying to the dice or the cards, aloud, 'Give me just one more six—just one. It's all I ask.' He's doing the same thing.

"The one who thinks he must be a comedian. Ten and twenty thousand dollars the hotel is paying for entertainers in the various rooms—but he has to furnish alleged comedy of his own.

"The 'red-board' player who bleeds all over everyone and informs the world what a sucker anyone is to gamble in a casino, while steadily contributing his bankroll to the house.

"The one who just can't keep his mouth shut about what a genius he is—as long as he's winning. He wants to tell everyone at his table how to gamble, and wants to tell the casino owners just how smart he is to be beating them. (Some people of this type can't be still even after they've lost their last dollar!)

"These obnoxious people are not the unique burden of the gaming halls.

"Look around you, every day.

"All of them are there, doing exactly the same thing in slightly different form, in every stratum of society and every division of human labor. They all share a common goal and a common failing.

"They believe that money is something far more than a handy scorekeeping device.

"And they are giving themselves excuses . . . to lose it!"

The Greek maintained that it was no difficult task to look at any given gaming table and mark the players—without regard to the size of the bankroll displayed in front of them—as losers or winners.

"Naturally," he said, "the losers will be in the majority. They are in the majority everywhere.

"However, as in business or personal relationships or anything else, the fact that the odds are against them in what they are doing has little or nothing to do with making them losers.

"Remember this: The house doesn't beat a player. It merely gives him the opportunity to beat himself!"

The winners, he said, are a different proposition entirely.

They give themselves no excuses.

"When you see a man walk into the casino with an air of quiet confidence and buy a specific amount of chips—without asking whether he can cash a check later should need arise—then proceed directly to one game and test his luck with small wagers until he's sure of how it's running, keep an eye on him.

"You can bet that the pit boss will.

"And so may the manager, before the night's out.

"This man will be playing one of the two or three games where the odds against him are lowest, and he will be making bets on those parts of the game which are most intelligent.

"He will show no hesitation, because he will not be guessing.

"He will know the game and how it's played *before* he risks his first chip. And when he wins he will increase his stakes, to take full advantage of his luck. And when he's losing, he will bet conservatively, to ride out the streak.

"Should he lose the chips he came in with, he will quit.

"But as long as he is winning . . . you'll have to close the table or set fire to the casino to get him away.

"He lets the luck quit him; he never quits his luck. . . ."

Naturally, Nick went on, this kind of player has little or no time for small talk—or big talk—or comedy, or crowing, or crying, or any of the other distractions which cause a man to interrupt concentration on his game.

The drinks which are sent by the management to his table will be largely ignored, unless he takes just one, a few minutes before he is ready to quit or take a breather anyway.

The food, too, will be rejected for the most part.

"Too much food," said Nick, "is a soporific. And the last thing any winning player ever needs is a soporific. Two hours of steady play at any table is deadly enough on the powers of concentration.

"Time enough to drink or eat when you're doing it on the money you've taken away from the house!"

Enlarging on this last point, Nick's personal advice for the player who finds himself becoming even slightly drowsy, which can happen to anyone, at any time, was to cure it by any means at hand.

Nick had once found himself in a predicament considerably more serious than any likely to be encountered by the average player.

His luck was running good. But his body was giving him trouble. A leg, swollen and painful, was intruding upon his consciousness and impairing his absorption with the game. It was obviously time to seek medical aid. At the same time he knew he could not expect to walk away from the table to a doctor's office and find the luck still waiting there for him when he returned a week later. A compromise seemed in order.

For 55 hours Nick stayed at the table, winning steadily, while the hotel's house doctor pumped penicillin into him.

"I wound up $54,000 to the good," he smiled reminiscently, "and the leg was cured, too, by the time the winning streak died and I could go home to get some rest."

For more mundane situations, his recommendations continued less of the heroic and more of the practical.

"If you feel drowsy after a couple of hours," he advised, "go into the bathroom and take a look at yourself in the mirror. Tell yourself it's time to show what you're really made of.

"Then clean your fingernails.

"Wash your face and hands.

"Comb your hair, blow your nose—hell, brush your teeth if you've got a toothbrush handy! In short, go over yourself as if you were just starting for the day. Make your mind a blank throughout this process. *Don't* keep thinking of the game, back there. Think of something beautiful . . . a sunset, perhaps, or the way the clouds hang over a mountain in the early morning. (Never of a woman; this is distracting.) And then, when you go back to the game, concentrate entirely on it once more.

"If the feeling comes back a few hours later, take another break. Go through the same process. Or, if weather permits, take a little stroll outside the casino in the fresh air. Fresh air won't kill you. Maybe what's wrong is just inhalation of too much conditioned, synthetic air. Or too much cigar smoke.

"The point is not *what* you do, specifically.

"The point is whether or not it relaxes you, refreshes you, and puts your mental equipment back in working order. If it does this, it would matter not at all whether your technique were to take a walk or meditate in the lotus position of Yoga for ten minutes."

Even the clearest and most refreshed mind, however, is of little use if its owner is lacking in understanding of the kind of game he is playing and the factors which can influence his ability to win or lose.

Nick conceded this failing, and went on to outline his personal plan of attack:

"The odds on all games," he said, "are, admittedly, stacked against the bettor, regardless of where he does his betting. However, as I have mentioned many times before, some of the games are a better bet than others.

"Faro, for instance, is an excellent game with a very low—sometimes nonexistent—house percentage. You can't ask better than an absolutely even bet, can you?

"Craps is next, if you stick to the Pass, Come (or, as I prefer, the Don't Pass and Don't Come), and then either lay or take the odds on the points.

"Blackjack, too, has a low house edge for the expert player.

"Shimmy is a game where the house p-c is low enough to be interesting.

"But even if a player sticks to these games, he has no guarantee of coming out a winner, or even of finishing even (which is nonsense, in any case). There is no method known to humanity that can change a minus expectation (a formal term for negative odds) to a plus expectation.

"Yet, it *is* possible to win!

"The secret—and the difference between winners and losers—is in discipline.

"That is, the winner manages his money.

"The loser lets the money manage him."

Money management, as Nick saw it, was one of the ultimate tests of human character and intelligence. It requires, first of all, the basic intention of winning.

"Remember what I told you before?" he inquired. "You can only win if you intend to do so. Don't laugh! The loser loses because, back in the part of the mind where he lives, he wants to do so.

"He is punishing himself, sometimes, for something or other. Or he is demonstrating to his own satisfaction the fact of his own unworthiness.

"Who knows how many reasons a man may have to want to lose?

"But the greatest run of luck in the world will be useless to him in this frame of mind. No matter how much he wins, he will be, literally, *afraid* to quit winners. He will stay at the table, hour after hour, until he finally gets what he wants—an empty pocket, and an empty checking account."

Nick was convinced that almost any player with any knowledge of a game knows when it's time for him to quit. Winners, he believed, heed this knowledge. Losers ignore it.

"It takes real character to quit winners," he said. "If you do this, you will have to submit to admiration and envy from other players—perhaps even from the management of the casino. Nobody would think of pitying a winner.

"So it comes down to a matter of what you'd rather have: Pity or admiration?

"Think it over. When you've made up your mind, half the work is done."

The rules for becoming a winner—and the explanation of how such a thing can happen in defiance of odds—seemed remarkably simple from Nick's point of view.

"Not that I always follow them," he admitted ruefully. "There is some evidence to indicate that I am a member of the human race, and thus prey to its follies and self-deceptions. But when I do *not* follow these rules, at least I try not to deceive myself about what I have done when I reexamine the matter, later."

The technique of winning he summed up in a simple thought-problem. It went this way:

Suppose a man enters a casino with $500 in his pocket once every month for six months, and refuses at any time to write a check for more or to borrow additional funds.

Suppose, further, that for the first five sessions he loses his $500 stake. That's a run of bad luck in anybody's book, but it can happen to the best gamblers in the world. And does.

But then suppose this same man makes his sixth foray—again with just $500 as the total stake he is willing to risk—and hits his first streak of good luck.

He can play it either one of two ways.

He can bet *exactly the same way and in the same amounts* as he did on his first trip—perhaps even cutting the amounts down a little, because he doesn't want to seem too eager—and win $500 or so.

Or he can increase the amounts of his bets and hit the tables for $5,000 or more.

The first way, he's still a $1,500 loser when he quits.

The second way, he's a $3,000 winner.

"Which way," Nick inquired, "would you rather see yourself?

"If your choice is the second way, there is only one method by which you can put yourself in the picture. That is to *limit your losses* to an amount which you determine *before you set foot in the casino*—but put *no limit of any kind* on your winnings.

"Peculiarly, this is exactly the opposite of the plan followed by a good 98 percent of all gamblers.

"They somehow fear to win.

"So when they have won a little bit—a pitifully little bit, in most cases—they stop playing. Well, certainly this is half a step in the right direction. At least they didn't just keep playing forever until they could collect sympathy as losers.

"But it still makes no sense, because had they lost they would have continued cashing checks and even borrowing money and losing that, too. They place no limit of any kind on how much they can lose—only on how much they can win.

"Naturally, nobody could expect to win on that basis."

The habit of increasing bets when losing fits in neatly with the loser's habit of allowing himself unlimited losses. As soon as he's a few dollars short, he begins raising his wagers in hopes of immediately recouping the loss.

Knowledgeable gamblers call this chasing your money.

It is a common error.

Considerably less common—and no error at all—is to decrease your bets when you're losing. (In a game where you're betting constantly on fast action, it is often difficult to be sure whether the weight of the luck is for or against you. But it's not hard to check. If your pile of chips is smaller than when you started, you're losing. If it's bigger, you're winning.)

"And," said Nick, "if by decreasing the size of your bets when losing you can ride out a streak of bad luck, you have survived the run—and given yourself a chance to win.

"As soon as you're winning, you increase the bets again.

"You ride the luck.

"In short, what you are doing is to exactly reverse the playing system of the loser."

Getting down to specifics, Nick said it was his idea that a bettor should never risk more than 5 percent of his original stake on any single bet until he is sure how his luck is running. In fact, Nick recommended a smaller amount for the first few bets.

"If it's running bad, don't run away immediately," he said. "Consider the money you brought in not as money per se but as a risk *in action*. Money that is in action does not belong to you anymore. It's become something else; it is now your handy bookkeeping system.

"Ride out the first few losing bets, and keep the losses small.

"Chances are, your luck may turn. In that case, you can recoup. And when you do, you bet the sky. And you keep it up—on an ascending scale I'll suggest later—until the winning streak's finally played out.

"If the luck *doesn't* turn from bad to good ... well ... that's the breaks. And it's not the end of the world. You'll come back and have another try some other day.

"On the other hand, if a player's luck starts good from his first few bets, there is no excuse at all for conservatism.

"Remember," said The Greek, "that old percentage is always back there, grinding away. The only way you can keep it from slowly grinding your bankroll to a pulp is to win as much as possible in as few bets as possible.

"Luck runs in cycles.

"You have to win big when it's running good or be caught in the whirlpool when it's running bad."

A horrible example, Nick said, was the case of the Las Vegas visitor —an otherwise intelligent young man from Kansas—who had lost a few dollars at the Craps table, and then started to pass when he got his own hands on the dice.

After a solid 17 passes, both sevens and points, the youngster gleefully told the pit boss:

"I'm almost even!"

The pit boss didn't know whether to laugh or cry.

"And neither did I," said Nick. "After his second pass, I'd come over to the table and started breaking my own rule (Nick usually played the "Don't Come" side of the layout) by betting with him. I'd won about $8,000, and would have made more than that if it hadn't been for the house limit.

"But the kid wasn't quite that far ahead.

"You know, he'd bet exactly one dollar to come, every single damned time!"

One method recommended by The Greek for telling a winning player when it's time to "quit winners" was a system of "plateaus" based on the stake with which he originally entered the casino.

"A man who comes in with $500 as his stake," he said, "should keep that money on the table and in play until he either loses it—and quits— or has $1,000 of the house's money to stack beside it.

"When that happens, the original stake should go right back in his pocket, and stay there. If he loses the $1,000 he's built up, well, all right. It just wasn't his night. He's losing, and it's no time to chase the money.

"On the other hand, if he gets still another $500 for a total of $1,500, another $500 ought to go into his pocket. And *not* come out *again that night*.

"Now he's still got $1,000 of the house's money on the table and ready to go into play as needed. He'll be bucking the house limit on most of his bets from then on, and anything he wins should stay in play. If he loses that $1,000, it's quitting time.

"But say he's won another $4,000, besides the $1,000 he left on the table. When his luck changes and he loses back $1,000, it is *time to quit*.

"He has established a 'plateau' of $1,000 for himself. That's *exactly twice* the amount he came in with, it's all he should permit himself to lose at any time before withdrawing from the game. I don't care if his winnings stack up to ten times that amount—the moment he loses $1,000, it is safe to assume that he is all through winning for the night.

"The man who has the self-control to quit right then, without trying 'just one more bet' with his money below that $1,000 plateau, is a man who will never need pity. Or want it.

"He is a winner."

As a sidelight on this advice, Nick also had something to say about just how that "plateau" $1,000 should be lost.

"As soon as you lose a couple of bets with the house's money," he advised, "it's a good idea to cut your betting back a bit. Just as you would do if you lost the first few bets when you originally sat down to play.

"See how the luck runs.

"If it's only a little streak, you can always nudge them up there again. If not—well—again, there's a chance you can ride out the bad time on small action, and the luck will return before you've hit the bottom of the plateau.

"Maybe, too, it might be a good time to take that little walk, or wash your face.

"The losses *might* be due to a drowsiness of which you're not aware.

"In any case, remember this: A winner can actually lose more than 50 percent of his bets and still come out thousands, even millions, of dollars ahead.

"Just one streak of luck, properly ridden and encouraged, can more than compensate for a large number of bad times at the table, if you have the sense to limit your losses on them.

"Whether it does this or not is entirely up to you.

"It's a matter of character . . . entirely."

A Professor Beats the Gamblers

When a mathematical genius named Edward O. Thorp had a whirl at the blackjack tables in Las Vegas in 1958, he was on the way to launching one of the great gaming revolutions of all time. A graduate of UCLA with a doctorate in mathematics, he was about to leave California to join the faculty of the Massachusetts Institute of Technology. At the heart of the system he developed later at MIT was the electronic computer which he used to analyze the millions of possibilities contained in a deck of cards. When he returned to Nevada to put his system to the test, his success stunned the gambling community to the point where, after the publication of his book *Beat the Dealer* (1962), the rules governing blackjack in the Nevada casinos were altered. Dr. Thorp is now a faculty member at the University of California at Irvine.

BY EDWARD O. THORP

GAMBLERS HAVE learned through experience that games of chance can be run in such a way that a certain percentage favors one side at the expense of the other side. That is, if the game is played a sufficient number of times, the winnings of the favored side are generally near a certain fixed percentage of the total amount of all bets placed by the opponent. The modern gambling casino takes the side of the gambling games which has proved in practice to be favorable. If necessary, the casino alters the rules of the game so that the casino advantage is sufficient to cover expenses and yield a desirable rate of profit on the capital which the owners have invested.

There have been many attempts to overcome the casino advantage. But all of them have the same flaw. The casino always sets a limit to the amount that may be bet. With this limit on bets, the casino wins the same percentage of the gross bets which it normally wins, even though a player uses a complicated betting scheme. It was no surprise, then, when it was proved, by using the mathematical theory of probability, that for *most* of the standard gambling games no betting scheme can ever be devised that will have the slightest effect upon the casino's long-run advantage. In view of this mathematical proof and the painful experience of millions of gamblers, informed people and uninformed people alike firmly believe that it is impossible to beat any of the modern casino gambling games.

I was well acquainted with these facts, and therefore I did not harbor the belief that gambling in the casinos was a likely way to make money. I was, however, a frequent visitor in Nevada. One Christmastime during school vacation, just before my wife and I left U.C.L.A. to spend a few days in Las Vegas, a professor called my attention to an article in one of the mathematics journals. The article described a strategy for playing blackjack which assertedly limited the house to the tiny edge of .62 percent. This allows the player an almost even break, so I made up a little card with the strategy on it and brought it along on our trip.

As played in the casinos, blackjack, or twenty-one, involves a dealer employed by the casino and one to six players. After players make their bets, hands of two cards each (hole cards) are dealt to each of the players and to the dealer. The players in turn, and then the dealer, are allowed to draw additional cards. The goal is a total as close to twenty-one as possible without exceeding it. The dealer's strategy is fixed: he must draw to (hit) totals of sixteen or less and may not draw to totals of seventeen or more. Players can draw or not, as they please. They also have the option of doubling down with their hole cards—that is, they can double their bet and draw exactly one more card.

The numerical value of cards is ten for all tens and face cards; it is as labeled for cards two through nine, and aces may be counted as either one or eleven, as desired. A pair of hole cards with the same numerical value may be split, to form two hands. An additional bet equal to the original one must be placed on the new hand.

Bets are usually paid off at even money. If the player's total exceeds the dealer's, he wins. If the totals are equal, it is a tie. If the player has a lower total, he loses. If the player's total exceeds twenty-one, he "busts" and immediately loses. If the two hole cards of either the player or the dealer total twenty-one, they are termed a natural, or blackjack. Naturals are immediately turned face up and win against all non-naturals. A player is paid at the rate of three to two for a natural. There are many details which have been omitted from this sketch of rules. Also, casinos often have minor variations in these rules.

When I arrived at the blackjack tables I purchased ten silver dollars. This was more than the total amount of all bets I had made in my life up to that time. I was resigned to losing, but I wanted to see how long my stack would last, as well as to try out the strategy under fire.

In a few moments the slowness of my play and the little card in my palm amused and attracted bystanders. The dealer could not conceal his scorn for one more system player. These sentiments were laced with pity when they saw me playing. Who ever heard of splitting a pair of lowly eights and doubling the amount of money being risked when the dealer's up card was the powerful ace? Who doubled down on ace, two against a five? Why stand on a piteous twelve against a four?

To add to this beginner's misery, the dealer was having a very strong run of luck. Every player at the table was losing heavily. Surely my ten crumbs would soon be swept away. Or would they? Somehow these weird plays kept turning out right. As the other players lost heaps of chips, my little stack held. It even inched up once.

And then a strange thing happened. I was dealt ace, two. I drew a two, then a three. I now had ace, two, two, three. The dealer had a nine up. The dealer might not have nineteen. Only a fool would draw again and risk the destruction of such a good hand. I consulted my card and drew. With no little satisfaction and several tsk-tsks, the amused on-lookers saw me draw a six for fourteen. Serves me right. I drew an ace for fifteen. Tough luck; I drew again. A six! I now held ace, two, two, three, six, ace, six—a seven-card twenty-one. This is an event so rare that it happens only once per several thousand hands.

After a moment of shock, some of the bystanders said I had a twenty-five-dollar bonus coming. The dealer said no, it was only paid at a few places in Reno. I was unaware of such a bonus. But I thought it might be amusing to create the impression that I'd sacrificed my soft eighteen because I foresaw the seven-card twenty-one. The amusement and pa-tronization of some bystanders changed to respect, attentiveness, and even to goose pimples.

After another fifteen minutes and the obliteration by the dealer of all my fellow players, I was behind a total of eight and one half silver

dollars and decided to stop. The atmosphere of ignorance and superstition that pervaded my little experience securely planted in my mind
the suggestion that even good players didn't know the fundamentals of
this game.

When I returned home, I carefully studied the mathematics article
by Baldwin, Cantey, Maisel, and McDermott on blackjack. In a flash of
mathematical intuition I realized that it must be possible for the player
to beat the game. The idea was this: the basic strategy by Baldwin was
a complete set of instructions telling the player the best possible way to
play. To simplify the calculations, it was assumed that the deck always
had its average composition—that is, that all hands were dealt from a
complete shuffled deck. However, when the game is actually played,
used hands are placed face up on the bottom of the deck, and subse-
quent rounds of play come from a progressively more depleted deck.
In general, the proportions of the various cards in the depleted deck
will not be the same as in a complete deck. Thus, the casino advantage
should fluctuate. Mathematical considerations suggested that the fluctuations should often be much larger than .62 percent, and further, the
player should have the advantage frequently. If the player were to bet
very heavily when he had an advantage and very lightly when he had a
disadvantage, he would not need to have the advantage very often
in order to make a handsome profit.

The basic problem, then, was to determine when the player has the
advantage and how large this advantage is. Baldwin's calculations had
taken four capable young men a total of twelve man-years of off-duty
army time, working with the aid of desk calculators. My first step was to
master every detail of these calculations.

The next step was to analyze the effect on the casino advantage when
changes were made in the proportions of various cards in the deck. For
example, suppose all the aces are removed from the deck. No naturals
are then possible, and there are a number of other changes in the game.
The result is that the player is seriously hurt.

It would be necessary to make a number of calculations similar to the
Baldwin calculation, but because greater precision was desirable, they
would each be many times as lengthy. Since ten thousand man-years at
desk calculators were required, the problem could be done only by an
electronic computer. I had access to the IBM 704 in the M.I.T. compu-
tation center. Writing up instructions for the computer turned out for
this problem to be a long and tricky business. However, when I finished,
it took the computer a mere seven hours to type out the answer—
enough numbers to fill an average-size book.

The answers amazed me. The typical casino advantage over a player using the best complete deck strategy, hereafter called the basic strategy, was less than .21 percent. I have since learned that, in fact, the player using the basic strategy has a small edge of about .16 percent over the house, *without* keeping track of the cards. If various groups of cards were used up in play, the advantage surged wildly back and forth between casino and player. (The player, if he only knew it, has the advantage about half the time.) The four fives cause a bigger swing than any other four cards. When they are gone, the player has an edge of more than 3.3 percent. The next largest effect occurs when the four aces are gone. Then the casino has an edge of about 2.7 percent. When I examined the effect of variations in the proportion of the sixteen ten-value cards present, I learned that player or house advantages of more than 10 percent were frequent. Occasionally the advantage approached 100 percent! I developed a detailed system of play which involved keeping count of the number of ten-value and non-ten-value cards remaining to be played. Experiments with several people showed that twenty hours of practice was generally adequate to train them as ten-count players for casino play.

I thought that the simpler but less efficient strategy based on counting fives might make an interesting talk at an upcoming annual meeting of the American Mathematical Society in Washington, D.C. A few days before the meeting, the society published abstracts of the two hundred or so talks that were to be given. Included was my abstract describing the fives strategy, "Fortune's Formula: A Winning Strategy for Black-jack."

Following my talk I was asked to give a press conference. Then I was televised by a major network and interviewed on a number of radio programs. Over the next few weeks I received hundreds of letters and long-distance phone calls. The bulk were requests for information. Interspersed among these were several offers to back me in a casino test of my system. The amounts proffered ranged from a few thousand dollars to as much as $100,000. Together they totaled a quarter of a million dollars.

The decision was being thrust upon me of whether or not to go to Nevada and test my ideas in play. I finally decided to go. Part of the reason was, I suppose, to silence that irritating question, "Well, if you're so smart, why aren't you rich?" Another was that I decided to write a book expounding my ideas, and I felt that the reader should know that in this case theory really works.

What may have finally clinched matters was scoffs and boasts from casinos that my claims were ridiculous. Their arrogance was succinctly summarized by a casino operator being interviewed on a nationwide television program. When he was asked whether the customers ever walked away winners, he said, "When a lamb goes to the slaughter, the lamb might kill the butcher. But we always bet on the butcher."

The most attractive offer was one of $100,000 made by two New York multimillionaires whom I will refer to as Mr. X and Mr. Y. They are both large-scale gamblers. Mr. Y has lost $100,000 in one of the casino games without being seriously hurt financially. Mr. X's gambling activities involve hundreds of thousands, and even millions in profit. At the invitation of Mr. X and Mr. Y, I flew from Boston to New York to discuss the system and to plan a trip to Nevada.

There were two main approaches we could adopt for betting. One, which I'll term "wild," involved betting the casino limit whenever the advantage to the player exceeded some small figure, say one percent. This method produces, on the average, the greatest gain in the shortest time. However, in a short run of a few days, the fluctuations in the player's total capital generally are violent, now favoring the player, now favoring the casino, so a large bankroll is required. Mr. X and Mr. Y said that they would back this to the extent of $100,000, and that they would go further if necessary.

I was not in favor of this approach, since there were too many things I did not know about the gambling world. I also had no idea how I would be affected if I were to get behind, say $50,000, and were betting each minute more than my monthly salary. Further, the purpose of the trip, from my point of view, was to test my system rather than to make big money for Mr. X and Mr. Y, so I preferred being certain of a moderate win, rather than a probable, but somewhat uncertain, big win. I therefore favored conservative play, betting twice the minimum bet I was making when the advantage was one percent, four times my minimum when it was 2 percent, and finally leveling off at ten times my minimum when it was 5 percent or more in my favor. If my bets ranged from $50 to $500 (the highest casino maximum generally available), $6000 or $7000 would probably be adequate capital. To be safe, we took along $10,000.

When the M.I.T. spring recess came, Mr. X and I flew to Reno, where Mr. Y was to join us. We checked into one of the large Reno hotels about 2 A.M. and immediately went to sleep. Early the next morning we investigated casinos.

Our plan was to start small betting, $1 to $10, and gradually increase the amount of the bets as I gained experience. Eventually we planned to bet $50 to $500, always using the ten-count system.

First we drove to a casino outside of town. In an hour or so of play I won a few dollars, and the establishment closed for three hours because of Good Friday, so we returned to Reno. We next investigated a number of casinos in Reno to determine which rules were most favorable. As a nice spot for practicing, we selected a casino that dealt down to the last card and allowed the player to double down on any hand, split any pair, and insure. This is a more favorable set of rules than is ordinarily found.

After a lavish dinner and a rest, I returned about 10 P.M. I began by playing for fifteen or twenty minutes at a time and then resting for a few minutes. When I sat down again, I always chose the table with the fewest players. I also paused for thought and stared at all the cards played. My behavior pattern made it apparent that I was using some system. But system players are frequent, if not common, in the casinos. They are welcome as long as they are losing. Playing $1 to $10, I gradually fell further behind, until at 5 A.M. I was down $100.

Then business fell off sharply, and I was able to get a table completely to myself. My new dealer was particularly unfriendly. When I asked to be dealt two hands, she refused, saying that it was house policy that I must bet $2 per hand to play two hands. This change in the scale of betting would have confused my records of the evening's play, so I refused. Besides, I was getting tired and irritable. After a sharp exchange of words, she dealt as rapidly as she could.

Just then a one percent advantage arose. I decided to go to the $2 to $20 scale and bet $4. I won, and the advantage coincidentally advanced to 2 percent. I let my $8 ride and won. My advantage rose to 4 percent. I let my $16 ride and won again. I left $20 on the table with the remark that it was time to take a small profit. I continued with $20 bets as the deck remained favorable. At the end of the deck, I had recouped my $100 loss and had a few dollars profit besides.

The doubling-up betting pattern I used in the last few minutes makes no sense in games where the house has the advantage, but in blackjack, with counting methods, it is as profitable as any other way of putting down money *at favorable times*. Further, since it is so widely and so unsuccessfully practiced, it makes excellent camouflage.

Sandy-eyed and stiff, I woke up early Saturday afternoon and had breakfast. Mr. X and I again visited the casino outside of town. Within minutes, playing $10 to $100, I won two or three hundred. Then Mr. X jumped in. After two hours, we had accumulated $650, and the house began to "shuffle up"—that is, they would shuffle the deck several cards before the end. Favorable situations arise with greatest frequency toward the end of the deck, so shuffling can sharply reduce the rate of profit. Since we were practicing, it seemed discreet to leave and hope we could come back later for a few full-scale hours.

Mr. Y arrived Saturday evening, and we set out to seek our fortune. First we visited one of the most famous clubs in the center of downtown Reno. We began play at the $500-maximum tables. (The maximum generally ranges from $100 to $500 in Nevada, varying from casino to casino, and frequently from table to table within a given casino. With our capital, we preferred the highest maximum possible.) In fifteen minutes we won $500 while warming up at $25 to $250. Then our dealer pressed a concealed button under the table with her foot. In a few minutes the owner and his son arrived. There were many pleasantries and politenesses exchanged, but they made their point: the deck would be shuffled as often as necessary to prevent us from winning.

The owners had learned, over the last decade, that some players wait for very special combinations of cards to arise at the end of the deck. Then they sharply up their bet, sometimes going from $1 to $500. These players are stopped by shuffling five or ten cards from the end of the deck.

To be safe, the owners instructed our dealer to shuffle twelve to fifteen cards from the end. Fortunately for them, they waited to see the results. The tens strategy locates favorable situations after the first hand has been played, even as early as after only four cards have been dealt.

A few minor situations appeared and were exploited by us. Then the deck was shuffled twenty-five cards from the end. Still, occasional minor favorable situations arose. Finally the dealer began shuffling forty-two cards from the end, after only two hands had been played. During this twenty minutes of fencing, bad luck in addition to this particular club's unfavorable rules and the shuffling allowed us to squeeze out only an additional $80, so we stopped.

We next visited the casino in one of the large hotels, where we had been told that a cheat dealer was used on big-money players. After being cheated on the very first hand, we moved on.

At our next stop, the maximum was $300, but this was compensated for by excellent rules: the player could insure, split any pair, and double down on any set of cards. We purchased $200 in chips from the cashier and selected an empty table. I lost steadily, and at the end of four hours of play I was $1700 behind and quite discouraged. However, I decided to wait for the deck to become favorable just once more so that I could recoup some of my losses.

In a few minutes the deck obliged, suddenly producing a 5 percent advantage calling for the maximum bet of $300. Curiously, my remaining chips amounted to precisely $300. As I tried to decide whether to quit if I lost this one, I picked up my hand and found a pair of eights. They must be split. I flung three $100 bills from my wallet onto the second eight. On one of the eights I was dealt a three. I had to double down. So I flung three more $100 bills onto this hand. Nine hundred dollars was now lying on the table, the largest bet I'd yet made.

The dealer was showing a six up and had a ten under and promptly busted. Now I was only eight hundred dollars down. This deck continued favorable, and the next deck went favorable almost at once. In a few minutes I wiped out all my losses and went ahead $255. Then we quit for the evening.

For the second time, the tens system had shown a feature that would appear again and again—moderately heavy losing streaks, mixed with "lucky" streaks of the most dazzling brilliance.

The next afternoon the three of us visited the casino outside of town again. Before sitting down to play, I made a phone call. When I came back my friends told me the casino had barred us from play, but that they would be only too happy to pick up our meal tab. I called the floor manager and asked him what this was all about. He explained, in a very friendly and courteous manner, that they had seen me playing the day before and were very puzzled at my steady winning at a rate that was large for my bet sizes. He said that they decided that a system was involved.

We returned to our hotel, and while my friends took care of business, I spent a couple of hours betting $5 to $50 at our hotel's tables. Despite the annoying presence of a shill, I won about $550. At this point, the pit boss asked me to stop playing at the hotel. He said that this also went for Mr. X and Mr. Y and any other friends.

It was almost suppertime Sunday when the three of us revisited the casino at which I had made the $900 bet. I was warmly remembered as the rich playboy of the night before who had been down $1700 before wriggling off the hook by some quirk of fate. We were invited to dine, courtesy of the house, as a prelude to the evening's gaming festivities. After two $4 entrées of assorted baked oysters on the half shell and various supporting dishes, capped with wine, I set out somewhat unsteadily for the gaming tables. Within a few minutes, however, I was at peak alertness. After four hours of betting $25 to $300, I was ahead about $2000. I was beginning to tire, so with the utmost reluctance I returned to my hotel.

I remember that casino fondly: the fine cuisine, the spacious attractive modern dining room, and the casino with its little clusters of blackjack tables, the favorable rules, the courtesy and hospitality, and, last but not least, the free money.

We were again ready for action early Monday afternoon. We decided to drive to the south end of Lake Tahoe. About 6 P.M. we arrived at a large brightly lighted gambling factory. It was jammed. I was barely able to get a seat at the blackjack tables.

A few minutes after I placed on the table $2000 worth of chips I had purchased from the cashier, a drooling pit boss rushed over to invite me to dinner and the show. I requested that my two friends be included. In a few minutes, I won $1300, and Mr. X, betting wildly, won $2000. Then we took time out for our free dinner—filet mignon and champagne. Within hours, destiny would present us with a bill for our free dinner. The charge? Eleven thousand dollars.

After dinner we strolled over to another casino. There was a $500 limit and acceptable rules. As usual, I purchased $2000 in chips from the cashier and selected the least busy table. From the beginning I was plagued by $1 bettors who came and went, generally slowing down the game and concealing cards so that they were hard to count.

Whenever one arrived, I pointedly reduced my minimum bet from $50 to $1. After a few minutes the pit boss got the message and asked me if I would like a private table. When I said it would transport me with ecstasy, he explained that the club didn't like the psychological effect of a private table on the other customers. With a trace of a smile, he said that a $25-minimum game could be arranged, and wondered if that would be satisfactory. I promptly agreed, and a sign to that effect was installed, clearing the table of all customers but me. A small crowd gathered. They were quiet, perhaps anticipating the imminent slaughter of their somewhat plumpish fellow lamb.

After I had won a few hundred, my friend Mr. X jumped in. I then took the responsibility for keeping the count and calling the signals for both of us. Within thirty minutes we had emptied the table's money tray—the blackjack version of breaking the bank. The smiles of the pit boss were replaced by signs of fear.

The employees began to panic. One of our dealers bleated to her boyfriend higher-up, "Oh, help me. Please, help me." The pit boss was trying to explain away our win to a nervous knot of subordinates. While the money tray was being restocked, the crowd swelled. They began to cheer their David on against the casino Goliath.

In two hours, we broke the bank again. The great heaps of chips in front of us included more than $17,000 in profits. I won $6000, and Mr. X, betting wildly, had won $11,000. I was tiring rapidly. The aftereffects of our huge dinner, the increased effort in managing two hands, and the strain of the last few days were telling. I began to find it very difficult to count properly and observed that Mr. X was equally far gone. I insisted that we quit, and I cashed in my $6000. As I did so, I was startled to find three or four pretty girls wandering back and forth across my path smiling affectionately.

After wending my Ulyssean way back to the tables, I watched horror-stricken. Mr. X, refusing to stop play, poured back thousands. In the forty-five minutes or so that it took to persuade him to leave, it cost the two of us about $11,000 of our $17,000. Even so, when we returned to our hotel that evening, we were ahead $13,000 so far on the trip.

Tuesday we paid a series of visits to a downtown club which had bad rules and shuffled five to ten cards from the end. We also had poor luck, and playing $50 to $500, we lost almost $2000.

We remembered that the club where I first practiced so lengthily had excellent rules and made a practice of dealing down to the last card in the deck. We decided to return there. I purchased $1000 in chips and began to win. Within minutes the owner was on the scene.

In a panic, he gave the dealer and the pit boss instructions. Whenever I changed my bet size, the dealer shuffled. Whenever I varied the number of hands I took (I could now play from one to eight hands at a time, and faster than the best dealers could deal), the dealer shuffled. The dealer whom I had played against last in my practice session was standing in the background saying over and over, in reverent tones, how much I had advanced in skill since the other night. Finally I happened to scratch my nose, and the dealer shuffled! Incredulous. I asked her whether she would shuffle each time I scratched my nose. She said she would. A few more scratches convinced me that she meant what she said. I then asked whether any change in my behavior pattern, no matter how minute, would cause her to shuffle. She said it would.

I was now playing merely even with the house, as the shuffling destroyed nearly all my advantage (except that gained from seeing the burned card). I then asked for some larger denomination chips—$50 or $100—as all I had were twenties. The owner stepped forward and said that the house would not sell them to us. He then had a new deck brought in and carefully spread, first face down, then face up. Curious, I asked why they spread them face down. Although the practice is a common one in the casinos, seldom do they examine the backs of the cards for a couple of minutes, as these people were doing. The dealer explained that it was believed that I had unusually acute vision (I wear glasses), could distinguish tiny blemishes on the backs of the cards, and that this was what enabled me to foretell what cards were going to be dealt. I scoffed, but the owner, still panicky, brought in four new decks in five minutes.

My behavior was unchanged, in spite of the new decks, so they gave up on that. In whispers, they formulated a new theory. I asked them, then, what they thought my secret was. The dealer claimed that I could count every card as it was played, so that I knew exactly which cards had not yet been played at each and every instant. It is a well-known fact to students of mnemotechny (the science of memory training) that one can readily learn to memorize in proper order a deck of cards as it is dealt. However, I am familiar enough with the method involved to know that the information, when so memorized, cannot be used quickly enough for play in blackjack. So I challenged the dealer by rashly claiming that no one in the world could watch thirty-eight cards dealt quickly off a pack and then tell me quickly how many of each type of card remained.

She answered by claiming that the pit boss, next to her, could do just that. I told them I would pay $5 on the spot for a demonstration. They both looked down sheepishly and wouldn't answer. I made my offer $50. They remained silent and ashamed. Mr. Y increased the offer to $500. There was no response. We left in disgust.

I had proved the system, and the millionaires had business elsewhere, so we agreed to terminate our little gambling experiment. In thirty man-hours of medium- and large-scale play, we built $10,000 into $21,000. At no point did we have to go into our original capital further than $1300 (plus expenses). Our experiment was a success, and my system performed in practice just as the theory predicted.

The day of the lamb had come.

❖❖❖❖❖❖❖❖❖❖❖❖❖❖❖❖❖❖❖❖❖❖❖❖❖❖❖❖❖❖❖❖❖❖❖❖

Omens and Superstitions

Variously a journalist, a radio scriptwriter, and an advertising agency executive, the late Stearn Robinson is admiringly remembered for her *The Dreamer's Dictionary* (1974), a work both scholarly and entertaining culled from dream interpretations dating from antiquity. The piece that follows is taken from what was to have been a book on superstition.

BY STEARN ROBINSON

❖❖❖❖❖❖❖❖❖❖❖❖❖❖❖❖❖❖❖❖❖❖❖❖❖❖❖❖❖❖❖❖❖❖❖❖

VIRTUALLY EVERY human activity, no matter how trivial, has its superstitions, with none more varied or ritualistic than those connected with gambling and games. Oddly enough, even those games which rely mainly on skill (rather than chance) are invested by serious players with "luck attracting" rites. Gamblers, as a class, are perhaps the most fervent believers in lucky charms and conversely in unlucky omens.

To pass another person on a staircase on the way to a gaming room is to be avoided like the plague as it is believed to signify a cross which offends the "Moody Goddess" and causes her to devitalize your luck for the following period of play.

When cutting cards you must never cut crosswise if you wish to win, and you should leave a game as quickly as you can after dropping (or flicking out) a card from the pack because this is a sign that "lady luck" is about to move elsewhere.

Frequently you will find players changing their seat or calling for a new pack of cards in the belief that the change will extend to their luck. You may also change your luck by walking around your seat from left to right which will invalidate the bad luck by enclosing it in a circle. Another method of changing your luck is to slip a handkerchief under yourself, thereby changing your base and making a new start.

Forms of defense against the devils of misfortune include "crossing out" your opponent's luck. To accomplish this you must quietly place a used match in the ashtray, then sneak another one in crosswise on top of it. Of course if you are involved with really knowledgeable players some wise guy will break up your cross with a cigarette end before you can say, "hit me," "Banco," or whatever the operative punt is.

Gamblers will carry an infinite variety of lucky charms on themselves, anything from a rabbit's foot to a rusty horseshoe nail. Amulets made from an endless variety of materials such as precious stones, worthless stones, scarabs, pixies, children's teeth, elephant's hair, you name it and no matter how bizarre, some superstitious gambler somewhere has got it in his (or her) pocket.

The hope of gain coupled with the fear of loss is the catalyst which creates a highly charged atmosphere in most gaming rooms. In this emotional climate you, as a player, are generally exposed to forces that are stronger than the rational thinking of your ordinary workaday world and you are thrown back to your ancestral belief in magic. Beginner's luck, for example, is based on the Stone Age superstitious belief in the "magic" of new things.

If you happen to be in a winning streak you will discover, if you look around you, that many other players are imitating your game or your gestures in the hope of attracting some of your luck.

When shooting craps you should try to become adept at surreptitiously touching some intimate part of your body with the dice in order to bestow "creative" power on them. There are many rules you must follow if you wish to stay on good terms with the Goddess of Chance.

You must never indicate she is with you, for this constitutes "boasting" and is a temptation for fate to intervene. Neither must you sing or whistle while gambling because using the vocal chords disperses your power whereas silence conserves it. You must always avoid transferring your luck to others and so you must not, if you wish to avoid disaster, lend money to another gambler as this symbolizes disposing of some of your luck by transmitting it to someone else.

Psychology
of Gambling

"Gaming is a principle inherent in human nature. It belongs to us all," said Edmund Burke, addressing the House of Commons on February 11, 1780. It should be a date recalled with gratitude by all casino operators, bookmakers, card and dice manufacturers (legitimate and otherwise), and not least of all by gamesters who may suffer a twinge of conscience when the grocery money goes down the drain. That is to say, what can they do about it when the universal urge acknowledged by the great Burke overcomes them? In any case, herewith a few insights, fictional and otherwise.

◇◇

The Gambler and His Motives

Compulsive gambler or occasional "punter": each has his reason for a flutter at the table or the wheel. But what is it? Very likely he himself doesn't know. But perhaps he will, after pursuing this research in one of the most comprehensive studies of gambling yet assembled, Alan Wykes's *The Complete Illustrated Guide to Gambling*.

BY ALAN WYKES

◇◇◇

GAMBLING IS a way of buying hope on credit. We are all the bonded slaves of the management that issues the credit cards. To realize the completeness of our bondage we have only to remember that each of us owes his existence to the chancy collaboration of two small fertile organisms; while an apparently chancy distribution of chromosomes, genes, and hormones influences our sex, coloring, and disposition. We press on through life toward a death whose manner and date depend entirely on chance. During our womb-to-tomb progress we never stop gambling, for we cannot know the outcome of each of the many decisions we have to make every day; we can only "hope for the best."

Even a man who sets out deliberately to free himself from the grip of chance is going to have a thin time. He can stop smoking because of the risk of lung cancer; he can give up alcohol for fear of damaging his liver; he can stay indoors to avoid the hazards of travel; he can keep his money in an old sock to avoid the risk of losing it. But if he carries his apprehensions to logical conclusions he will atrophy in bed, while his risk-taking nephew grabs the sock, spends the money on riotous living, and dies happily at the age of 94. With chance, as with many things, there is little justice.

Sensible people don't expect justice from chance. If they did, they would give up breeding children in a world that can't support them; they would not drink before driving or speed when sober; they would choose selfless leaders instead of maniacs. As it is, they propagate *ad libitum*, have a last drink for the road, and risk everything on the leadership of a Genghis Khan or a Hitler.

In 1949—to press home my point about the injustice of chance—a man was haranguing the multitude at England's Ascot racecourse. His purpose was sincere: to discourage the gamblers. He had set up an iron-railed podium under a sheltering tree and had attracted an amused crowd. While he ranted away with many an apocalyptic gesture, black clouds gathered and heavy rain began. He turned the storm to his advantage. "The wrath of God is made manifest," he boomed. "The heavens are displeased by the evil of gambling." Perhaps, however, the heavens were more displeasesd by the lecturer's presumption. As the storm built up and the audience scattered to shelter, lightning struck the tree and the iron rail of the podium and gave the anti-gambler severe shock and burns.

Statesmen are for the most part thought of as cautious people. But every international conference is hedged about with the risks of crackpot challenges and diplomatic bluffs. And it would have been impossible to advance even to our present state of world relations without political leaders chancing their arms. Guillaume Dubois, a court favorite during the reign of Louis XIV, sought England's help in shoring up the crumbling morale of his decadent country. In doing so he risked his own somewhat pockmarked career and the future of France. But his gamble led to the first *entente cordiale* among England, France, and Holland, and eventually gained him an archbishopric, a cardinal's red hat, and appointment as prime minister. Today, statesmen hold the destruction of the world at arm's length by risky diplomatic maneuvers that offer odds that few steady gamblers would accept.

Inevitably, then, we ourselves gamble, and we entrust our future to the hands of gamblers. But in this book I am not especially concerned with our unavoidable daily risks as we cross a busy street or cast a vote. I am concerned with one of the most persistent—and perhaps forgivable—of human failings: The pleasure that so many of us take in placing bets, however small or large, on the uncertain outcome of events.

The paraphernalia of the gambler is varied and extensive. Cards, dice, mah-jongg tablets, rings, and many another cryptic shape or design; animals of every kind (from insects to primates) in competitive events; men and women in every manifestation of human conflict; pawnbrokers' tickets in squalid back-street shops or ticker-tape machines in Wall Street; airplanes, motorcars, and water craft; electric hares, computing machines, newspapers, and telephones; wheels to spin and drums to mix lottery tickets; firearms, slot machines, matchsticks. One could go on interminably. The point is that all this apparatus merely offers variety of interest and a chance to develop skill. None of it is strictly necessary.

Determined gamblers will bet on which of two raindrops will first reach the bottom of a window pane, or on the number of hairs growing on a hirsute mole. Nor need the stakes necessarily be financial or even useful. The 16th-century English historian Stow reports that one Sir

Miles Partridge played at dice with King Henry VIII for the bells of St. Paul's Church, and won them. The annals of the town of Chester le Street, in the north of England, record that in 1735, "a child of James and Elizabeth Leesh was played for at cards by Henry and John Trotter, Robert Thomson and Thomas Ellison, won by the latter pair and delivered to them accordingly." From China in the fourth century B.C. comes a poem telling the story of two gamblers who, having nothing else to stake, bet their ears on which side of a birch leaf would lie uppermost after its fall from the tree; the loser honorably severed the lobes of his ears and presented them on the leaf to the winner.

The annals of gambling are full of such anecdotes—some spectacular, some not. All of them substantiate the fact that there must be complex motives behind such compulsive urges to lose (which is what those of us who gamble a great deal inevitably do in the long run).

Incidentally, there is no evidence to suggest that gambling is a natural instinct. The games of very young children are purely competitive and carry no reward but triumph and, occasionally, token "prizes." The competitive spirit apparently is born with the baby; but fascination with the elements of risk and the chance of gain develops later in the child's life, and therefore seems to be an extra provided by experience. In other words, gambling, in the sense of placing bets, is apparently part of a cultural pattern (though an exceedingly ancient one),

Why, then, do people gamble? What is it that makes the placing of a bet and the awaiting of its outcome so very exciting to most of us? It isn't easy to answer these questions. You won't find the answers by trying to observe your own reactions to the turning wheel at Monte Carlo; you'll soon be far too busy observing the wheel. But change the ethnological scene, and watch a couple of Africans playing mbao (a game with board and pieces, like chess, and involving some skill); you will witness a scene of emotional intensity, the players' eyes rolling and limbs jerking as they prostrate themselves and make appeals to gods of fortune. (But in this case the stakes are likely to be higher than you'd play for—a favorite wife, perhaps, or a herd of goats.)

In neither Monte Carlo nor the African bush, though, will you discover exactly what lies behind the fascination exerted by the whimsical turns of fortune. Actually, it is more than mere fascination for the really confirmed gambler; it is a necessity. Those of us who think ourselves jaunty devils whenever we place a small bet on a horse certainly feel excitement; we yell as loudly as anyone else when our horse makes a final spurt for the post. But such exhilaration isn't so demanding that we would fling our families into penury to repeat it.

*   *   *   *

To test my shaky faith in gamblers' knowledge of their own motives, I recently singled out 128 inveterate (as opposed to occasional) gamblers—all known to me personally. To each I sent a questionnaire—perhaps it should have been called a suggestionnaire—that suggested eight possible reasons for excessive gambling and invited the recipients to indicate any that they felt might apply to others if not themselves (an invitation designed to relieve the exercise of its resemblance to a confessional). The reasons I suggested were:

1. The acquisition of unearned money—i.e., a form of greed.
2. Social cachet—or, more bleakly, snobbery.
3. Sexual compensation.
4. Masochism.
5. Boredom: the refuge of an empty mind.
6. Intellectual exercise.
7. The desire to prove one's superiority to the forces of chance.
8. Inexplicable excitement.

A quick riffling through the replies to the suggestionnaire confirmed my suspicion that only reasons 6 and 8 would be seen by the recipients applicable to themselves. Reasons 1 (greed) and 2 (snobbery) were attributed to gamblers other than the recipients. Reasons 3 (sexual compensation) and 4 (masochism) got me nothing but some unprintably ribald comments. And only a very few respondents even bothered to consider 5 (boredom) or 7 (the desire to prove one's superiority to the forces of chance).

So much for my own probing (though I shall be returning to it later, to prove how seriously based its premises were). One might as well ask a pyromaniac why he finds so much joy in fire. An objective investigation is needed, based on a knowledge of the human mind. Inevitably, one turns to the psychologist and the psychiatrist.

In the early part of the 19th century, a Swedish doctor, Erik Kröger, set up what he called a "study spa" in Zurich and began collecting drunks and compulsive gamblers. A report on his observations, which he sent to a medical colleague, is enlightening (I have straightened out the doctor's somewhat difficult English):

"I now have my inebriates separated from my gamblers. Each room has a spyhole so that I can watch them unobserved.... I found my gamblers in Wiesbaden, where they had been thrown out of various gambling houses for unpaid debts and quarrelsome natures. One of them is greedy (he plays only for small stakes and snatches his winnings impatiently); another clever and conceited, for he plays only games in which he can prove his own intellectual superiority; another so empty-headed that he can give his mind to nothing but cards and can't understand even the simplest book; and yet another crazy with superstition, making him amusing to watch as he performs his ceremonies of mumbo-jumbo, rising from his chair and encircling it, bowing and whispering to his cards and dice, and working out complex formulae to control his luck. There are also two who display symptoms of great emotion—tearing their hair, grinding their teeth, and shrieking out in passion whether they win or lose. They will continue in this manner sometimes for 48 hours before falling into an exhausted sleep."

Unfortunately, Dr. Kröger's studies petered out when the law gripped him for confining people against their wills. But, given the chance, he might have got in ahead of Freud with a study of one particular kind of behavior. In any case, he apparently uncovered at least three of the motives I suggested to my gambling friends—greed, boredom, and the desire to prove oneself superior to the forces of chance.

Freud, when he came along, suggested that sexual compensation was very much at the back of the gambler's urges. "The fluttering movements of a card dealer's hands," he wrote, "the thrust and withdrawal motions of the croupier's rake, and the shaking of the dice box can all be identified with sublimations of copulation or masturbation."

As we all know, Freud had an unsettling tendency to find sexual symbols in almost everything. But his idea has been supported by evidence from a good many later psychiatrists. Three whom I have questioned produced among them seven case histories involving marriages that had gone adrift—all of them featuring husbands who were heavy and insistent gamblers, five of them arraigned by their wives for sexual frigidity. One psychiatrist told me: "Of course I'm not saying that gambling is a consciously selected alternative to sexual activity; but it can be an outlet for sexual activity that has been frustrated—for any of a dozen reasons—in its normal form. Compulsive gamblers do exhaust themselves emotionally, and evidence sifted from a good many case histories suggests that they also incline to sexual frigidity."

Dostoevski wrote to his wife that he actually experienced orgasm on losing (not winning, please note) a large sum at roulette one night. And the American psychologist Robert M. Lindner has written a paper on "The Psychodynamics of Gambling" in which he cites the case of one of his own patients whose symptoms almost exactly paralleled Dostoevski's, and whose motive, Lindner found upon analysis, was simply a more satisfying alternative to masturbation caused by childhood frustrations. Chronic gamblers, Lindner states, "seem all to be strongly aggressive persons with huge reservoirs of unconscious hostility and resentment...." Another psychiatrist, Ralph Greenson, says: "The gambler masochistically enjoys his fear of losing and continues it as long as possible, because when he leaves the table or racecourse to take up his ordinary life some really intolerable fear awaits him; the smaller fear of losing his money is by comparison a pleasure. The mock struggle is a sublimation of a real struggle."

*   *   *   *

It can hardly be denied, then, that gambling often gratifies a basic emotional or sexual urge. I am convinced that this type of satisfaction is more often sought (whether consciously or unconsciously) by the dedicated gambler than is material gain. For him, the winnings are a bonus added to the excitement of the gamble itself. Indeed, his *losses* may be equally a bonus. I believe that in the gamblers' world only the professional cheats and swindlers . . . are motivated by avarice.

Of course, one occasionally comes across a really grasping character in gambling as elsewhere—the man who, having won a hundred thousand in a lottery, will sell his story to a newspaper for a few hundred more, even though the publicity can only bring beggars in droves to his door; or the skilled poker player who will ruthlessly take your last penny, not because he enjoys the game but because he enjoys counting his winnings. But these are not true gamblers. The true gambler is notoriously open-handed. It is certainly hard to see how such addicts as Dostoevski and Richard Minster could be motivated by greed, when they kept hammering away at the excitement that they invariably gained by *losing* money.

*   *   *   *

To move on to motive 5 in my suggested list: Because every kind of risk-taking is exciting in some degree, there is a strong probability that a good many of us do gamble as a refuge from boredom. One respondent to my suggestionnaire wrote: "It was certainly boredom in the first place that sent me to the poker table. While I was in the army, I suppose I had a completely empty mind, and when I saw a game going I joined in. I'd never even played cards before, except kids' games, and I'd certainly never gambled beyond an office sweep ticket. But after that I never looked back. Boredom certainly started it with me, and I sometimes think I go on because I'm still bored with life in general." But though boredom may drive some people to gamble in the first place, they would probably drop it quickly if they didn't eventually find more positive satisfactions in it.

Intellectual exercise, for instance. Surely such a splendid game as poker (which involves, among other skills, a knowledge of psychology) provides a man with plenty of brain-tingling activity. Or a woman, for that matter.

Incidentally, lots of women have been—and still are—more than a match for men at the gaming tables. The Greek biographer Plutarch mentions Parysatis, queen of Persia, who diced for the life of a slave and, after winning him, had him tortured to death. The English novelist and playwright Oliver Goldsmith writes of an old lady who on her deathbed played cards with the curate and, having won all his money, went on to play him for the costs of her own funeral. Her continued winnings gained her a much grander burial than she would otherwise have been able to afford. Between these two extremes, women abound in the field of gambling as thick as leaves in Vallombrosa. But save for one possibility, there doesn't seem to be any strong case for thinking they might be motivated differently from men.

That possibility is my suggested gambling motive number 7: the desire to prove one's superiority to the forces of chance. In this motivation I think women may have the edge on men. Capricious creatures themselves, they may well be fascinated by the so-called caprices of fortune, and may enjoy some close in-fighting with them. (Not for nothing is fortune supposed to be a goddess.) Of course, some women ignore the fact that the laws of probability take no heed of the sex of the gambler. They have their illogical fancies and may often be found backing a horse for the color of its jockey's shirt or a boxer for the color of his eyes. A hunch that pays off reinforces the women's belief in their own intuition; one that fails tends to be taken as a personal affront from another woman, and they gird themselves up for battle accordingly. On the other hand, a considerable number of women gamblers take a strictly "professional" approach. Ignoring "intuition," they attack with expertise; if their game is horse racing, they are vastly knowledgeable about horses' and jockeys' past records. Others may "play the percentages" in casinos; as an American friend once told me, "the hardest eyes and the coolest brows around a Las Vegas craps table belong to the women."

* * * *

To generalize summarily:

The word "gambling" derives from the Anglo-Saxon *gamenian* (to sport or play), and of course there were contests of skill and strength before there was any betting on them. But as soon as the delectable hazards of chance were revealed to men, they saw rich new opportunities for battle. A whole new world offered itself for exploration, complete with richer rewards than any childish game could promise, and requiring less effort.

"If you climb that wall, Son, the chances are that you'll fall in the sea and drown."

"No, I shan't," says Son, climbing the wall. "I shall see the sea."

Which of course he does. He has won his first round against the laws of probability. Who but Son can gauge the egocentric pleasure of knowing that it's important that he doesn't tumble into the deep? And who but he can sense the excitement that pleasure may bring him in further bouts with chance—in daily life or at the gaming tables?

This, then, is the bedrock of the psychological side of gambling. Egocentricity plus hope (which is as instinctive as egocentricity in human nature) equals the necessity all of us have to take risks. Egocentricity plus hope, plus any one of eight or more motives as an individual compulsion, equals the psychological equipment of the serious gambler —the man who knowingly knots himself up with chance more tightly than he need.

◇◈◈◇

James Pethel

When George Bernard Shaw resigned as drama critic for the English *Saturday Review* in 1898, he introduced his successor in a memorable valedictory: "The younger generation is knocking at the door; and as I open it there steps spritely in the incomparable Max." This was, of course, Max Beerbohm. Incomparable he remained, as essayist, caricaturist, and storyteller until his death in 1956.

BY MAX BEERBOHM

◇◈◈◇

September 17, 1912

THOUGH SEVEN years have gone by since the day when last I saw him, and though that day was but the morrow of my first meeting with him, I was shocked when I saw in my newspaper this morning the announcement of his sudden death.

I had formed, in the dim past, the habit of spending August in Dieppe. The place was less popular then than it is now. Some pleasant English people shared it with some pleasant French people. We used rather to resent the race-week—the third week of the month—as an intrusion on our privacy. We sneered as we read in the Paris edition of the New York Herald the names of the intruders. We disliked the nightly crush in the baccarat room of the Casino, and the croupiers' obvious excitement at the high play. I made a point of avoiding that room during that week, for the especial reason that the sight of serious, habitual gamblers has always filled me with a depression bordering on disgust. Most of the men, by some subtle stress of their ruling passion, have grown so monstrously fat, and most of the women so harrowingly thin. The rest of the women seem to be marked out for apoplexy, and the rest of the men to be wasting away. One feels that anything thrown at them would be either embedded or shattered, and looks vainly among them for a person furnished with the normal amount of flesh. Monsters they are, all of them, to the eye (though I believe that many of them have excellent moral qualities in private life); but, just as in an American town one goes sooner or later—goes against one's finer judgment, but somehow goes—into the dime-museum, so, year by year, in Dieppe's race-week, there would be always one evening when I drifted into the baccarat room. It was on such an evening that I first saw the man whose memory I here celebrate. My gaze was held by him for the very reason that he would have passed unnoticed elsewhere. He was conspicuous, not in virtue of the mere fact that he was taking the bank at the principal table, but because there was nothing at all odd about him.

Between his lips was a cigar of moderate size. Everything about him, except the amount of money he had been winning, seemed moderate. Just as he was neither fat nor thin, so had his face neither that extreme pallor nor that extreme redness which belongs to the faces of seasoned gamblers: it was just a clear pink. And his eyes had neither the unnatural brightness nor the unnatural dullness of the eyes around him: they were ordinarily clear eyes, of an ordinary grey. His very age was moderate: a putative thirty-six, not more. ("Not less," I would have said in those days.) He assumed no air of nonchalance. He did not deal out the cards as though they bored him. But he had no look of grim concentration. I noticed that the removal of his cigar from his mouth made never the least difference to his face, for he kept his lips pursed out as steadily as ever when he was not smoking. And this constant pursing of his lips seemed to denote just a pensive interest.

His bank was nearly done now. There were but a few cards left. Opposite to him was a welter of parti-coloured counters which the croupier had not yet had time to sort out and add to the rouleaux already made; there were also a fair accumulation of notes and several little stacks of gold. In all, not less than five hundred pounds, certainly. Happy banker! How easily had he won in a few minutes more than I, with utmost pains, could earn in many months! I wished I were he. His lucre seemed to insult me personally. I disliked him. And yet I hoped he would not take another bank. I hoped he would have the good sense to pocket his winnings and go home. Deliberately to risk the loss of all those riches would intensify the insult to myself.

'Messieurs, la banque est aux enchères!' There was some brisk bidding, while the croupier tore open and shuffled the two packs. But it was as I feared: the gentleman whom I resented kept his place.

'Messieurs, la banque est faite. Quinze mille francs à la banque. Messieurs, les cartes passent! Messieurs, les cartes passent!'

Turning to go, I encountered a friend—one of the race-weekers, but in a sense a friend.

'Going to play?' I asked.

'Not while Jimmy Pethel's taking the bank,' he answered, with a laugh.

'Is that the man's name?'

'Yes. Don't you know him? I thought every one knew old Jimmy Pethel.'

I asked what there was so wonderful about old Jimmy Pethel that every one should be supposed to know him.

'Oh, he's a great character. Has extraordinary luck. Always.'

I do not think my friend was versed in the pretty theory that good luck is the unconscious wisdom of those who in previous incarnations have been consciously wise. He was a member of the Stock Exchange, and I smiled as at a certain quaintness in his remark. I asked in what ways besides luck the 'great character' was manifested. Oh, well, Pethel had made a huge 'scoop' on the Stock Exchange when he was only twenty-three, and very soon doubled that, and doubled it again; then retired. He wasn't more than thirty-five now. And? Oh, well, he was a regular all-round sportsman—had gone after big game all over the world and had a good many narrow shaves. Great steeple-chaser, too. Rather settled down now. Lived in Leicestershire mostly. Had a big place there. Hunted five times a week. Still did an occasional flutter, though. Cleared eighty thousand in Mexicans last February. Wife had been a bar-maid at Cambridge. Married her when he was nineteen. Thing seemed to have turned out quite well. Altogether, a great character.

Possibly, thought I. But my cursory friend, accustomed to quick transactions and to things accepted 'on the nod,' had not proved his case to my slower, more literary intelligence. It was to him, however, that I owed, some minutes later, a chance of testing his opinion. At the cry of 'Messieurs, la banque est aux enchères' we looked round and saw that the subject of our talk was preparing to rise from his place. 'Now one can punt!' said Grierson (this was my friend's name), and turned to the bureau at which counters are for sale. 'If old Jimmy Pethel punts,' he added, 'I shall just follow his luck.' But this lodestar was not to be. While my friend was buying his counters, and I wondering whether I too would buy some, Pethel himself came up to the bureau. With his lips no longer pursed, he had lost his air of gravity, and looked younger. Behind him was an attendant bearing a big wooden bowl—that plain but romantic bowl supplied by the establishment to a banker whose gains are too great to be pocketed. He and Grierson greeted each other. He said he had arrived in Dieppe this afternoon—was here for a day or two. We were introduced. He spoke to me with some *empressement*, saying he was a 'very great admirer' of my work. I no longer disliked him. Grierson, armed with counters, had now darted away to secure a place that had just been vacated. Pethel, with a wave of his hand towards the tables, said, 'I suppose you never condescend to this sort of thing?'

'Well——' I smiled indulgently.

'Awful waste of time,' he admitted.

I glanced down at the splendid mess of counters and gold and notes that were now becoming, under the swift fingers of the little man at the bureau, an orderly array. I did not say aloud that it pleased me to be, and to be seen, talking, on terms of equality, to a man who had won so much. I did not say how wonderful it seemed to me that he, whom I had watched just now with awe and with aversion, had all the while been a great admirer of my work. I did but say (again indulgently) that I supposed baccarat to be as good a way of wasting time as another.

'Ah, but you despise us all the same!' He added that he always envied men who had resources within themselves. I laughed lightly, to imply that it *was* very pleasant to have such resources, but that I didn't want to boast. And indeed, I had never, I vow, felt flimsier than when the little man at the bureau, naming a fabulous sum, asked its owner whether he would take the main part in notes of mille francs? cinq mille? dix mille? quoi? Had it been mine, I should have asked to have it all in five-franc pieces. Pethel took it in the most compendious form and crumpled it into a pocket. I asked if he were going to play any more to-night.

'Oh, later on,' he said. 'I want to get a little sea-air into my lungs now'; and he asked with a sort of breezy diffidence if I would go with him. I was glad to do so. It flashed across my mind that yonder on the terrace he might suddenly blurt out, 'I say, look here, don't think me awfully impertinent, but this money's no earthly use to me: I do wish you'd accept it, as a very small return for all the pleasure your work has given me, and . . . *There!* PLEASE! Not another word!'—all with such candour, delicacy, and genuine zeal that I should be unable to refuse. But I must not raise false hopes in my reader. Nothing of the sort happened. Nothing of that sort ever does happen.

We were not long on the terrace. It was not a night on which you could stroll and talk: there was a wind against which you had to stagger, holding your hat on tightly and shouting such remarks as might occur to you. Against that wind acquaintance could make no headway. Yet I see now that despite that wind—or rather because of it—I ought already to have known Pethel a little better than I did when we presently sat down together inside the café of the Casino. There had been a point in our walk, or our stagger, when we paused to lean over the parapet, looking down at the black and driven sea. And Pethel had shouted that it would be great fun to be out in a sailing-boat to-night and that at one time he had been very fond of sailing.

As we took our seats in the café, he looked around him with boyish interest and pleasure. Then, squaring his arms on the little table, he asked me what I would drink. I protested that I was the host—a position which he, with the quick courtesy of the very rich, yielded to me at once. I feared he would ask for champagne, and was gladdened by his demand for water. 'Apollinaris? St. Galmier? Or what?' I asked. He preferred plain water. I felt bound to warn him that such water was never 'safe' in these places. He said he had often heard that but would risk it. I remonstrated, but he was firm. 'Alors," I told the waiter, 'pour Monsieur un verre d'eau fraiche, et pour moi un demi blonde.' Pethel asked me to tell him who everyone was. I told him no one was any one in particular, and suggested that we should talk about ourselves. 'You mean,' he laughed, 'that you want to know who the devil I am?' I assured him that I had often heard of him. At this he was unaffectedly pleased. 'But,' I added, 'it's always more interesting to hear a man talked about by himself.' And indeed, since he had not handed his winnings over to me, I did hope he would at any rate give me some glimpses into that 'great character' of his. Full though his life had been, he seemed but like a rather clever schoolboy out on a holiday. I wanted to know more.

'That beer does look good,' he admitted when the waiter came back. I asked him to change his mind. But he shook his head, raised to his lips the tumbler of water that had been placed before him, and meditatively drank a deep draught. 'I never,' he then said, 'touch alcohol of any sort.' He looked solemn; but all men do look solemn when they speak of their own habits whether positive or negative, and no matter how trivial; and so (though I had really no warrant for not supposing him a reclaimed drunkard) I dared ask him for what reason he abstained.

'When I say I never touch alcohol,' he said hastily, in a tone as of self-defence, 'I mean that I don't touch it often—or at any rate—well, I never touch it when I'm gambling, you know. It—it takes the edge off.'

His tone did make me suspicious. For a moment I wondered whether he had married the barmaid rather for what she symbolized than for what in herself she was. But no, surely not: he had been only nineteen years old. Nor in any way had he now—this steady, brisk, clear-eyed fellow—the aspect of one who had since fallen. 'The edge off the excitement?' I asked.

'Rather! Of course that sort of excitement seems awfully stupid to you. But—no use denying it—I do like a bit of a flutter—just occasionally, you know. And one has to be in trim for it. Suppose a man sat down dead drunk to a game of chance, what fun would it be for him? None. And it's only question of degree. Soothe yourself ever so little with alcohol, and you don't get quite the full sensation of gambling. You do lose just a little something of the proper tremors before a coup, the proper throes during a coup, the proper thrill of joy or anguish after a coup... You're bound to, you know,' he added, purposely making this bathos when he saw me smiling at the heights to which he had risen.

'And to-night,' I asked, remembering his prosaically pensive demeanour in taking the bank, 'were you feeling these throes and thrills to the utmost?'

He nodded.

'And you'll feel them again to-night?'

'I hope so.'

'I wonder you can stay away.'

'Oh, one gets a bit deadened after an hour or so. One needs to be freshened up. So long as I don't bore you——'

I laughed, and held out my cigarette-case. 'I rather wonder you smoke,' I murmured, after giving him a light. 'Nicotine's a sort of drug. Doesn't it soothe you? Don't you lose just a little something of the tremors and things?'

He looked at me gravely. 'By Jove,' he ejaculated, 'I never thought of that. Perhaps you're right. 'Pon my word, I must think that over.'

I wondered whether he were secretly laughing at me. Here was a man to whom (so I conceived, with an effort of the imagination) the loss or gain of a few hundred pounds could not matter. I told him I had spoken in jest. 'To give up tobacco might,' I said, 'intensify the pleasant agonies of a gambler staking his little all. But in your case—well, frankly, I don't see where the pleasant agonies come in.'

'You mean because I'm beastly rich?'

'Rich,' I amended.

'All depends on what you call rich. Besides, I'm not the sort of fellow who's content with 3 per cent. A couple of months ago—I tell you this in confidence—I risked practically all I had, in an Argentine deal.'

'And lost it?'

'No, as a matter of fact I made rather a good thing out of it. I did rather well last February, too. But there's no knowing the future. A few errors of judgment—a war here, a revolution there, a big strike somewhere else, and—' He blew a jet of smoke from his lips, and looked at me as at one whom he could trust to feel for him in a crash already come.

My sympathy lagged, and I stuck to the point of my inquiry. 'Meanwhile,' I suggested, 'and all the more because you aren't merely a rich man, but also an active taker of big risks, how can these tiny little baccarat risks give you so much emotion?'

'There you rather have me,' he laughed. 'I've often wondered at that myself. I suppose,' he puzzled it out, 'I do a good lot of make-believe. While I'm playing a game like this game tonight, I *imagine* the stakes are huge, and I *imagine* I haven't another penny in the world.'

'Ah! So that with you it's always a life-and-death affair?'

He looked away. 'Oh, no, I don't say that.'

'Stupid phrase,' I admitted. 'But,' there was yet one point I would put to him, 'if you have extraordinary luck—always—'

'There's no such thing as luck.'

'No, strictly, I suppose, there isn't. But if in point of fact you always do win, then—well, surely, perfect luck driveth out fear?'

'Who ever said I always won?' he asked sharply.

I waved my hands and said, 'Oh, you have the reputation, you know, for extraordinary luck.'

'That isn't the same thing as always winning. Besides, I *haven't* extraordinary luck—never *have* had. Good heavens,' he exclaimed, 'if I thought I had any more chance of winning than of losing, I'd—I'd—'

'Never again set foot in that baccarat room to-night,' I soothingly suggested.

'Oh, baccarat be blowed! I wasn't thinking of baccarat. I was thinking of—oh, lots of things; baccarat included, yes.'

'What things?' I ventured to ask.

'What things?' He pushed back his chair, and 'Look here,' he said with a laugh, 'don't pretend I haven't been boring your head off with all this talk about myself. You've been too patient. I'm off. Shall I see you to-morrow? Perhaps you'd lunch with us to-morrow? It would be a great pleasure for my wife. We're at the Hôtel Royal.'

I said I should be most happy, and called the waiter; at sight of whom my friend said he had talked himself thirsty, and asked for another glass of water. He mentioned that he had brought his car over with him; his little daughter (by the news of whose existence I felt idiotically surprised) was very keen on motoring, and they were all three starting the day after to-morrow for 'a spin through France.' Afterwards, they were going on to Switzerland, 'for some climbing.' Did I care about motoring? If so, we might go for a spin after luncheon, to Rouen or somewhere? He drank his glass of water, and, linking a friendly arm in mine, passed out with me into the corridor. He asked what I was writing now, and said that he looked to me to 'do something big, one of these days,' and that he was sure I had it 'in' me. This remark (though of course I pretended to be pleased by it) irritated me very much. It was destined, as you shall see, to irritate me very much more in recollection.

Yet was I glad he had asked me to luncheon. Glad because I liked him, glad because I dislike mysteries. Though you may think me very dense for not having thoroughly understood Pethel in the course of my first meeting with him, the fact is that I was only conscious, and that dimly, of something more in him than he had cared to reveal—some veil behind which perhaps lurked his right to the title so airily bestowed on him by Grierson. I assured myself, as I walked home, that if veil there were I should to-morrow find an eyelet.

But one's intuition when it is off duty seems always so much more powerful an engine than it does on active service; and next day, at sight of Pethel awaiting me outside his hotel, I became less confident. His, thought I, was a face which, for all its animation, would tell nothing—nothing, at any rate, that mattered. It expressed well enough that he was pleased to see me; but for the rest, I was reminded, it had a sort of frank inscrutability. Besides, it was at all points so very usual a face—a face that couldn't (so I then thought), even if it had leave to, betray connexion with a 'great character.' It was a strong face, certainly. But so are yours and mine.

And very fresh it looked, though, as he confessed, Pethel had sat up in 'that beastly baccarat room' till 5 A.M. I asked, had he lost? Yes, he had lost steadily for four hours (proudly he laid stress on this), but in the end—well (he admitted), he had won it all back 'and a bit more.' 'By the way,' he murmured as we were about to enter the hall, 'don't ever happen to mention to my wife what I told you about that Argentine deal. She's always rather nervous about—investments. I don't tell her about them. She's rather a nervous woman altogether, I'm sorry to say.'

This did not square with my preconception of her. Slave that I am to traditional imagery, I had figured her as 'flaunting,' as golden-haired, as haughty to most men but with a provocative smile across the shoulder for some. Nor indeed did her husband's words prevent me from the suspicion that my eyes deceived me when anon I was pre-sented to a very pale small lady whose hair was rather white than grey. And the 'little daughter'! This prodigy's hair was as yet 'down,' but looked as if it might be up at any moment: she was nearly as tall as her father whom she very much resembled in fact and figure and heartiness of hand-shake. Only after a rapid mental calculation could I account for her. 'I must warn you, she's in a great rage this morning,' said her father. 'Do try to soothe her.' She blushed, laughed, and bade her father not be so silly. I asked her the cause of her great rage. She said 'He only means I was disappointed. And he was just as disappointed as I was. Weren't you, now, Father?'

'I suppose they meant well, Peggy,' he laughed.

'They were *quite* right,' said Mrs. Pethel, evidently not for the first time.

'They,' as I presently learned, were the authorities of the bathing establishment. Pethel had promised his daughter he would take her for a swim; but on their arrival at the bathing-cabins they were ruth-lessly told that bathing was 'défendu à cause du mauvais temps.' This embargo was our theme as we sat down to luncheon. Miss Peggy was of opinion that the French were cowards. I pleaded for them that even in English watering-places bathing was forbidden when the sea was very rough. She did not admit that the sea was very rough to-day. Besides, she appealed to me, what was the fun of swimming in ab-solutely calm water? I dared not say that this was the only sort of water I liked to swim in. 'They were *quite* right,' said Mrs. Pethel yet again.

'Yes, but, darling Mother, you can't swim. Father and I are both splendid swimmers.'

To gloze over the mother's disability, I looked brightly at Pethel, as though in ardent recognition of his prowess among waves. With a movement of his head he indicated his daughter—indicated that there was no one like her in the whole world. I beamed agreement. Indeed, I did think her rather nice. If one liked the father (and I liked Pethel all the more in that capacity), one couldn't help liking the daughter: the two were so absurdly alike. Whenever he was looking at her (and it was seldom that he looked away from her) the effect, if you cared to be fantastic, was that of a very vain man before a mirror. It might have occurred to me that, if there were any mystery in him, I could solve it through her. But, in point of fact, I had forgotten all about that possible mystery. The amateur detective was lost in the sympathetic observer of a father's love. That Pethel did love his daughter I have never doubted. One passion is not less true because another predominates. No one who ever saw that father with that daughter could doubt that he loved her intensely. And this intensity gauges for me the strength of what else was in him.

Mrs. Pethel's love, though less explicit, was not less evidently profound. But the maternal instinct is less attractive to an onlooker, because he takes it more for granted, than the paternal. What endeared poor Mrs. Pethel to me was—well, the inevitability of the epithet I give her. She seemed, poor thing, so essentially out of it; and by 'it' is meant the glowing mutual affinity of husband and child. Not that she didn't, in her little way, assert herself during the meal. But she did so, I thought, with the knowledge that she didn't count, and never would count. I wondered how it was that she had, in that Cambridge bar-room long ago, counted for Pethel to the extent of matrimony. But from any such room she seemed so utterly remote that she might well be in all respects now an utterly changed woman. She did preeminently look as if much had by some means been taken out of her, with no compensatory process of putting in. Pethel looked so very young for his age, whereas she would have had to be quite old to look young for hers. I pitied her as one might a governess with two charges who were hopelessly out of hand. But a governess, I reflected, can always give notice. Love tied poor Mrs. Pethel fast to her present situation.

As the three of them were to start next day on their tour through France, and as the four of us were to make a tour to Rouen this afternoon, the talk was much about motoring—a theme which Miss Peggy's enthusiasm made almost tolerable. I said to Mrs. Pethel, with more good-will than truth, that I supposed she was 'very keen on it.' She replied that she was.

'But darling Mother, you aren't. I believe you *hate* it. You're *always* asking Father to go slower. And what *is* the fun of just crawling along?'

'Oh, come, Peggy, we never crawl,' said her father.

'No, indeed,' said her mother, in a tone of which Pethel laughingly said it would put me off coming out with them this afternoon. I said, with an expert air to reassure Mrs. Pethel, that it wasn't fast driving, but only bad driving, that was a danger. 'There, Mother!' cried Peggy. 'Isn't that what we're always telling you?'

I felt that they were always either telling Mrs. Pethel something or, as in the matter of that intended bath, not telling her something. It seemed to me possible that Peggy advised her father about his 'investments.' I wondered whether they had yet told Mrs. Pethel of their intention to go on to Switzerland for some climbing.

Of his secretiveness for his wife's sake I had a touching little instance after luncheon. We had adjourned to have coffee in front of the hotel. The car was already in attendance, and Peggy had darted off to make her daily inspection of it. Pethel had given me a cigar, and his wife presently noticed that he himself was not smoking. He explained to her that he thought he had smoked too much lately, and that he was going to 'knock it off' for a while. I would not have smiled if he had met my eye. But his avoidance of it made me quite sure that he really had been 'thinking over' what I had said last night about nicotine and its possibly deleterious action on the gambling thrill.

Mrs. Pethel saw the smile that I could not repress. I explained that I was wishing *I* could knock off tobacco, and envying her husband's strength of character. She smiled too, but wanly, with her eyes on him. 'Nobody has so much strength of character as he has,' she said.

'Nonsense!' he laughed. 'I'm the weakest of men.'

'Yes,' she said quietly. 'That's true, too, James.'

Again he laughed, but he flushed. I saw that Mrs. Pethel also had faintly flushed; and I became horribly conscious of following suit. In the sudden glow and silence created by Mrs. Pethel's paradox, I was grateful to the daughter for bouncing back into our midst and asking how soon we should be ready to start.

Pethel looked at his wife, who looked at me and rather strangely asked if I were sure I wanted to go with them. I protested that of course I did. Pethel asked her if *she* really wanted to come: 'You see, dear, there was the run yesterday from Calais. And to-morrow you'll be on the road again, and all the days after.'

'Yes,' said Peggy, 'I'm sure you'd much rather stay at home, darling Mother, and have a good rest.'

'Shall we go and put on our things, Peggy?' replied Mrs. Pethel, rising from her chair. She asked her husband whether he were taking the chauffeur with him. He said he thought not.

'Oh, hurrah!' cried Peggy. 'Then I can be on the front seat!'

'No, dear,' said her mother. 'I am sure Mr. Beerbohm would like to be on the front seat.'

'You'd like to be with Mother, wouldn't you?' the girl appealed. I replied with all possible emphasis that I should like to be with Mrs. Pethel. But presently, when the mother and daughter reappeared in the guise of motorists, it became clear that my aspiration had been set aside. 'I am to be with Mother,' said Peggy.

I was inwardly glad that Mrs. Pethel could, after all, assert herself to some purpose. Had I thought she disliked me, I should have been hurt; but I was sure her desire that I should not sit with her was due merely to a belief that a person on the front seat was less safe in case of accidents than a person behind. And of course I did not expect her to prefer my life to her daughter's. Poor lady! My heart was with her. As the car glided along the sea-front and then under the Norman archway, through the town and past the environs, I wished that her husband inspired in her as much confidence as he did in me. For me the sight of his clear, firm profile (he did not wear motor-goggles) was an assurance in itself. From time to time (for I too was ungoggled) I looked round to nod and smile cheerfully at his wife. She always returned the nod, but left the smile to be returned by the daughter.

Pethel, like the good driver he was, did not talk: just drove. But he did, as we came out on to the Rouen road, say that in France he always rather missed the British police-traps. 'Not,' he added, 'that I've ever fallen into one. But the chance that a policeman may at any moment dart out, and land you in a bit of a scrape, does rather add to the excitement, don't you think?' Though I answered in the tone of one to whom the chance of a police-trap is the very salt of life, I did not inwardly like the spirit of his remark. However, I dismissed it from my mind; and the sun was shining, and the wind had dropped: it was an ideal day for motoring; and the Norman landscape had never looked lovelier to me in its width of sober and silvery grace.

I presently felt that this landscape was not, after all, doing itself full justice. Was it not rushing rather too quickly past? 'James!' said a shrill, faint voice from behind; and gradually—'Oh, darling Mother, really!' protested another voice—the landscape slackened pace. But after a while, little by little, the landscape lost patience, forgot its good manners, and flew faster, and faster than before. The road rushed furiously beneath us, like a river in spate. Avenues of poplars flashed past us, every tree of them on either side hissing and swishing angrily in the draught we made. Motors going Rouen-wards seemed to be past as quickly as motors that bore down on us. Hardly had I espied in the landscape ahead a château or other object of interest before I was craning my neck round for a final glimpse of it as it faded on the backward horizon. An endless up-hill road was breasted and crested in a twinkling and transformed into a decline near the end of which our car leapt straight across to the opposite ascent, and—'James!' again, and again by degrees the laws of Nature were re-established, but again by degrees revoked. I didn't doubt that speed in itself was no danger; but when the road was about to make a sharp curve why shouldn't Pethel, just as a matter of form, slow down slightly and sound a note or two of the hooter? Suppose another car were—well, that was all right: the road was clear. But at the next turning, when our car neither slackened nor hooted and was, for an instant, full on the wrong side of the road, I had within me a contraction which (at thought of what must have been if . . .) lasted though all was well. Loth to betray fear, I hadn't turned my face to Pethel. Eyes front! And how about that wagon ahead, huge hay-wagon plodding with its back to us, seeming to occupy the whole road? Surely Pethel would slacken, hoot? No. Imagine a needle threaded with one swift gesture from afar. Even so was it that we shot, between wagon and road's edge, through; whereon, confronting us within a few yards—inches now, but we swerved—was a cart, a cart that incredibly we grazed not as we rushed on, on. Now indeed had I turned my eyes on Pethel's profile. And my eyes saw there that which stilled, with a greater emotion, all fear and wonder in me.

I think that for the first instant, oddly, what I felt was merely satisfaction, not hatred; for I all but asked him whether by not smoking to-day he had got a keener edge to his thrills. I understood him, and for an instant this sufficed me. Those pursed-out lips, so queerly different from the compressed lips of the normal motorist, and seeming, as elsewhere last night, to denote no more than pensive interest, had told me suddenly all that I needed to know about Pethel. Here, as there—and oh, ever so much better here than there!—he could gratify the passion that was in him. No need of any 'make-believe' here! I remembered the strange look he had given when I asked if his gambling were always 'a life-and-death affair.' Here was the real thing—the authentic game, for the highest stakes! And here was I, a little extra-stake tossed on to the board. He had vowed I had it 'in' me to do 'something big.' Perhaps, though, there had been a touch of his make-believe about that. . . I am afraid it was not before my thought about myself that my moral sense began to operate and my hatred of Pethel set in. But I claim that I did see myself as no more than a mere detail in his villainy. Nor, in my just wrath for other sakes, was I without charity even for him. I gave him due credit for risking his own life—for having doubtless risked it, it and none other, again and again in the course of his adventurous—and abstemious—life by field and flood. I was even rather touched by memory of his insistence last night on another glass of that water which just *might* give him typhoid; rather touched by memory of his unsaying that he 'never' touched alcohol—he who, in point of fact, had to be *always* gambling on something or other. I gave him due credit, too, for his devotion to his daughter. But his use of that devotion, his cold use of it to secure for himself the utmost thrill of gambling, did seem utterly abominable to me.

And it was even more for the mother than for the daughter that I was incensed. That daughter did not know him, did but innocently share his damnable love of chances. But that wife had for years known him at least as well as I knew him now. Here again, I gave him credit for wishing, though he didn't love her, to spare her what he could. That he didn't love her I presumed from his indubitable willingness not to stake her in this afternoon's game. That he never had loved her —had taken her, in his precocious youth, simply as a gigantic chance against him—was likely enough. So much the more credit to him for such consideration as he showed her; but little enough this was. He could wish to save her from being a looker-on at his game; but he could, he couldn't not, go on playing. Assuredly she was right in deeming him at once the strongest and the weakest of men. 'Rather a nervous woman'! I remember an engraving that had hung in my room at Oxford—and in scores of other rooms there: a presentment by Sir Marcus (then Mr.) Stone of a very pretty young person in a Gainsborough hat, seated beneath an ancestral elm, looking as though she were about to cry, and entitled 'A Gambler's Wife.' Mrs. Pethel was not like that. Of her there were no engravings for undergraduate hearts to melt at. But there was one man, certainly, whose compassion was very much at her service. How was he going to help her?

I know not how many hair's-breadth escapes we may have had while these thoughts passed through my brain. I had closed my eyes. So preoccupied was I that, but for the constant rush of air against my face, I might, for aught I knew, have been sitting ensconced in an arm-chair at home. After a while, I was aware that this rush had abated; I opened my eyes to the old familiar streets of Rouen. We were to have tea at the Hôtel d'Angleterre. What was to be my line of action? Should I take Pethel aside and say 'Swear to me, on your word of honour as a gentleman, that you will never again touch the driving-gear (or whatever you call it) of a motor-car. Otherwise I shall expose you to the world. Meanwhile, we shall return to Dieppe by train'? He might flush—for I knew him capable of flushing—as he asked me to explain. And after? He would laugh in my face. He would advise me not to go motoring any more. He might even warn me not to go back to Dieppe in one of those dangerous railway-trains. He might even urge me to wait until a nice Bath chair had been sent out for me from England...

I heard a voice (mine, alas) saying brightly 'Well, here we are!' I helped the ladies to descend. Tea was ordered. Pethel refused that stimulant and had a glass of water. I had a liqueur brandy. It was evident to me that tea meant much to Mrs. Pethel. She looked stronger after her second cup, and younger after her third. Still, it was my duty to help her, if I could. While I talked and laughed, I did not forget that. But—what on earth was I to do? I am no hero. I hate to be ridiculous. I am inveterately averse from any sort of fuss. Besides, how was I to be sure that my own personal dread of the return-journey hadn't something to do with my intention of tackling Pethel? I thought it had. What this woman would dare daily because she was a mother, could not I dare once? I reminded myself of Pethel's reputation for invariable luck. I reminded myself that he was an extraordinarily skilful driver. To that skill and luck I would pin my faith...

What I seem to myself, do you ask of me?

But I answered your question a few lines back. Enough that my faith was rewarded. We did reach Dieppe safely. I still marvel that we did.

That evening, in the vestibule of the Casino, Grierson came up to me: 'Seen Jimmy Pethel? He was asking for you. Wants to see you particularly. He's in the baccarat room, punting—winning hand over fist, of course. Said he'd seldom met a man he liked more than you. Great character, what?' One is always glad to be liked, and I plead guilty to a moment's gratification at the announcement that Pethel liked me. But I did not go and seek him in the baccarat room. A great character assuredly he was; but of a kind with which (very imperfect though I am, and no censor) I prefer not to associate.

Why he had particularly wanted to see me was made clear in a note sent by him to my room early next morning. He wondered if I could be induced to join them in their little tour. He hoped I wouldn't think it great cheek, his asking me. He thought it might rather amuse me to come. It would be a very great pleasure for his wife. He hoped I wouldn't say No. Would I send a line by bearer? They would be starting at 3 o'clock. He was mine sincerely.

It was not too late to tackle him, even now. Should I go round to his hotel? I hesitated and—well, I told you at the outset that my last meeting with him was on the morrow of my first. I forget what I wrote to him, but am sure that the excuse I made for myself was a good and graceful one, and that I sent my kindest regards to Mrs. Pethel. She had not (I am sure of that too) authorised her husband to say she would like me to come with them. Else would not the thought of her have haunted me so poignantly as for a long time it did. I do not know whether she is still alive. No mention is made of her in the obituary notice which woke these memories in me. This notice I will, however, transcribe, because (for all its crudeness of phraseology) it is rather interesting both as an echo and as an amplification. Its title is—'Death of Wealthy Aviator.' Its text is—'Widespread regret will be felt in Leicestershire at the tragic death of Mr. James Pethel, who had long resided there and was very popular as an all-round sportsman. In recent years he had been much interested in aviation, and had become one of the most enthusiastic of amateur airmen. Yesterday afternoon he fell down dead quite suddenly as he was returning to his house, apparently in his usual health and spirits, after descending from a short flight which despite an extremely high wind he had made on his new biplane and on which he was accompanied by his married daughter and her infant son. It is not expected that any inquest will be necessary, as his physician, Dr. Saunders, has certified death to be due to heart-disease, from which, it appears, the deceased gentleman had been suffering for some years. Dr. Saunders adds that he had repeatedly warned deceased that any strain on the nervous system might prove fatal.'

Thus—for I presume that his ailment had its origin in his habits—James Pethel did not, despite that merely pensive look of his, live his life with impunity. And by reason of that life he died. As for the manner of his death, enough that he did die. Let not our hearts be vexed that his great luck was with him to the end.

<<<<<<<<<<<<<<<<<<<<<<<<<<<<<<<<<<<<<<<<<<<<<<<<<<<<

Fiodor's Last Game

One of the greatest of all novelists was an inveterate gambler—and, to compound his problem, he preferred roulette, in which the odds against the player are forbidding. Following their marriage in 1867 he and his second wife, Anna, spent most of the next four years in Germany and Switzerland where he occasionally won but more often lost. In her fascinating *Reminiscences* we see the agony they endured until, all but incredibly, Dostoevsky scored his greatest victory: to be precise, on April 28, 1871, as recorded in a letter written from Wiesbaden to his wonderful and understanding wife.

BY ANNA DOSTOEVSKY

<<<<<<<<<<<<<<<<<<<<<<<<<<<<<<<<<<<<<<<<<<<<<<<<<<<<

FIODOR so often spoke of the certain "ruin" of his talent, if we remained any longer abroad, and was so tormented by the thought that he would not be able to keep his family, that as I listened to him I, too, was driven to despair. To relieve his anxious mood and to disperse his gloomy thoughts, which prevented him from concentrating on his work, I had recourse to the device which always helped to distract his mood and to amuse him. As we possessed then about three hundred thalers, I said that it would be worth while to try once more our luck at roulette; I pointed out that as he had occasionally happened to win, there was no reason why we should not hope that our luck would turn this time, and so on. I certainly did not entertain any hope of his winning at roulette, and I also was very sorry to part with a hundred thalers, which it was necessary to sacrifice, but I knew by the experience of his former visits to the tables that, after receiving new and exciting impressions, after satisfying his craving for risk, for gambling, Fiodor would return home calmed, and realising the futility of his hopes of winning at the tables, would sit down with renewed strength to his novel, and in a couple of weeks would make good his losses. My idea of his going to play roulette pleased my husband very much, and he did not oppose it. Taking with him 120 thalers and stipulating, if he lost them, that I should send him money for his return fare, he left for Wiesbaden, where he stayed for a week. As I had supposed, his playing resulted disastrously, and his travelling expenses included,

Fiodor spent 180 thalers—quite a considerable sum of money in our circumstances. But the cruel torments which he experienced during that week, as he blamed himself for robbing me and our child, had such an effect upon him that he decided never again in his life to play roulette. And this is what my husband wrote me on April 28, 1871: "A great thing has happened to me; the filthy fancy, which has tormented me for ten years (or truer, since the death of my brother, when I found myself suddenly crushed by debts) has vanished. I kept on dreaming of winning; I dreamt seriously, passionately. Now it is all over and finished. This was actually the last time. Do you believe me, Anya, that now my hands are untied? Gambling was a tie on me; but now I shall think of work and shall not dream of gambling for nights on end as I used to do."

I, of course, could not all at once believe in such a great happiness as Fiodor's indifference to roulette. Surely he had promised me not to play so many times before, and yet he had not found the strength to keep his word. But this time the happiness was realised, and indeed that was the last time he played roulette. Later on, during his travels abroad (in 1874, 1875, 1876, 1879) Fiodor never once went to a casino. It is true that roulette was soon forbidden in Baden, but roulette tables were to be found in Saxony and in Monte Carlo. The distance would not have prevented my husband from going there, if he had wished to play. But he was no longer drawn to it. It was as though Fiodor's "fancy" of winning at roulette was a sort of diabolical suggestion or disease, of which he suddenly and for ever cured himself. He returned from Wiesbaden cheerful and calm, and immediately sat down to the continuation of his novel The Devils. He foresaw that our going back to Russia, settling in a new place and the expected increase of our family would not allow him to do much work there. All my husband's thoughts were turned to the new period opening before us, and he speculated on how he would find his old friends and relations, who, according to him, might have changed considerably in the last four years. In himself he was conscious of a certain definite change of views and convictions.

Skulduggery

In convention assembled, the reprobates waiting in the wings and about to step onstage were of many types, temperaments, and degrees of talent, but all of them must have shared the credo enunciated by one of the most prestigious in the company. "It's morally wrong to allow suckers to keep money," Canada Bill Jones declared flatly. As a working philosophy, this was a complete statement.

◇◇

Shenanigans on the Mississippi

Among all the rogues who worked the Mississippi steamers, George H. Devol must have been the outstanding prodigy. Born in Marietta, Ohio, in 1829, he ran away from home at the age of ten. At seventeen he was an accomplished card cheat and a master of the art of "stocking" (stacking) a deck. Not yet twenty, he was bilking American soldiers by the score aboard a boat on the Rio Grande during the Mexican War. His great days, however, were spent as guest of the Father of the Waters, where his specialties were poker, three-card monte (the immediate predecessor of the carnival shell game), and rough-and-tumble fighting. (No man was known ever to beat him in a head-butting match.) Occasionally he "reformed," but not for long, and ultimately he lost most of his three-card monte fortune playing faro, to which he was hopelessly addicted. He died at seventy-three, with more respect for his fellow gamblers, as he tells us, than for the so-called respectable but greedy businessmen they fleeced so handily.

BY GEORGE H. DEVOL

WE WERE going up with Captain Bill Harrison on board the *Doubeloon*, and just after leaving the wharf I took a look around to find some good-looking suckers. I had not found anything that I thought suited me, and was standing at the bar talking to Captain Bill, when he asked me if the fellows in the barber shop were with me. I said, "What fellows?" For I could see my partners, Brown and Chapple, sitting out on the guards. He said, "Go back and take a peep at them." I did go back, and I saw some fellows with two tables covered all over with jewelry and silverware. They had a wheel with numbers on it, and the corresponding numbers were on the table under the jewelry, etc. They were just getting started, and had some customers who were paying their dollar, and trying their luck turning the wheel. I looked on until I thought I understood the game, and then I went to the pantry and came back. I saw a nice looking watch on one of the numbers, but the space on the wheel that had the same number on it was so very narrow that the wheel would not stop on it one time in a thousand. I asked the boss if the watch was good; and he told me that any one that won it could have $100 in gold if he did not want the watch. I fooled around a little while, then I put down my dollar, and gave the wheel a pretty heavy whirl. She went around about twice, and stopped on the number that called for the watch. The fellow was all broke up, but he gave me $100 in gold, and I put up another dollar. I started the wheel again, and I hope I may never see the back of my neck if she did not stop on the watch again. The boss was dumbfounded. He looked at the wheel, paid me another $100 in gold, and as he paid over the money he looked at me as if he did not like me; and as I make it a rule not to stay where I am not wanted, I went out to see the boys. I told them how it was done, and they went in and got $100 in gold. As they were coming out they heard the fellow say, "Who in the h—l put this molasses on the wheel?"

We opened monte, and caught the wheel man for his entire stock, and we had more Christmas presents than anybody in the State. Molasses will catch more suckers than soft soap.

*   *   *   *

Before the war they had an old steamer fitted up as a wharf-boat and lodging-house at Baton Rouge, to accommodate people that landed late at night, or would be waiting for a boat. This old boat was head-quarters for the gamblers that ran the river. Many a night we have played cards in the old cabin until morning, or until our boat would arrive. When thoroughbred gamblers meet around the table at a game of cards, then comes the tug of war. We would have some very hard games at times, and we found it pretty hard to hold our own. My partner proposed that we fix up some plan to down the gamblers that played with us on the old boat, so we finally hit upon a scheme. We bored a hole under one of the tables, and another under one of the beds in a state-room opposite. Then we fixed a nail into a spring, and fastened the spring on the under side of the floor, so that the nail would come up through the floor under the table. Next we attached a fine wire to the spring, and ran it up into the state-room. Then we bored a hole in the bulkhead of the state-room, just over the top berth, so that a person could lie in the berth and look out into the cabin. Now we were ready for the thoroughbreds. When we would get one of our smart friends, we would seat him at our table in his chair, which was always on the side of our state-room. We called it ours, for we had fitted it up just to suit us; and for fear some one would use it when we were out traveling for our health, we paid for it all the time. We had a good boy that liked to lie down and make money, so we would put him in the upper berth while the game was in progress. He would looked through the peep-hole, and if our friend had one pair he would pull the wire once; if two pair, twice; if threes, three times; if fours, four times, etc. We would kick off one boot and put our foot over the nail, and then we would be able to tell what hand our friend held. One day I was playing a friend at our table, and he was seated in his chair. I got the signals all right for some time, and then the under-current seemed to be broken. I waited for the signals until I could not wait any longer, for I was a little behind (time), so I picked up a spittoon and let fly at our room. That restored communications, and I received the signals all right. My friend wanted to know what I threw the spittoon for. I told him the cards were running so bad that I got mad; and that an old nigger had told me once it was a good sign to kick over a spittoon when playing cards; so I thought I would not only kick it over, but would break the d——d thing all to pieces. He replied, "I noticed that your luck changed just after you threw her, and I will try it the next time I play in bad luck."

* * * *

We were on board a Red River packet called the *F. K. Bell*, and we had not made any preparations to gamble. After a while a gentle-man came up and asked me if I ever played poker. My partners, Tom Brown and Holly Chappell, and some of the officers of the boat, were sitting there and heard the conversation. They had to put their hand-kerchiefs in their mouths to keep from laughing, when they heard my answer, "No, I did not." "Well," said he, "I will teach you if you will sit down." He got a deck of cards at the bar, and commenced to show me which were the best hands. I at last agreed to play ten-cent ante. We played along, and I was amused to see him stocking the cards (or at least trying to do so). He gave me three queens, and I lost $10 on them, for he beat them with three aces. Presently he beat a full hand and won $25. That made him think his man was a good sucker. I always laughed at my losing, and kept telling him that after a while I would commence to bet higher. I pulled out a big roll of bills and laid it on the table. Finally I held out four fives, and then I went a big blind on his deal, so that if he did not come in I would throw down my hand, and perhaps there would be no pair in it. About this time, he commenced to work with the cards, but I paid very little attention to his work. After playing a while I got three jacks, and then we commenced to bet high. He raised me, and I raised him back, and at last he thought we had enough up. Then I got away with the hand he gave me, and pulled up the four fives. Then the betting became lively. I made him call me; and when he saw my hand, and I had got the money, he grabbed at me and said, "That is not the hand you had."

"How the d—l do you know what I had?" "Well," says he, "where are the other five cards?" "I don't know what you are talking about." He counted the cards and found the jacks, for I had palmed them on top of the deck. Then he pulled out his knife and said, "You are a gambler, and I want my money back." "Oh, is that all? I did not understand. I will give it back, as I don't want to keep your money if you think I did not win it fairly." I let on as though I was taking out the money, when I pulled out old Betsy Jane. He saw her looking him in the face, and he wilted like a calf. I made him apologize, and you never saw a man get such a turning over as they all gave him. They told him he must not pick out such apt scholars, for they learn too quickly. What hurt my feelings more than anything else was, that he would not speak to me all the way up to where I got off. As I was leaving the boat I said to him, "Good-bye, sir. We are never too old to learn."

* * * *

Some men are born rascals, some men have rascality thrust upon them, others achieve it. This is a story of a chap that I think must have had a birthmark of knavery somewhere concealed about his body. It was during the war, and I was going up on the steamer *Fashion*, Captain Pratt. I was dealing red and black, and had a big game, as there were a number of cotton buyers on board. One of them was a fine appearing gentleman from New York, who was soon $3,800 loser; then he began to play reckless, and was still followed by his bad luck. I noticed his nervousness, and came to the conclusion that he was not playing with his own money.

Finally looking up, he said, "How much will you turn for?"

Noticing his excited condition, I said, "Put down as much as you think proper, and if you go too high I'll tell you." With that he pulled out a long pocket-book, and drawing forth a roll of hundred-dollar bills threw them on the red. I picked up the money and counted it, and found there were thirty-three one-hundred-dollar bills.

"That's beyond my limit," I said; "but as I know you are a great deal heavier loser than that, I'll give you a chance to get even, so crack her down."

I made a turn, he lost. With a trembling hand and wild eye he counted out the balance of his money and laid it before me, saying: "This is my last bet; if I lose, there is $4,000, and there is $200 more. Will you turn for it?"

"Lay her up," was all I said.

Down it went, just as any high-roller would do if he had some one else's money; he lost, and fell back in his chair in a dead faint; ice water was brought and he was revived. After the game he came to me and said, "Not a dollar of that money was my own; it belonged to a wealthy New York firm, one of the members of which I was to meet in New Orleans, and render an account." I told him that he would have to say that the money was invested in cotton that would be shipped in a few days. "That will give you time to skip," I said, "for the affair is bound to come out, and then you will be in trouble."

"No," he said, "I won't run away. I have thought of a plan that will let me out of the scrape. There is another man on the boat who is buying for the same firm. I will go to him and get a bundle of money which I will hand to you privately, and then you come before the passengers and hand it to me. You can say, 'I don't want your money, so here it is, take it.' I will thank you kindly, and there will be plenty of witnesses to say that I did not lose the money gambling." I did exactly as the fellow wanted, much to the astonishment of the passengers, who said that I must either be the biggest-hearted man in the country, or the biggest fool that ever ran unhung, to give a man back that much money after fairly winning it.

When New Orleans was reached I was arrested, but easily proved that I had returned the money, or rather refused to take it, and was discharged; but the good old greenbacks were safe in my inside pocket, all the same.

* * * *

When a sucker sees a corner turned up, or a little spot on a card in three-card monte, he does not know that it was done for the purpose of making him think he has the advantage. He thinks, of course, the player does not see it, and he is in such a hurry to get out his money that he often cuts or tears his clothes. He feels like he is going to steal the money from a blind man, but he does not care. He will win it, and say nothing about how he did it. After they have put up their money and turned the card, they see that the mark was put there for a purpose. Then they are mad, because they are beat at their own game. They begin to kick, and want their money back, but they would not have thought of such a thing had they won the money from a blind man, for they did think he must be nearly blind, or he could have seen the mark on the winning card. They expected to rob a blind man, and got left. I never had any sympathy for them, and I would fight before I would give them back one cent. It is a good lesson for a dishonest man to be caught by some trick, and I always did like to teach it. I have had the right card turned on me for big money by suckers, but it was an accident, for they were so much excited that they did not get the card they were after. I have also given a big hand in poker to a sucker, and had him to knock the ginger out of me, but this would make me more careful in the future. I've seen suckers win a small amount, and then run all over the boat, telling how they downed the gambler; but they were almost sure to come back and lose much more than they had won.

I have often given a sucker back his money, and I have seen them lose it with my partner, or at some other game on the same boat. I have won hundreds of thousands from thieves who were making tracks for some other country to keep out of jail and to spend their ill-gotten gains. I enjoyed beating a man that was loaded down with stolen money more than any one else. I always felt as if it was my duty to try and keep the money in our own country.

Young men and boys have often stood around the table and bothered me to bet. I would tell them to go away, that I did not gamble with boys. That would make some of the smart Alecks mad, and they would make a great deal of noise. So, when I was about to close up, I would take in the young chap. He would walk away with a good lesson. But when I had to win money from a boy to keep him quiet, I would always go to him and return the money, after giving him a good talking to.

I meet good business men very often now that take me by the hand and remind me of when I won some money from them when they were boys, and returned it with a good lecture. I have sometimes wished I had one-tenth part of what I have returned to boys and suckers, for then I would have enough to keep me the balance of my life.

I had the niggers all along the coast so trained that they would call me "Massa" when I would get on or off a boat. If I was waiting at a landing I would post some old "nig" what to say when I went on board, so while the passengers were all out on the guards and I was bidding the "coons" good-bye, my "nig" would cry out:

"Good-bye, Massa George; I's goin' to take good care of the old plantation till you comes back."

I would go on board, with one of the niggers carrying my saddle-bags, and those sucker passengers would think I was a planter sure enough; so if a game was proposed I had no trouble to get into it, as all who play cards are looking for suckers that they know have money; and who in those old ante-bellum times had more money than a Southern planter? I have often stepped up to the bar as soon as I would get on board and treat every one within call, and when I would pay for the drinks I would pull out a roll that would make everybody look wild. Then I was sure to get into the first game that would be started, for all wanted a part of the planter's roll.

I have downed planters and many good business men, who would come to me afterwards and want to stand in with my play; and many are the thousands I have divided with them; and yet the truly good people never class such men among gamblers. The world is full of such men. They are not brave enough to take the name, but they are always ready for a part of the game. A gambler's word is as good as his bond, and that is more than I can say of many business men who stand very high in a community. I would rather take a true gambler's word than the bond of many business men who are to-day counted worth thousands. The gambler will pay when he has money, which many good church members will not.

Wilson Mizner

No one who knew him is on record as saying that he ever knew another man remotely like Wilson Mizner (1876–1933). The reasons are clear. Here, in one person, were a crook, a savage wit, a compassionate friend, a superb anecdotalist, a playwright and screenwriter when the need to work overwhelmed him, a maker of still-remembered epigrams, a gambler of sorts when his end of a bet was as carefully prearranged as he could make it.

BY ALVA JOHNSTON

DAMON RUNYON called Wilson Mizner the greatest man-about-town that any town ever had. He was referring to the period when Mizner was Broadway's leading wit and one of Broadway's successful playwrights and confidence men. But years before that Mizner had been the greatest man-about-town in Dawson City and Nome. He was the world's foremost authority on the hot side of the frozen north. Nobody was ever snugger and cozier than he was at sixty below zero. The star writers of the Arctic school—Robert W. Service, Jack London, Rex Beach, and others—raved about the snowscapes, the glittering stars, and the aurora borealis. Mizner liked the crackling wood stoves, flickering candles, and smoking kerosene lamps. The literary artists painted the lonely immensities of the great outdoors. Mizner mixed with the gang in stuffy interiors. "Flesh beats scenery," he said. The average Yukon literary artist found that the Arctic was God's Country, and then ducked out as quick as he could. Mizner found the place overrun with crooks, con men, fugitives from justice, cardsharps, adventuresses, and sporting ladies, and stayed there six years.

* * * *

Mizner was twenty years old when he started for the Yukon Territory, in 1897. He left San Francisco with the fervent God-bless-yous, and don't-hurry-backs of his relatives. All they knew about the Yukon was that it was a remote and inaccessible region, and that no place could be too remote and inaccessible for Wilson. For years, he had brought only scandal and notoriety to his family. The Mizners were perhaps too grand and too genteel for their day and age. For three generations, they were State Department diplomats. The Mizner forebears had married themselves into a solid system of cousinships with the old Knickerbocker and Huguenot families of New York. Wilson's people had founded three California towns—Benicia, Colusa, and Vacaville. They had an aristocratic maxim that no gentleman works at anything except the dignified and honorable professions. Of Wilson's five older brothers, the first, Lansing, was a lawyer; the second, Edgar, was a diplomat and mining engineer; the third, William, was a physician; the fourth, Henry, was a clergyman; and the fifth, Addison, was an architect. Wilson was the most aristocratic of the lot. He abbreviated the family maxim to "No gentleman works." As a boy, he refused to study, because he regarded lessons as a form of work; he held, with Molière, that a gentleman knows everything without having to learn anything. His father was an old and sick man when he suddenly discovered that he had a fairly well-developed problem child on his hands.

The family's opportunity to catapult Wilson into sub-zero oblivion came through his brother Edgar, the mining engineer, who took a post as representative in the Yukon Valley of the Alaska Commercial Company. Activity had been increasing along the Yukon for years before the great gold strike, on the Klondike River, in 1896. Prospectors had been drifting in. The fur trade had come to have some importance.

Anticipating a boom in the region, Alaska Commercial had bought a series of trading posts, and Edgar was sent there to supervise the company's affairs. He induced Wilson to accompany him, and all San Francisco congratulated the family on its good luck. The two brothers started north when news of the Klondike bonanza was still believed to be a nonsensical rumor, but they soon learned that millions were actually being taken out of the old creek beds. Edgar wrote to San Francisco urging all other able-bodied Mizners to head for the Klondike and infinite riches. He sent Wilson to Skagway, Alaska, the chief gateway to the Klondike, to handle company business and prepare for the Mizner expedition to the gold fields.

By that time, Skagway was seething. Through the freemasonry of desert rats, news of the gold strike had been spread to prospectors all over the West. Skagway had become a roaring log-and-tent frontier town, with saloons, gambling joints, and a thriving red-light colony. Wilson had already received training from good underworld masters. At Skagway, he received a polishing and finishing from the greatest American professor of sharp practice, gentle larceny, and all-around crime—the celebrated Jefferson Randolph (Soapy) Smith, the real-life American version of the Man Who Would Be King. Soapy and Mizner were attracted to each other by the natural law that causes celebrities to gravitate into one another's society.

Of all Mizner's idols and mentors, none had a greater influence on his life than Soapy.

Born in 1860, Soapy started out in life as a peanut boy with a small travelling circus. A circus is a little nation all by itself, and it probably implanted in Soapy his ambition to run a little nation of his own. At any rate, it taught him the shell-and-pea game and other methods of skinning suckers and getting ahead in the world. He got the name of Soapy in Denver, where, in the eighties, he used to drive up in a buggy to a busy street corner, set a tray of soap on a tripod, and start to sing ballads in a pleasing baritone. When he had a crowd, he would tell funny stories while he folded dollar bills around some of the cakes of soap and then wrapped them all in blue paper. He sold them for fifty cents a bar, many of the customers getting dollar bills with their purchases. Then he began wrapping up soap with twenty-dollar bills and auctioning the cakes off to the highest bidders, prices going to five dollars or more. Occasionally, with whoops of joy, a lucky customer would pull out a twenty-dollar bill. When the soap market was saturated, Soapy would auction off bottles of an all-curing elixir the same way. Now and then, a rumor would start that the twenty-dollar bills were either palmed or slipped to Soapy's confederates.

Whenever trouble threatened, Soapy would sweep his merchandise into a suitcase, or "keister," leap into his buggy, and drive off at a rapid pace.

Soapy occasionally had trouble with the police. Mizner told how Soapy was once arrested in Chicago on a charge of operating with confederates and obtaining money under false pretenses. According to Mizner, the judge was confused. "I can't make head or tail out of this testimony," he exclaimed. "Let the defendant show me how it works, and let the police officers tell me how the law is violated." Soapy wrapped up several cakes of soap, first putting a fifty-dollar bill around one of them. "Now, Your Honor," said Soapy, "you give me twenty-five cents and choose one of these cakes." The judge handed over a quarter and chose the fifty-dollar cake. He shook his right fist at the police officers as his left folded up the bill and placed it in his vest pocket. "You!" he shouted. "You have been hounding an honest businessman for pursuing his lawful calling. His merchandising methods are obviously fair and honorable. Case dismissed."

Mizner studied the soap game under Soapy Smith in Skagway and practiced it occasionally in later life for amusement. In 1928, a Hollywood producer dragooned Mizner into going to Palm Springs, then a desert outpost, to write a motion picture. Mizner said that he had been kidnapped and that he couldn't write until he had restored his self-respect by trimming a few suckers. He went out in the street with a tray of soap, singing and shouting and waving twenty-dollar bills. Nobody paid the slightest attention to him. He was deeply wounded and felt that he was losing his talent. He comforted himself with the theory that Palm Springs people were all invalids and didn't have life enough in them to be suckers. He took revenge in a short story, "You're Dead," in which he stated that the entire population of Palm Springs was *in extremis*.

*   *   *   *

In preparation for their second play, "The Greyhound" written in 1911 [Paul] Armstrong took Mizner on a transatlantic voyage. "The Greyhound" was a melodrama about ocean-going crooks—"sea serpents," "deep-sea fishermen," or "pearl divers," as they used to be called. Mizner had a scholarly grasp of this subject. He knew international low life as Henry James knew international high life. For years, he had been practically a commuter from New York to London and Paris, and had made a total of thirty transatlantic round trips. He had dabbled in the theatre in London, and he called himself "the father of free lunch in Paris," because, with the help of some international characters, including the Broadway Polonius Swiftie Morgan and the colored heavyweight Sam McVey, he induced the proprietor of Ciro's to give away lobster, goose liver, caviar, ham, and anchovies in order to lure an American clientele to his place. Mizner was also something of a sea serpent or deep-sea fisherman himself. He said he was always able to win the confidence of strangers by warning them against strangers. He knew every twist of fraud and larceny on the high seas, but Armstrong didn't, and Armstrong insisted on the trip so that Mizner could brief him on background and atmosphere for their drama of deviltry on the steamship lanes.

Mizner usually won when he played games of chance, by land or by sea, but he never claimed to be a really great cardsharp. He was, however, a supreme artist at taking a lot of people thrown together by chance and quickly converting them into one big, happy family. His power to produce mirth in a small or moderate-sized group of people is said to have been unequalled. On the first night out, he would have the whole ship's population of prospective suckers bellowing. His function was to deprive them of their reason with Mizner gags; once the brain was completely abstracted, it was time for the cardsharps, dice wizards, and con men to go to work. Mizner, his mission accomplished, might then disport himself as he pleased for the rest of the trip. If his crooked friends prospered, they would make a suitable recognition of his contribution to the success of the voyage. One of the few survivors of the happy days on the high seas is Swiftie Morgan, who had a special talent for breaking down the reserve of upper-class Englishmen. Being small and wiry, Swiftie was introduced as the coming wonder of the American turf. Great jockeys were irresistible to British swells. According to Swiftie, Mizner seldom joined the big card games, but he would sometimes amuse himself by playing bankers-and-brokers. He would start it as a sort of solitaire, dividing a pack of cards into several small stacks. He would scratch his head, mutter to himself, and then finally pick up the cards and examine them with little exclamations of joy or chagrin. If anybody asked questions, he would explain that he was trying to guess the number of high cards in each pile. He would never invite another man to join in a game, but he would never churlishly reject the suggestion if it came from a likely-looking prospect. Swiftie says that Mizner relieved the Pittsburgh steel baron William E. Corey of fifteen thousand dollars at this pastime. Corey didn't know that Mizner always took the precaution of bending the high cards lengthwise and the low cards crosswise before he started to amuse himself. The curvature was microscopic, and would never catch the eye of an unsuspecting opponent, but Mizner could tell by a glance at the side of a pile how many high cards it contained.

* * * *

Wilson Mizner was fond of moralizing. When younger men came to him for advice, he told them that the great rule of life was "Never gamble except with a little the best of it."

He was at times content with a very small advantage. In the Klondike, he had trouble with the Northwest Mounted because he had five deuces in a deck, the minutest possible degree of dishonesty. His approach to any topic was a calculation of odds. Writhing with agony from an attack of appendicitis, he was told that he was to be operated on by a surgeon who had performed eighteen successful appendectomies in a row. Mizner handed a roll of bills to his pal Lew Lipton, of Broadway and Hollywood, saying, "See what odds you can get that I don't break his run."

He preferred odds of 100 to 0 in his favor and often made arrangements that insured those odds. He was also ready to accept odds of 51 to 49 in his favor, and he would rather gamble honestly than not at all. When he became a celebrity in New York in 1906, through his marriage to the wealthy Mrs. Yerkes, a news dispatch from San Francisco gave an idea of his range and versatility as a gamester. A ferryboat had stopped in San Francisco Bay at the cry of "Man overboard!" A lifeboat was lowered and the sailors found Mizner treading water, a stopwatch in his hand. He had a bet on the length of time necessary for his rescue. He was walking across Times Square once with Honest John Kelly, the famous gambler and referee, when a streetcar knocked over a fish wagon. A lobster and a crab landed side by side on the pavement and started for the streetcar tracks. "A hundred on the lobster," said Mizner, but Kelly wouldn't bet.

Mizner won a good deal by betting on Jess Willard to beat Jack Johnson in their bout in Havana in 1915. By a simple device, he had convinced himself that the fight was fixed. A few days before the bout, he cabled, "WHAT SHALL I DO?" to Jack Johnson. Johnson and Mizner were close friends. Mizner reasoned that if the fight was on the level, Johnson would cable enthusiastically about his chances of winning, and that if it was a fake, Johnson would not reply at all. After two days without word from the black champion, Mizner bet everything he had on Willard.

Mizner won $10,000 on a big race in England by characteristic foresight. On the day of the race, Mizner, who was living at the Hotel Claridge, at Forty-fourth and Broadway, had a late breakfast in his apartment with a New York businessman who was famous for his eagerness to back his judgment on any subject that came up. The two men began to deplore the fact that they had failed to bet on the race. Mizner offered to put up $200 just to increase their interest in the event. His guest snorted at such a picayune sum, and said, "Let's make it ten thousand." Mizner said he didn't have that much; his guest insisted on trusting him for it. Mizner sipped highballs, talked, and studied the entries for a long time. Finally, he chose the horse listed in the newspapers as No. 7. An hour or two later, they went downstairs. The evening papers were out with the news that No. 7 had won. Mizner had picked No. 7 advisedly. Across the court from his room, he had a confederate whose telephone was connected with a poolroom. When the confederate got the news that the horse had won, he went to his window and held up five fingers of one hand and two of the other. Mizner then made the bet on No. 7.

He won a roll of bills at Atlantic City once by a game that was halfway between a lucrative practical joke and a crooked gamble. He and some other sports were lounging along the boardwalk betting on anything in which they could find an element of chance, such as which of two sunbathers would be the first to go into the water or which of two swimmers would be the first to come out of it. One of the party noticed a pair of gigantic feet sticking out of a window on the first floor of a boardwalk hotel. The owner of the feet was out of sight, apparently lying back in a chair. Mizner and his friends began to guess how tall the man was, from the evidence of his feet. Finally, they backed their guesses with money. Most of the bettors placed the man's height at well over six feet. Mizner made the lowest estimate. With a curious disregard of the principles of human symmetry, he guessed five feet one. When the money was up, they called on the man in the hotel room. He was a dwarf, four feet six inches tall, with No. 11 shoes. Mizner had brought him from New York and planted him there, figuring he could probably win a few bets on the man's paradoxical physique.

Mizner once employed a practical joke for the purpose of giving Nat Goodwin, the famous comedian, a lesson in ethics. Goodwin had pleaded to be allowed to be Mizner's confederate in a crooked card game. The comedian didn't want ill-gotten money, but he craved experience. Mizner explained that he was playing on the level at the time because all his fellow-players were as sophisticated as he was. Goodwin, a hero-worshipper, would not believe that Mizner would stoop to honesty under any circumstances. He continued to plead for a chance to help swindle somebody, and Mizner finally gave in. He promised to bump Goodwin's knee under the table at the point when the crooked work started. After the game had been going for three or four hours, Mizner bumped him and then handed over a new deck for Nat to deal. The actor dealt the first three cards but failed to get the fourth off the deck. He struggled furiously with the fourth card. Finally, he noticed that everybody was grinning at him. In order to instruct the actor in the principle of honor among thieves, Mizner had driven a nail through forty-nine cards leaving only the three top cards loose.

*　*　*　*

Whether he was playing on the level or had a little the best of things, Mizner was a pretty consistent winner at gambling. But even when he was taking large pots and enjoying considerable royalties from Broadway hits, he succeeded in living up to his revenue. At some periods of his career, women kept him solvent; at others, they kept him broke. When he was in luck, he was a prodigal buyer of furs, diamonds, and other antidotes to indifference. He held his own with the big spenders back in the pre-income-tax, champagne-for-the-house days. His resourcefulness in getting rid of money was illustrated by a front-page scoop in the World on December 19, 1912, describing a poker game played by Mizner, John Shaughnessy, Nat Evans, and George Young Bauchle. With stakes running into tens of thousands on the table. Mizner said, "I can't bear to spend Christmas in New York. If I win this hand, I'll take you all to Europe and show you around as long as the money lasts, provided you go to the boat with me as soon as the hand is played." Mizner won. He, Shaughnessy, and Evans hurried to the Mauretania and boarded it without baggage. Bauchle remained behind.

Evening it up with the World, the New York Press got a front-page scoop by cabling to Mizner on his arrival in London for an account of the expedition. It was an Iliad of hardship. According to Mizner, there had been only one toothbrush and one mustache cup among the three. He added that they were in a tramplike state because of their inability to buy clothes and other equipment in London on Christmas Day. "ALL THE STORES AND THEATRES, NOT EXCEPTING WESTMINSTER ABBEY, ARE CLOSED," he cabled. Serious trouble arose, he reported, because Shaughnessy's racial prejudice against Englishmen took the form of a blanket announcement at a big Christmas party: "If there's any battle of the Revolutionary War that remains undecided, I'd like to fight it over again."

Later, in Paris, Mizner took his guests out for a nine-course dinner at nine different restaurants, each course being something for which one particular dining place was especially noted. Correspondents in Paris and elsewhere on the Continent kept New York readers posted on such activities. Toward the end of the trip, Mizner was accused of trying to drive his companions home before all the money was spent. He failed to move them, even though he bribed orchestra leaders to play "Home, Sweet Home" incessantly. They stayed with him until his money was gone.

*   *   *   *

Mizner denied on the witness stand in a Magistrates' Court on August 28, 1918, that he lived entirely by gambling. He testified that he had a half interest in a tannery in Newark and did scenarios on the side. The charge against him was that of assaulting Herman Frank, an actor, in a Times Square restaurant. Frank had accused Mizner of stealing a Ziegfeld beauty from him. According to the testimony, Frank had sent Mizner a challenge to a duel in Van Cortlandt Park and Mizner had neglected to reply. On cross-examination, Mizner said that he didn't write scenarios but that he telephoned them. Referring to a screen drama of which Mizner was the author, the opposing lawyer said, "Do you mean to say that you gave that to the motion-picture company by telephone?" "Yes," said Mizner, "and they paid me by telephone." Like most of the criminal charges against Mizner, the assault charge evaporated somewhere in the judicial processes.

*   *   *   *

Men who were in Wilson's confidence tell of the wide range of devices by which he raised money. A rich young man of Seattle, on a visit to New York, complained to Mizner of a hangover and a complete inability to remember the events of the preceding night. Mizner hopped over to confer with the maître d'hôtel of a reigning lobster palace, concocted an itemized bill for nearly two thousand dollars, to be split two ways, and had it collected from the Westerner, who was informed that during the period about which his mind was a blank he had thrown one of the biggest and wildest parties of the season. Once, on a visit to a prosperous underworld establishment, Mizner faked the symptoms of scarlet fever. A confederate, masquerading as a physician, notified the proprietress that he would have to quarantine the place for a month. He settled, however, for a thousand dollars. On one occasion, Mizner sold a selling-plater for ten times its value by the simple device of moving back the six-furlong post in an early-morning workout, thereby shortening the course so that a stopwatch indicated the horse had broken the six-furlong record.

He was twenty-five or twenty-six when he executed one of the most profitable of his coups. A close pal of his was a member of a San Francisco family that had gained enormous wealth in Nevada silver mines. Mizner took the young scion of the Comstock Lode to New Orleans; their mission was to clean out a poolroom with the help of inside racing information. What the young silver millionaire didn't know was that the poolroom, with its entire personnel, customers and all, had been organized by Mizner solely for the purpose of getting a slice of the silver millions. Mizner's net profit at the expense of his bosom friend was more than $100,000, and in those simple days it lasted him more than a year. Mizner never had the slightest compunction about this informal method of redistributing the wealth. On their return to San Francisco, the young silver millionaire became suspicious and accused Mizner of fraud. Mizner gave him a beating, after which they became comrades again.

On other occasions, Mizner opened poolrooms and gambling houses, each for the purpose of fleecing a man of great wealth. For the exclusive benefit of the son of one of New York's richest bankers, he rented a house in Great Neck and installed a small stock company of underworld characters, who went through the motions of gambling for large sums in order to make the sucker feel that he was only one of many wealthy patrons. The Great Neck establishment failed with a considerable loss. The sucker had lost more than $200,000 when the operator applied too much magnetism and arrested the roulette ball in mid-career. The sucker grabbed his money. Mizner fled.

A trip on an ocean liner usually produced a substantial bank roll for Mizner, whether he played honestly or otherwise. On rare occasions, he picked the wrong man. He once drew a simple-looking stranger into a poker game and let him win for a while. Suddenly they began raising each other wildly, and the stakes became enormous. Mizner laid down four queens and reached for the pot. The stranger laid down four kings. Mizner pushed the pot back across the table. "You win, stranger," he said, "but those are not the cards I dealt you."

Although Mizner preyed on suckers most of his life, he was never appreciative. He seemed to have a genuine hatred of them. He regarded them as a corrupting influence. He never showed regret for his misspent life, but his bitterness on the subject of suckers apparently reflected a deep conviction that he would have been a credit to society if he had not fallen into their company. He asserted that confidence men did not discover suckers. The suckers, he said, hunted up the confidence men and usually brought them suffering and disgrace. He regarded the sucker as an unconscious *agent provocateur*. The police were never known, he asserted, to catch a confidence man until the suckers found him for them.

Mizner had a social philosophy on this subject. He particularly objected to Gold Coast punks who dangled inherited bank rolls before the eyes of resourceful men, and he disapproved of a government that allowed such things to be. He said that he had already been "sucker-sour" at the age of twenty-two. Texas Guinan's "Hello, sucker" was borrowed from Mizner. Other lines of his on this subject were "A sucker is born every minute, and two to take him" and "Boost a booster, knock a knocker, and use your own judgment with a sucker." Some authorities credit him with "Never give a sucker an even break," but this is disputed.

◇◇

A Great Card Swindle

The masterly bit of larceny described below is abridged from *Sharps and Flats*, by John Nevil Maskelyne (1830–1917), whose source was the famous nineteenth-century French conjurer, Jean Eugene Robert.

BY JOHN NEVIL MASKELYNE

◇◇

ONE OF the most immense frauds ever perpetrated in connection with card-sharping, and in which the fewest persons were concerned, was that recorded by Houdin. At the outset it was entirely conceived and executed by one sharp alone, although another took part in it at a later stage, much to the disappointment of the original promoter of the scheme.

At the date of the narrative, Havana, according to the historian, was the place most addicted to gambling of any in the world. As he also observed, that was not saying a little.

A Spanish sharp, named Bianco, purchased in his own country a tremendous stock of playing cards; and, in view of the undertaking in which he was about to embark, he opened every one of the packs, marked all the cards and sealed them up again in their wrappers. This he did so skillfully that there was no evidence of the fact that the packages had ever been tampered with. The stupendous feat involved in a proceeding of this kind being successfully accomplished, the cards were shipped off to Havana and there disposed of to the card-dealers at a ruinous sacrifice. So good indeed were these cards, and so cheap, that in a very little while the dealers could not be induced to purchase those of any other make.

The sharp, it may be imagined, was not long in following upon the track of his cards; and being a man of good address he contrived to obtain introductions into the best society. He played everywhere, of course, and where he played he won.

Among the various clubs in Havana was one which was of the most exclusive kind. The committee was so vigilant, and such great precautions were taken to prevent the admission of doubtful characters, that hitherto it had been kept free from the contamination of cheating. Into this club, however, Bianco contrived to effect an entrance, and carried on his operations therein with much success. He was destined, notwithstanding the zeal of the committee, to remain alone in the field but a very short time. Another sharp, a Frenchman this time, contrived also to obtain admission to the club; and he, too, set to work to prospect the country, thinking that he had possessed himself of a gold mine as yet unexploited.

Accordingly, this second adventurer, Laforcade by name, seized a favourable opportunity of appropriating a quantity of the club cards. These he took home with him for the purpose of marking them, intending to return them when marked to the stock from which they had been taken. One may imagine the man's surprise upon opening the packs to find that every card had already been marked.

Evidently, then, somebody had been before him, and Laforcade determined to find out who it could be. He made inquiries as to where the cards were obtained, and, purchasing some at the same place, found that these also were marked. In fact, every pack that he could procure had been tampered with in like manner. Here, then, was a gigantic swindle, and he determined to profit by it. He would let the other man do all the work, but *he* would share in the profits. If the other man, whoever he might be, would not listen to reason, he would threaten to hand him over to the police.

Having arrived at this decision, he set to work to watch the play of the various members of the club, and, naturally, the invariable good fortune of Bianco could not fail to attract his attention. Keeping strict watch upon that gentleman's proceedings, Laforcade soon arrived at the conclusion that Bianco, and no other, was the man of whom he was in search. He therefore took an early opportunity of engaging his brother swindler in a quiet game of écarté, whilst no other members of the club were present.

The game was played, and Bianco won, as a matter of course. Then, as usual, the winner asked his opponent if he was satisfied, or whether he would prefer to have his revenge in another game. Much to his surprise, however, instead of saying simply whether he preferred to play again or not the loser coolly rested his elbows on the table, and regarding his adversary composedly, gave him to understand that the entire secret of the cheerful little deception which was being practised was in his possession. This, of course, came rather as a bomb-shell into Bianco's camp, and reduced him at once to a condition in which any terms of compromise would be acceptable, in preference to exposure and imprisonment.

Matters having arrived at this point, Laforcade proposed terms upon which he was willing to come to an understanding with the Spaniard. These were, briefly, that Bianco should continue his system of plunder, on condition that he handed over to his fellow-cheat one-half of the proceeds. These terms were agreed to, and upon that basis of settlement the agreement was entered into.

For some time after this all went well with the two swindlers. Laforcade established himself in luxury, and gave his days to pleasure. Bianco ran all the risk; the other had nothing to do but sit at home and receive his share of the profits. It is true he could keep no check upon his associate, to see that he divided the spoils equitably; but, holding the sword of Damocles over him, he could always threaten him with exposure if the profits were not sufficiently great.

At length, however, Bianco began to tire of the arrangement, which perhaps was only natural. Besides, the supply of marked cards was beginning to run short, and could not be depended upon much longer. This being so, the prime mover of the plot having won as much as he possibly could, promptly vacated the scene of his exploits.

The unfortunate Laforcade thus found himself, as the Americans say, 'left.' The prospect was not altogether a pleasant one for him. He had acquired expensive tastes which he might no longer be enabled to indulge; he had accustomed himself to luxuries he could no longer hope to enjoy. He had not the skill of the departed Bianco; yet nevertheless, he was compelled to (metaphorically) roll up his sleeves and work for his living. Things were not so bad as they might have been. There was still a good number of falsified cards in use: so he determined to make the best possible use of his opportunities while they remained.

He therefore set to work with ardour, and success largely attended his efforts. At last, however, the crash came. He was detected in cheating and the whole secret of the marked cards was brought to light.

Even in this unfortunate predicament Laforcade's good fortune, strange to say, did not desert him. He was taken before the Tribunal, tried and acquitted. Absolutely nothing could be proved against him. It is true the cards were marked, but then, so were nearly all the others in Havana. Laforcade did not mark them as was proved in the evidence. He did not import them. To all intents and purposes he had nothing to do with them whatever. It could not even be proved that he knew of the cards being marked at all. Thus the case against him broke down utterly, and he got off scot free. It is, nevertheless, presumable that he did not long remain in that part of the world. As to what became of Bianco, nothing is known. Possibly his record concluded with the familiar words 'lived happily ever after'; but most probably not. The end of such men is seldom a happy one.

The recital of the above-mentioned circumstances will serve to accentuate the contention that it is impossible wholly to guard against cheating. Here was a case in which the utmost caution was observed, in order to exclude cheats and impostors from a club; and yet it is seen that, within a very short time, two men of the sharp persuasion contrived to effect an entrance.

There is only one course to pursue of which it can be said that it is absolutely safe. It is an extremely objectionable one, no doubt; but we are speaking, just now, of absolute safety. There is nothing for it but to suspect your best friend, *if he is a gambler.*

◇◇

Canada Bill

Founder of the still-continuing Pinkerton investigative agency, Allan Pinkerton (1819–1884) was an early abolitionist and Underground Railroad operator, foiled a plot to assassinate President-elect Abraham Lincoln, was a major figure in the Union's intelligence service in the Civil War, went on to be the nemesis of counterfeiters and train robbers, and finally wrote of his eventful life in *Criminal Reminiscences and Detective Sketches*, where this portrait of a talented rapscallion appears.

BY ALLAN PINKERTON

◇◇

THERE ARE some men who naturally choose, or, through a series of unfortunate blunders, drift into the life of social outlaws, who possess so many remarkably original traits of character that they become rather subjects for admiration than condemnation when we review their life and career.

On first thought it could hardly be imagined that one who has been all his life, so far as is known, a gambler and a confidence man, whose associates were always of the same or worse class than himself, who had no more regard for law than a wild Indian, and who never in his entire career seemed to have an aspiration above being the vagabond, par excellence, could move us to anything beyond a passing interest, the same as we would have for a wild animal or any unusual character among men and women.

But here is a man who, from his daring, his genuine simplicity, his great aptitude for his nefarious work, his simple, almost childish ways, his unequaled success, and a hundred other marked and remarkable qualities, cannot but cause something more than a common interest, and must always remain as an extraordinarily brilliant type of a very dangerous and unworthy class.

Such was "Canada Bill," whose real name was William Jones. He was born in a little tent under the trees of Yorkshire, in old England. His people were genuine Gypsies, who lived, as all other Gypsies do, by tinkering, dickering, or fortune-telling, and horse-trading. Bill, as he was always called, grew up among the Romany like any other Gypsy lad, becoming proficient in the nameless and numberless tricks of the Gypsy life, and particularly adept at handling cards. In fact, this proficiency caused him finally to leave his tribe, as, wherever he went among them, he never failed to beat the shrewdest of his shrewd people on every occasion where it was possible for him to secure an opponent willing to risk any money upon his supposed superiority in that direction.

Having become altogether too keen for his Gypsy friends, he began appearing at fairs and traveling with provincial catchpenny shows in England. Tiring of successes in that field, he eventually came to America, and wandered about Canada for some time in the genuine Gypsy fashion. This was about twenty-five years ago, when Bill was twenty-two or twenty-three years of age, and when thimble-rigging was the great game at the fairs and among travelers.

Bill soon developed a great reputation for playing short-card games, but finally devoted his talents entirely to three-card monte under the guise of a countryman, and may be said to have been the genuine original of that poor, simple personage who had been swindled by sharpers, and who, while bewailing his loss and showing interested people the manner in which he had been robbed, invariably made their natural curiosity and patronizing sympathy cost them dearly.

Himself and another well-known monte-player, named Dick Cady, traveled through Canada for several years, gaining a great notoriety among gamblers and sporting men; and it was here that this singular person secured the sobriquet of "Canada Bill," which name clung to him until his death, in the summer of 1877; and he was known by everybody throughout the country who knew him at all by that name, it being generally supposed that he was of Canadian birth.

As a rule, three-card monte men are mong the most godless, worthless, unprincipled villains that infest society anywhere; but this strange character, from his simplicity, which was genuine, his cunning, which was most brilliant, his acting, which was inimitable, because it was nature itself, created a lofty niche for himself in all the honor there may be attached to a brilliant and wholly original career as a sharper of this kind; and however many imitators he may have—and he has hundreds —none can ever approach his perfection in the slightest possible degree.

Any deft person, after a certain amount of practice, can do all the trickery there is about the sleight-of-hand in three-card monte; but the game is so common a dodge among swindlers, that unless the confidence of the dupe is first fully secured, he seldom bites at the bait offered.

This must either be confidence, on the part of the person being operated on, that he is smarter than the dealer, if his real character is known; or, in case it is not known, a conviction that he is a genuine greenhorn who can easily be beaten the second time.

It was here that Canada Bill's peculiar genius never failed to give him victory; and it is said of him that he never made a mistake and never failed to win money whenever he attempted it.

His personal appearance, which was most ludicrous, undeniably had much to do with his success. He was the veritable country gawky, the ridiculous, ignorant, absurd creature that has been so imperfectly imitated on and off the stage for years, and whose true description can scarcely be written. He was fully six feet high, with dark eyes and hair, and always had a smooth shaven face, full of seams and wrinkles, that were put to all manner of difficult expressions with a marvelous facility and ease. All this—coupled with long, loose-jointed arms, long, thin, and apparently a trifle unsteady legs, a shambling, shuffling, awkward gait, and this remarkable face and head bent forward and turned a little to one side, like an inquiring and wise old owl, and then an outfit of Granger clothing, the entire cost of which never exceeded fifteen dollars —made a combination that never failed to call a smile to a stranger's face, or awaken a feeling of curiosity and interest wherever he might be seen.

*   *   *   *

One November night, several years since, I started on a hurried trip over the Pittsburgh and Fort Wayne road from Chicago to the East, for the transaction of some important business of such a nature that I did not desire the fact of my presence known there; and, noticing several eastern and western people of my acquaintance in the sleeper and throughout the cars, before the train started, I quietly entered the smoking-car, and took a cigar and a seat in a quiet corner, with the object of avoiding my friends as much as possible, and remaining where I was until everything had got quiet in the sleeper for the night so that I could safely retire without observation.

Being very tired, after a casual glance at several other persons in front of me in the car, I settled myself snugly in my seat, hoping to be able to get a little nap; but I had scarcely got myself comfortably arranged, when the train halted at Twenty-second Street, and my attention was attracted by the entrance into our car of a tall, stumbling fellow, dressed in some cheap, woolen, home-spun stuff, that hung about his attenuated frame like a dirty camp-meeting tent around a straggling set of poles.

Pausing just inside the door for a moment, he deposited on the floor a valise whoses size and cavernous appearance would have won the heart of an audience at a minstrel show, and then, giving his big hand a great ungainly wave as if to clear away the smoke immediately in front of him, peered into the murky distance, and ejaculated, "Gaul-darned thick!"

By this time there was a broad smile on the faces of all the passengers, and many mirthful references were made in an undertone to the wild "Hoosier," some of which he evidently overheard, but which were received in the best of humor, the subject of such witticism turning a benign and smiling farmer face upon all, but holding on to his big, though evidently nearly empty valise with both hands, as if indicating that he was quite ready for any good-natured joke with "the boys," so long as none of them attempted any sharp city tricks upon him.

We had been bowling along for but a short time, however, before the conductor made his appearance.

His was mere business—to collect fares; that was all. He came through the car like an "old campaigner," with no favors to ask and none to give.

He got along to where our bucolic friend was sitting without trouble, when that lively individual seemed ready for an argument.

"You're the conductor?" he remarked dryly.

"Yes."

"You takes the money for ridin' on this machine?"

"Yes; where ye goin' ? "

"Fort Wayne, God willin'."

The countryman clumsily produced a bill from out a huge roll, and then remarked:

"Lots of good boys on the train?"

"Dunno; guess so," replied the conductor. The conductor gave the innocent party his change, when that ubiquitous individual remarked:

"Lots of funny fellows on this train?"

The conductor had passed, but he took the time to turn and say:

"Don't trust 'em, my Granger friend."

"D——d if I will," said he, as he took a stronger and firmer hold of his priceless "grip-sack." "D——d if I will, fur I've been thar! I've been thar!"

A roar of laughter followed this sally from the "Injeanny Granger," and I noticed at the time, without giving it any particular attention so far as this countryman and his immediate remarks were concerned, that, at various intervals throughout the car, the laughing which followed his remark was extremely well distributed; but being tired, I received all this merriment as a common occurrence, and, after the conductor passed, fell into a heavy drowse.

I was of course unconscious of what passed for a little time, but was eventually disturbed by renewed laughter through the car, and noticed that quite a group had gathered around the Granger, whose members were evidently greatly interested in whatever he was doing and saying: while his great, honest face, all alive with enthusiasm, was wreathed with smiles at being such an object of general interest.

As before stated, up to this time I had given the matter no thought; but when I now heard one of a couple in front of me remark: "Very quaint character; very quaint character. I believe some of those Chicago rascals have victimized him, and he is telling the passengers about it," which was followed by a request to his companion to "come along and see the fun," I immediately understood that we were to be given an exhibition of three-card monte of a very interesting character, and that many of the persons in the car were "cappers," or those members of the gang who are used to persuade fools to bet upon the game.

By this time so much interest was being exhibited in the uncouth fellow's manipulations, that two seats had been given him; and there he sat in one corner of the space thus made, with his legs crossed under him like a tailor's, his huge valise lying across this framework in such a manner that a most neat, level, and glossy surface was made, and all this with a nicety of calculation really remarkable, while his whole form, manner, and action showed him to be the simplest, most honest of men, who, out of the pure goodness of his heart,—rough, ignorant, and un-kempt as he was,—proposed giving the crowd about him his experi-ences merely for what benefit it would certainly prove to them.

"Yaas," he said in an indescribably droll tone of voice, "yaas, them doggoned Chicago skinners cum nigh a ruinin' me. Now, I do 'low them fellers beat the hull tarnal kentry. But gosh! I found 'em out!"

He then reached his long, skinny fingers down into his huge valise and brought out a handful of articles of various kinds, among which were a couple of sickle-teeth, tied together with a string, a horn husking-pin, and a "snack" of chicken covered with bread-crumbs. These caused another laugh, but were suddenly returned to their resting place and several other dives made into the greasy cavern, evidently to the great discomfiture of the gawky; but he chattered and grinned away, until finally a brand-new pack of cards had been secured.

To any casual observer it was more than apparent that the poor silly fellow was not more than half-witted, and the fun of it all seemed to lie in his sincerity, which the passengers took for one of the hugest of jokes.

After things had been got to rights—which took the clumsy fellow a long time, during which he enlivened his listeners with his idea of Chi-cago as a city, its people as sharpers of the first order, and the grandeur of his own great State, Indiana—he selected three cards from the pack, and, wrapping the balance in a dirty bit of brown paper, put them away carefully in the valise.

The three cards selected were the five of spades, the five of clubs and the queen of hearts, and the gentleman from Indiana now began his exposition in real earnest.

"Wy, d'ye know, the durn skunks said they knowed me, 'n' 'fore I knowed what I was a doin' these old friends, as they said they wus, had me bettin' that *I* could jerk up the joker. Now, yer see, fellers," remarked the dealer, as he held up the queen, "they called this keerd the joker, fur why I can't tell yer, lest it's a joke on the dealer if yer picks it up."

"Of course you picked it up," remarked a flashy gentleman, who had the appearance of a successful commercial traveler on a good salary.

Such a look as the dealer gave the man.

"Picked it up!—picked it up? My friend, mebby you think you're smart enough to pick it up! Don't you ever squander yer money like I did a-tryin'! Pick her up! Pick up hell! 'Tain't in her to git picked up. She can't be got. Them cussed coons has worked some all-fired charm on that durned keerd, so that no man can raise her. Mebby you kin lift the keerd? She allers wins, she does; but don't bet nuthin'."

Here the dealer bunglingly shuffled the cards, and made such a mess of it that the effort only brought forth more peals of derisive laughter.

"Now, ye see, fellers," pursued the imperturbable dealer, "this is the five uv spades, hy'r is the five uv clubs, and thar is the rip-roarin' female that wins every time she kin be got. I'm jest a-goin' to skin the boys down hum in Kos-cus-ky County; fur it's the beautifullest and deceivenst game out; but," he added, with the solemnity of a parson at a funeral, "fellers, d'ye know I wouldn't hev a friend o' mine bet on this yer game fur anything—not fur a good hoss!"

He closed this admonitory remark with such a droll wave of his long arm and hand, that a palpable snicker greeted the performance; and the flashy gentleman who had suggested that the greeny must have been able to pick up the card when being entertained by his Chicago friends, bent forward, and after a moment's hesitation over the three cards, which were lying face downward upon the valise, picked up one, which, with an air of triumph, he held aloft for a moment and then slapped down with a great flourish.

This was the "rip-roarin' female that wins every time!" and his honor, the gentleman from Kosciusco County, Indiana, turned white as he observed how neatly her ladyship could be brought to the surface by one of a miscellaneous crowd.

"Jehosiphat!" he exclaimed, as he grabbed the cards and began another bungling shuffle of them—"Jehosiphat! Stranger, d'yer know I've pea-green scrip in my pocket as says as yer can't do that agin?"

"Oh, I wouldn't take your money!" the flashy man replied, as he nudged a man near him. " 'Twouldn't be fair, you know."

"Now—now, see hy'r, stranger," answered the Indianian, "I've told ye already that ye hadn't ought to bet on this deceitful game; but yer is too sassy and bold. Yer thinks yer knows it all, 'n' yer doesn't. Jist wait till I fix the keerds. Thar now! Old Injeanny agin the field!"

The dealer had rearranged the cards in a reckless wild fashion; but there they lay, and the passengers crowded closer and closer about the group to see all the fun that might happen.

Slowly and ungainly enough the dealer reached down into the outside pockets of his homespun suit with both hands. Finding nothing there, he tremulously went into his pantaloons pockets; but he found nothing there.

"Oh, he's a fraud!" suggested a big-bellied man near me, turning to a rural-looking fellow at his side. "Do you know," he continued warmly, "you and I could go in together, and clean that 'old Jasey' out—if he's got any money. But," he added, confidentially, to his companion, "I don't believe he's got a copper."

His companion, whom I had already taken for a country merchant, or something of that kind, as he afterward proved to be, looked nervous, and only replied:

"Wait a bit; let's see what he can find in his clothes. Perhaps these gentlemen wouldn't let us win anything anyhow."

I did not catch the answer, only observing that a pretty good understanding had been arrived at between the two. The party from Indiana by this time, after going through nearly every pocket in his clothing, had brought out from an inside vest-pocket a great, rough, dirty-looking wallet that contained, as could be seen at a glance, a very large though loosely arranged package of green backs, which he had denominated "pea-green scrip," and which he shook out into his broad-rimmed hat at his side in an alarmingly careless way.

"Thar's what I got left, after comin' outn' that d——d Gomorer, Chicager!" the dealer said feelingly. "Stock's down, 'n' grass is dry, but I'll be gol-walloped ef I don't believe for a hundred-dollar pictur the female boss can't be lifted agin!"

"I'm your sweet potato—just for once, mind you, just for once, for I ain't a betting man. But I'll risk that much just to show you how easily you can be beat at your own game!" remarked the flashy man, carelessly, at the same time covering the hundred-dollar "pictur" with ten ten-dollar bills.

"Can't I go halves on that?" eagerly asked a rough-looking fellow, who stood on a seat peering over the heads of the passengers, and at the same time holding up a fifty-dollar bill.

I saw that the scheme for getting outside parties to bet, and divide chances with those who considered themselves "up to the game," was being given a fine impetus.

"Well, I don't mind, although I'm sure of the whole," said the flashy party, as he received the fifty dollars nonchalantly.

The honest Granger from Indiana looked dumbfounded at this new evidence of a want of confidence in his ability, but spoke up cheerily: "Wall, thar's the keerds; yer kin take yer pick!"

Upon this the flashy party pushed his way into the open space, sat down opposite the dealer, and, without any further ado, reached forward with one hand and turned the queen in a twinkling, and raked in the money with the other, immediately rising and handing the party who had taken half the bet the one-hundred-dollar bill, and pocketing the ten ten-dollar bills, and then immediately leaving the luckless dealer, to communicate and comment upon his good fortune to his friends throughout the car and tell them how easily the thing was done.

"Gaul darn the keerds, anyhow!" blurted out the dealer; "the hull cussed thing's gone back on me; but I swon ef I don't keep the fun a-goin' !"

Suddenly there was a movement near me, and I heard the country merchant remark to his friend:

"Well, I'll go in five hundred with you. Be careful now, be careful!"

Another "capper" in the crowd, having a Jew in tow, now bet a hundred dollars, and won, dividing the winnings with that party, who received his share with rapturous delight; and it could be easily seen he was in a fine condition to be "worked."

The large man with the country merchant now stopped and turned to his friend, saying in an undertone: "No, you're a stranger to me, and I'd rather you'd bet the money. We will fix it this way: I'm certain of picking up the card, but I might be mistaken. I'll make two or three small bets first, or enough, so that I can pick up the card. While I have it in my hand, I'll turn one corner under, so that the card, after it is dealt, won't lay down flat. You'll see it plainly, and you can't make a mistake. Now, watch things!"

With this fine piece of bait, the corpulent fellow, who was none other than a "capper," sat down opposite the dealer and made a few small bets. He lost three in quick succession, but on the fourth trial he turned up the queen, and won.

I watched him closely, for I had overheard him state to his dupe that he would mark the card by turning one corner of the same under toward the face. Surely enough, he did so very deftly, and I noticed that the country merchant had also seen the action, for he immediately stepped forward and took the place made vacant for him.

"Careful now!" said the stout man, as they passed each other.

An answering look from the merchant showed that he considered himself up to a thing or two; and, as he seated himself, he inquired of the ignorant dealer if he limited his bets.

"Ye kin jist bet yer hull pile, or a ten-cent pictur, stranger!" replied that worthy, with a silly, childish chuckle, as he tossed the cards back and forth in a seemingly foolishly-reckless way.

The crowd now pressed forward, all interest and attention.

"Two hundred dollars on the queen!" said the country merchant, laying that amount on the old valise. I noticed that a quick look of intelligence passed between the stout man and the Hoosier dealer. The stout fellow was mistaken in his man. He was betting too low. I made up my mind that his look to the dealer expressed all this with the additional advice: "Let him win a little!"

The money was covered, and the merchant's hands fluttered tremulously over the cards for a moment. But he picked up the queen and won. A buzz of excited comments followed.

"Be ye one o' them Chicager skinners?" asked the dealer. "Confound it! I'm a-gittin' beat right an' left!"

"You don't limit bets?" asked the merchant eagerly.

"Nary time, nary time. Hyr's a hatful of picturs as backs the winnin' keerd, which is always the queen."

"Well, then," said the dupe with painful slowness, while the corners of his mouth drew down and his lips became colorless, "I'll bet fifteen hundred dollars I can pick up the queen!"

There laid one of the cards, showing it had been doubled enough to prevent its resting flatly upon the old valise. The merchant counted out the money in a husky voice, making several errors, and being corrected by some of the passengers. The dealer, who might have had just a trace of a glitter in his black, fishy eyes, groped around among his "picturs" and provided an equal amount. Every person in the car bent forward, and in a painful, breathless silence awaited the result.

"Yer pays yer money, 'n' yer takes yer choice!" remarked the dealer, leaning back in his seat, and whistling as unconcernedly as if at a town-meeting.

The merchant leaned forward. He looked at the cards as though his very soul had leaped into his eyes. He suddenly grasped the card that refused to lie flatly upon the valise, and turned it over.

He had picked up the five of clubs, and had lost!

Something like a moan escaped the poor victim's lips. My own blood boiled to rescue him from this villainous robbery. I could not do it without jeopardizing far greater interests, but my heart bled for him in his misery.

"I'm a ruined man!" he gasped, and then staggered through the crowd to sink into a vacant seat.

Even then he could not be left alone. His stout friend, the "capper," sought him out and upbraided him for his foolishness in picking up the wrong card and losing *his* five hundred dollars with his own. He even begged him to try again, and, finding that he had a few hundred dollars left out of what he was going to New York to buy goods with, cursed him because he would not risk that in order to retrieve himself and pay him back his money, which the reader will readily understand already belonged to the honest, simple-hearted Hoosier who was manipulating the cards.

But the game went on. The loss of so great a sum of money put rather a dampener upon it; but the "cappers" came to the rescue with twenty, fifty, and one hundred dollar bets, which were so rapidly won that the Jew was at last "worked" out of six hundred dollars in two quick bets of three hundred cash; and amid a great row and racket which he made over his loss, the voice of the brakeman could be heard, crying out:

"Valparaiso! Twenty minutes for supper!"

Not a minute more had passed, and the train had not even come to a halt, when every one of the nefarious gang had disappeared.

The flashy man, with the look of a successful commercial traveler, was gone; the stout man, who had "stood in" with the country merchant, had gone; the party who had entertained the Jew was gone; and the honest, simple, cheery countryman from Kosciusko County, Indiana, with his cavernous valise half full of loose bills, which he had not even taken time to arrange in the old book for carrying in his side-pocket—and who was none other than the notorious "Canada Bill"—was gone. They were all gone, and they had taken from their dupes from eighteen hundred to two thousand dollars.

I could not but pity the poor victims, who were left on the train to brood over their foolishness; but at the same time a sense of justice stole in upon my sympathy. Every one of these dupes had got beaten at his own game. They were just as dishonest as the men who fleeced them. They would not have risked a dollar had they not, one and all, believed that they had the advantage of a poor, foolish fellow. If he *had* been what they believed, and they had won his money, it would have been robbery just as much as it was robbery to take their money as neatly and easily as it was taken.

How to Beat the Horses

The pride of Chicago's con game community was Yellow Kid Weil, the most amiable of operators in that elite school of ·felony and certainly one of the most successful. He managed to stay out of jail until he reached his seventies, and consistently maintained that he practiced his art in defense against those who were out to rob *him*. "You don't get taken unless you have larceny in your heart," the Kid used to say patiently, as if explaining an equation in geometry.

BY YELLOW KID WEIL
AS TOLD TO W. T. BRANNON

THERE IS a widely accepted theory that crime does not pay. This may be true in many cases, but it was not always true in Chicago. Numerous forms of amusement and so-called vice that are now illegal once operated wide open and with the full blessing of the law.

For example, anybody could make book on the races, whether he operated at the tracks or a thousand miles away. Today bookmaking is unlawful even at the racecourse, the only legal wagering being at the pari-mutuel windows.

Betting on the races always fascinated me. Not that I ever believed for a moment that there was any such thing as "smart money" on a horse. As long as I can remember I've known that you can't beat them by any orthodox method. But the very fact that there are so many people who think they can beat the horses is the chief reason for my interest.

On every hand people clamored to bet their money. They sought "inside tips" and "sure things." Perhaps a few have actually tried to win by a study of past performances and careful analysis of the facts. I have never met anyone who did. True, there are more or less expert handicappers; but they sell their advice to others and bet very little of their own money on their selections.

The impression among horse players has been that some races are fixed. Even today many are eager to put their money on a race they think has been fixed.

Up to now the major part of my activities had been concerned with schemes to make money on the horses. My fake wire-tapping scheme was extremely profitable and I was quite happy to continue it.

However, Joe Moffatt, who operated the electrical shop where the suckers parted with their money for expensive-appearing gadgets for tapping telegraph wires, dealt with only a few of us. There were not more than a dozen top con men who had entree to Moffatt's shop. I might add that his business was legitimate. The laws relating to confidence games were different in those days.

Today almost any sort of conspiracy to separate a man from his money is illegal under the confidence laws. But in those days a confidence game was defined under the law as taking "unfair advantage of an unwary stranger." This was generally interpreted as a person from the bucolic areas. Any Chicago business man, presumably acquainted with city life and its pitfalls, was presumed to have entered a deal such as a wire-tapping scheme with his eyes open, and the courts refused to recognize him as an "unwary stranger."

Every profitable idea I ever originated for trimming wealthy men was sooner or later copied by others. This was the case with wire-tapping to get race information. At one time hundreds of small-time con men were working it in one form or another. They advertised openly for victims. I recall one day when a leading Chicago paper ran more than two hundred of these ads in its classified section.

These men did not have access to Joe Moffatt's place. The equipment they put together was crude and makeshift. Some of them actually believed that they could stop messages by attaching a wire to a telegraph line. Their suckers were barbers, waiters, bartenders, and others who could raise only a few hundred dollars at most.

The effect of all this was to arouse both the Western Union and the police. I had accumulated a tidy sum and decided to change my modus operandi, though I had no particular desire to change my clientele. Horse-race suckers were—or so I thought at the time—the most gullible of all. Without exception, everyone was interested in making a killing, though each knew that the big profit he hoped for would be strictly dishonest.

After purchasing a couple of horses, I arranged to enter them in competition at the Chicago racecourses: Hawthorne, Harlem, Washington Park, and Robey.

I stabled my horses at Jackson Boulevard and Homan Avenue, not far from the Garfield Park course. This was a five-eights track for trotters, but owners who wished to pay the fee could exercise their horses there. The five-eights track served my purpose admirably.

From the start I did not become a horse owner because of a notion that I might win purses. I had already learned that it could be more profitable to lose. That is the system I devised for "beating the horses."

I always maintained the finest tack-room at any racecourse where my horses were running. A tack-room is a place where an owner keeps his saddles, weights, jockey uniforms, etc. Mine was outfitted solely for show purposes. Anybody who saw it immediately concluded that the owner certainly must have fine horses.

As a matter of fact my horses seldom ran in the money. One of them, Mobina, was an old plater that would never even show. But I put fine saddles and a well-dressed jockey on him and to the uninitiated, he looked like a good bet.

There was a man whom I shall call Epping who lived on Jackson Boulevard and was a frequent visitor to the Garfield Park race track. He saw my boy exercising Mobina and became interested.

Knowing Epping's background, I was interested in him, too. He was wealthy and had a prosperous business on Chicago Avenue. In those days a man could keep all his money. There was no income tax and he did not have to account for where he got his money or how he disposed of it.

Epping's employees were often hard pressed for ready cash. They had a habit of going to the paymaster for an advance until payday. This gave Epping an idea. Why not set up a place where anybody who was regularly employed could obtain a small loan?

Until then the only people who made loans were the banks and the "loan sharks." This latter group not only made you mortgage your life but charged unbelievable rates. Epping altered this by making regular employment the chief qualification. And he charged rates that were considered reasonable—six per cent a month. His lending business was the beginning of the present-day small loan concern.

I already knew of Epping's wealth, and it did not take me long to discover that his chief aim in life was to accumulate more. He was interested in my horses because he had heard that there was considerable money to be made in winning purses. I soon learned that he knew very little about race horses. I told Epping that the five-eights course at Garfield Park was a three-quarter track, and he didn't know the difference. But what a difference it made in the running time of a horse like Mobina!

"That horse will make me a lot of money," I told Epping, "if I can raise the money to get him in shape."

"How much money do you need?" he asked.

"I'd have to do some figuring," I replied. "Why?"

"Would you be interested in a partner?"

"I hadn't thought of that. What do you suggest?"

He proposed that he make me a loan, to be repaid out of the profits. He would get a cut of the winnings. We discussed this at some length and decided that 20 per cent would be a fair split for Epping. I did some figuring, and explained that it was an expensive proposition to stable a horse and to pay a trainer and jockey. I finally arrived at a figure— $3,700.

Epping was a hard-headed business man and insisted that we draw up a contract. He agreed that it could be done by my own lawyer, who was in on the deal and knew the kind of contract that I would need. It was duly signed and witnessed, and Epping advanced the money. Then he waited for Mobina to start winning purses.

But there was no chance that Mobina would win. I didn't even enter him in a race. After about thirty days, Epping began to get impatient and asked for an accounting.

I told him that it takes time to get a horse in shape to race and reminded him that I was waiting for a good purse. This stall did not satisfy him. A few days later he demanded that I repay the loan.

I pointed to the contract. It provided that "When Mobina shall have raced and won, then the monies advanced by Party of the First Part (Epping) shall be paid by Party of the Second Part (Weil), plus 20 per cent of the gross winnings."

Epping saw the joker in the contract and knew that he couldn't get anything by bringing suit. But he did swear out a warrant charging me with operating a confidence game.

The judge threw the case out, holding that "the contract was based on a future event and that no crime had been committed or could be committed until the event had taken place."

Epping didn't bother me any more, and I don't recall that I ever saw him again. As a matter of fact, I never saw most of my victims again, once I had taken their money. This is strange, too, considering that I have been around Chicago for all these years. I probably have passed them on the street many times.

Meanwhile I met a man named A. B. Watts, who was a breeder of blooded horses. I made a deal with him to increase my stable, and thereafter all the horses I bought came from Watts. These included Title, Black Fonso, Thanksgiving, St. Durango, Sir Christopher, Dan Joe, Meddlesome, and Zibia.

These were fine-looking horses and made an excellent showing when I had exercised them for the benefit of suckers. The latter fell into several categories. Those like Epping advanced money to help train the horses and win purses. Others were led to believe that we were training a "ringer" which would later win and make it possible for them to clean up on wagering. The most gullible were those at the tracks who went for "inside tips" on betting.

At the track, I frequently posed as a jockey. I had to employ a stooge, and on many occasions was helped by William J. Winterbill. He was tall, broad-shouldered, and well-built, with fine features. He dressed conservatively.

Here is an example of the way we worked:

Winterbill and I selected a victim from the crowd of men standing near the betting ring. Program in hand, Winterbill approached the sucker and struck up an acquaintance while talking about the day's entries.

"My name is Winterbill," he introduced himself. "William J. Winterbill." He stuck out his hand.

"Mine is Harper," responded the other man. "Glad to know you, Mr. Winterbill."

Winterbill was an impressive-looking fellow. He had little trouble getting the victim to believe that he was a business man, taking a day off at the races.

"What horse are you betting on?" Winterbill asked.

"Haven't made up my mind," Harper replied. "Have you any suggestions?"

"No, I haven't decided either." Then his eye wandered away from the betting ring. "Say! Do you see that fellow standing there?"

He pointed to me. I had a pad of paper in my hand and was busily jotting down figures. "Yes, I see him," said Harper. "What about him?"

"Don't you know who he is?"

"Can't say that I do."

"Why, that's Willie Caywood, the jockey. He rides for Sam Hildreth, the famous trainer."

Of course, Harper had heard of Sam Hildreth. We always picked the names of a famous trainer. (Hildreth later raced Zev, one of the greatest horses of all time.) I was slight and young and could pass for a jockey.

"Wonder what he's figuring up?" Harper mused.

"I wonder, too," said Winterbill. "If there was only some way we could get to know him."

Just then, I dropped my pencil. It rolled some distance from where I was standing.

"Quick!" hissed Winterbill. "Now's your chance. Pick up his pencil. That's your chance to meet him. Maybe he will give you a tip."

Harper hurriedly retrieved my pencil. I was properly grateful.

"Thank you, Mr.—"

"Harper. Don't mention it."

"My name is Willie Caywood."

"Not the jockey?" asked Harper.

"Yes," I admitted.

Winterbill came up. Harper introduced us.

"We were just wondering what you were figuring," Harper ventured.

"Why—ah—I was just figuring up how much I would win today."

"What makes you so sure you'll win anything?" Harper asked.

I glanced about furtively, and lowered my voice. "I know I'm going to win. You gentlemen look like you can be trusted. I'll tell you the truth, but it must be strictly confidential. The boss is going to make a killing today. So he let me in on it."

"I don't suppose you'd be willing to tell us the name of the horse?" said Winterbill.

"No," I replied. "I couldn't do that. I promised the boss that I wouldn't. And if it got around, the odds would go down on the horse. My boss is going to spread his bets. He'll wire them around the country just before post time, so that nobody will get suspicious."

"Too bad," grunted Harper, obviously disappointed. "We hoped you might give us a tip."

"I'll tell you what," offered Winterbill, as if an idea had suddenly struck him. "If you won't give us a tip, maybe you'll make our bets for us."

I considered this a moment. "Yes, I guess I could do that. But I still can't tell you the name of the horse."

"I don't care," said Winterbill, "just so I clean up. Here's $2,500. Put it on the nose for me."

Harper had already dug into his pocket. "Here's $1,500 for me."

"All right," I agreed, taking their money. "I'll meet you gentlemen right here after the fifth race."

Winterbill was enthusiastic and Harper seemed well pleased. They left me and went into the grandstand, chatting and speculating on what horses in the fifth race was to make the killing. Winterbill excused himself from Harper on some pretext. He met me a short time later and we worked the same game on as many suckers as we could find.

But by the time the fifth race had been run, we were far away from the track. Mr. Harper and the others who kept the rendezvous were doomed to a long wait and to a sad disappointment.

Fleecing the Fleecers

The gambler who turns to virtue after years of skillful theft is not held in high esteem by his former fellows in the lodge. One such was Jonathan Harrington Green, who made a good thing of it on the Western waters for some years, and then greatly annoyed his old cronies by writing such books as *An Exposure of the Arts and Miseries of Gambling* and *Gambling Unmasked!* This passage from the latter volume suggests that while he was indulging in the iniquity he later deplored, he was also having a good deal of fun. We see him here just after he has boarded a boat at Natchez and is casting about for some profitable entertainment.

BY J. H. GREEN

I SOON found that my prospects were dull enough, for I could not start a game, even for amusement. So I took my berth, thinking I would sleep upon it. A curious set of passengers, thought I, afraid to play with a beardless boy. But as I lay in my berth, thinking over the matter, the boat stopped her engines—passengers had hailed her. The yawl was sent out, and two elderly men, planters in appearance, came on board. They were evidently under the influence of liquor. They had scarcely reached the boat before they sung out, "Bar-keeper, have you any cards on board?" Being answered in the affirmative, they asked if there were any gentlemen that would play? The bar-keeper could not inform them; but remarked they could satisfy themselves by inquiry. Upon this, they advanced to where several persons were seated, whom I had annoyed very much, by urging them to play. They all refused again. "But you must play," said one of the old men; "we will have a game." Some one of them pointed to my berth, and said there was a gentleman there who would probably be happy to accommodate them. He was right, and if they had not called upon me, I would soon have called upon them, to accommodate them with a game of poker. The old man turned round and felt his way along to the berth where I lay, as he supposed, asleep. But "all men do not sleep when their eyes are shut." He gave me a hearty shake, crying out, "Halloo! get up, get up." I affected the sleeping man, muttered out my surprise, asked him if the boat was

247

sinking, and so forth. He was perfectly deceived, and continued to bawl out, "Get up, get up, and play poker."

"Well, if I must, I must," said I. "Go and get the table and cards ready, and I will be with you as soon as possible." I soon heard him giving orders to the steward to bring a table and cards. While things were making ready, I was very busy in finding and arranging my wearing apparel, and saw, from the run of their conversation, that they were expecting a rich treat, and had agreed to play against me in partnership. Their agreement I overheard. Said one of them, "You, sir, set your foot on mine, and for one pair, kick me once; for two pairs, twice; for three, three times; for four, four times; and for 'a full,' once very hard." I knew that, with this arrangement, unless I should counterplay, they would soon fleece me. Soon after the game began, I found them feeling for feet, and being of an accommodating disposition, I gave them a foot a piece. Kick after kick did I get, and answer; and soon found myself winner by six hundred dollars, and my opponents in a very disagreeable mood for amusement players, as they assured me they were. We had about forty dollars in silver to play with, and as fast as I won it, they would give me bank-notes in exchange. When I had won the six hundred dollars, and all the silver, they wished to play upon credit. This I refused; and as they were getting very quarrelsome, I determined to close. They objected to this, and insisted that if I did quit, I should leave the silver. I did so, and they soon were playing high against each other. It is a natural consequence that, when two gamblers in partnership have been unsuccessful, they will turn upon one another. I lay in my berth, well pleased with my night's work. Unpleasant and harsh words passed between the old men.

"You did not play the game according to bargain, Mr. ——."

"I not play! Do you mean me, Mr.?"

"I mean you, ——."

"Don't say that, Mr. ——. No, sir, it will not do to accuse me, when you did not kick me right one time during the whole night."

"Hold! hold! Did you kick me according to the arrangement? Mr. ——, we are neighbors, and I thought friends, till this evening's play; but I must confess I am somewhat——"

"Ashamed of yourself, I suppose," said ——, taking the words out of his mouth.

"No, sir; one proposition, and leave the balance until to-morrow."

"Propose," said ——.

"That we settle our play to-night, and leave the matter of the incorrect kicking to be settled at another time."

"Very willing; how do you say we stand?"

"I owe you one hundred and seventy-five dollars," said ——.

"You are a correct man, sir."

"That I am, and this settlement will prove it; but let me ask how you like our night's play?" said ——.

"Don't like it at all," said ——.

"And the boy that played, what do you think of him?"

"I think just this, Mr. ——; I think we waked up the wrong passenger!"

"I think so, too; we are perfectly agreed, Mr. ——. And now, neighbor ——, you know I have a great respect for you, and hope you may not lose; but I must cast up my account against you, and see how much you are indebted to me."

"Account against me!" exclaimed ——; "I will submit to no such thing, I assure you."

"Just look over that list, and—keep cool, friend ——, keep cool, sir—it says you owe me two hundred and twenty-five dollars; bringing you in my debt fifty dollars. Is not that right?"

"Too late to rectify mistakes, sir."

"But you are bound to rectify this one. What do you think of that?"

"I think as I did of the boy—that I waked up the wrong passenger," said he, at the same time sliding his claim from the table, badly beaten.

Those two old men had come on board on purpose to fleece some inexperienced card-player, while they pretended that amusement was all they wanted in playing. I was, probably, the only individual on board whom they could not have beaten. Beware of the men who say they play merely for amusement. Beware, too, of those who advocate such playing; for, while here and there one may do it from ignorance, it is generally done by dishonest, unprincipled men, as a cloak for their own knavery and crime. The only safe course is total abstinence. Touch not, handle not the implements of the gambler.

The Rake of Piccadilly

As renowned as any gambler in eighteenth-century England was the Scot who was born William Douglas, went on to be the 3rd Earl of March and 4th Duke of Queensberry, and while still in his twenties joined the aristocratic young scamps at White's Club in London. Like them, he would bet on virtually anything. Unlike most of them he wagered with such prudence and creative imagination that in his old age he wound up ahead of the game—or so close to it that he could look back with no regrets.

BY HENRY BLYTHE

THE MEMBERS [of White's] greatly liked a flutter on some form of death or disaster. When they walked down the road to Mrs Comyns' brothel, they would lay bets as to whether or not they would contract venereal disease during intercourse, and one member even wagered that he would, and then went to a great deal of trouble to discover a pox-ridden young harlot who could ensure that he won his bet. They also enjoyed backing on whether elderly members of the Old Club would survive the year, or even the month; or on how many of the present members of Parliament would still be alive at the end of the session.

'Lord Montfort wagers Sir Jon Bland one hundred guineas that Mr. Nash outlives Mr. Cibber,' is another entry in the book around this period, and it is interesting to note that the bet was rendered void because both of the backers committed suicide before it was decided. This is a reminder that not only was death a favourite subject of conversation of the period, but that suicides were also frequent; in fact, suicide was known as 'the English malady'.

There was also a strong streak of cruelty to be noted running through these wagers at White's and elsewhere. Backers would nail some poor old watchman up in his wooden 'sentry box' and roll it down the hill, betting on whether he would emerge alive. Horace Walpole recounted how the members of White's once came to wager heavily on whether or not a complete stranger to them was alive or dead. It seemed that a man was walking down St James's Street one day when he collapsed suddenly in a fit outside the Club and was carried into the hall. The members crowded round excitedly at this unexpected diversion and promptly started to gamble on his condition. Some reckoned that he was either dead or dying, whilst others considered that he might recover. Out came the betting books, and odds were freely laid and taken. When one of the members suggested that a surgeon should be sent for, he was quickly shouted down, for those who had wagered on the man's dying had no desire to see a doctor arrive. In view of the inefficiency of doctors in those days, and their invariable remedy of bleeding for almost every form of illness, it is quite possible that the services of a surgeon would have hastened the man's death rather than prevented it.

This was the world of callous and irresponsible youth through which William Douglas now moved with growing assurance and authority. In his pocket was his betting-book, with each wager carefully outlined, and also in his pocket was a sum of exactly £50. This was the amount which he was prepared to lose during an evening's gaming, and he never exceeded it. When it was gone he went home, and he never chased his losses. Thus does the professional gambler operate, and William was a professional from the day he first arrived at White's. His opponents, who were reckless and inexperienced novices, never really stood a chance against him. William was an expert, too, in the despised field of 'gardening pursuits', by which was meant the ways of 'hedging' a bet so that the possibility of losing one's money was reduced or even eliminated altogether.

The members of the Young Club at White's welcomed William into their midst. They did not resent his shrewdness and certainly did not consider it unethical that he should seek out the stupidest or the wildest gamblers among them in order to try to 'fleece' them. The portrait of William at this time which Thackeray gave in *The Virginians* was condemnatory, but had these contemporaries of William's lived to read it, they would have considered it to be not only accurate but flattering, and would have been delighted if it had been applied to themselves.

> My Lord March has not one devil, but several devils. He loves gambling, he loves horse-racing, he loves betting, he loves drinking, he loves eating, he loves money, he loves women; and you have fallen into bad company, Mr. Warrington, when you lighted upon his lordship. He will play you for every acre you have in Virginia.

William's attitude to money was evident to all. He was trying to make as much as he could, as quickly as he could, cleverly and without sentiment. Yet although he was so business-like in his methods, his code of friendship could still predominate over all else. George Selwyn and he were friends. This meant, to both of them, that each stood by the other in moments of financial adversity. When the luck ran out for one, the other came forward with what help he could until the luck had changed. William would criticise George in private for his recklessness but in public he stood by him and paid George's debts when George could not pay them himself.

* * * *

Not that things went too well for [William] when he first settled down in England. In 1747 he suffered a setback when an Act for the abolition of hereditary jurisdictions of Scottish Peers came into force. William professed high indignation and promptly claimed double what he thought he ought to receive as compensation for the loss of the Sheriffship of Peebles and for the regality of Linton and Newlands. His demand for £5,000 was rejected, and instead he received £3,200 for the sheriffship and £218-4-5 for the regality. He complained bitterly and took the money with alacrity.

In the same year his mother, now the Countess of Ruglen, decided to marry again, having endured the privations of widowhood for some 15 years. Her choice fell upon a former Paymaster to the Forces named Anthony Sawyer, who may or may not have been after her money, for her dowry was substantial. William viewed this second incursion into marriage with strong disapproval and was pained to see money which he had earmarked for himself being spent by someone else. The marriage was not a success and was cut short by the sudden death of the Countess three months [later].

* * * *

His mother's death, however, was yet of considerable benefit to William, both financially and socially, for he now inherited the Earldom of Ruglen, and with it estates in the counties of Edinburgh and Linlithgow. He became known as the Earl of March and Ruglen, and his social status in Mayfair rose accordingly.

Meanwhile his hopes of ultimately acceding to the Dukedom of Queensberry had not increased. Henry Douglas, the Earl of Drumlanrig and the 3rd Duke's heir, had left Oxford and had embarked upon the dangers of a military career abroad. But courage and good fortune saw him safely through two campaigns, and his health remained excellent, as did that of his father. Charles Douglas, the younger son, still suffered from a delicate constitution, but watched over it with care. Thus the odds against William ever becoming a Duke of Queensberry and thereby one of the richest men in Europe seemed longer than ever.

He therefore continued to bet freely, but only when the odds were in his favour. He was well aware that the young bucks at White's admired him for his shrewdness, and William was flattered by the respect which they now began to show him.

This delight which he took in both winning money and proving his cleverness also aroused in him a love of breaking records. It pleased him to be told that such and such a thing could not be done, and then to prove that it could. One of his most celebrated wagers was made within a few years of his arrival in London. On it he founded his reputation.

How fast could a man travel in a wheeled vehicle? This was the question. Coaches and post-chaises lumbered along the badly constructed roads of the period at only a few miles an hour. A gentleman's carriage, drawn by fast horses, could travel at ten or more. William Douglas, examining the problem in detail, announced one day that he could produce a four-wheeled carriage, drawn by four horses, which would carry a man nineteen miles in one hour.

The claim was thought ridiculous. Nothing like this speed had ever been achieved before, and when William showed his willingness to back his claim with hard cash, some heavy bets were at once entered in his betting-book. The main bet was with a certain Theobald Taaffe, known also as Count Taaffe, and Andrew Sprowle; and it was for a thousand guineas—a very large sum for a young Scots peer of seemingly moderate means. However, William Douglas shared the bet with one of his Old Wykehamist cronies, the Earl of Eglinton, who also helped him with his plans. Taaffe, who had once been an M.P. for Arundel, was a wild Irishman and a noted gambler. Walpole described him as 'a gamester, usurer, adventurer'. In fact, he was very near to being a crook. William's associate Lord Eglinton was also something of a ne'er do well. No one concerned in the wager was a fool.

Numerous side bets were struck over the event, and William began to make his plans with his accustomed thoroughness.

In those days the techniques of carriage building were still surprisingly undeveloped. A gentleman's carriage might well be ornately fitted and lavishly decorated, but mechanically it was usually an indifferent piece of work. Little had been discovered about springing, and nothing at all about pneumatic tyres. English coachbuilders produced heavy and cumbersome vehicles which were immensely strong and stood up well to the violent treatment they received on the bad roads of the period; but they were not fast.

William Douglas approached one of the best and least conservative craftsmen, Wright, of Long Acre, and set him to work designing a coach on completely original lines. The terms of the wager were that the vehicle should 'carry a man', but they did not state that he had to be carried in a carriage as such. William decided that a body was therefore unnecessary. All that was required were four wheels joined by the lightest possible framework. Weight, in fact, was the crux of the whole matter, and every ounce that could be dispensed with was sacrificed. What Wright finally produced was really no more than two sets of wheels joined by a central bar, which was of thinnest wood bound with wire. The driver was slung on leather straps between the two rear wheels, on a tiny seat covered with velvet. The harness, usually a fairly weighty item in carriage equipment, was in this case constructed out of whalebone and silk. Silk was also used for the traces. Thus weight was reduced as far as possible whilst strength was still preserved, for the vehicle had to cover nineteen miles on a far from even surface.

After being tested and found satisfactory, the vehicle was weighed. The total weight of carriage and harness was two and a half hundredweight.

The next problem was the selection and training of the horses. Fortunately for William Douglas and his partner the terms of the wager gave them ample time to carry out their tests. But they had to give two months' notice of the date of the match.

The best horses were obtained and rigorously trained. So rigorously, indeed, that seven of them died under the severity of the trials to which they were subjected. This was a matter of no consequence to William, to whom horseflesh was always expendable; but their defection caused him much additional expense. Finally he was able to assemble a team of four he considered strong enough and fast enough. (Three, in fact, were ex-racehorses.) Trained reserves were also available in case of any last-minute accident. Each of the four horses carried a rider on his back, whilst the driver, or 'passenger', carried William's colours of red and black. The riders, or postilions as they really were, wore blue satin waistcoats, buckskin breeches, white silk stockings and black velvet caps, for William Douglas was nothing if not a showman.

The day fixed for the great event was 29 August 1750. The time, seven o'clock in the morning. The place, Newmarket Heath. The course was via the Warren and Rubbing Houses, through the Ditch—the gap in the ancient mound known as The Devil's Dyke, which runs north and south across the Heath—then to the right, three times round a staked piece of ground of four miles, and then back to the starting point.

A large crowd collected to watch the event, and wagering on the outcome continued while the final preparations were being made. A well-known Newmarket character named Tuting was appointed as official course-clearer, and he led the parade, wearing a jacket of crimson velvet. Three umpires had been appointed. Armed with stop watches, they took up different positions to ensure that there was no cheating—a necessary precaution when the gamesters involved were known to be so astute.

William Douglas had no doubt about the outcome. His plans had been carefully made, and he knew that only an unforeseen accident could prevent him from winning his wager. His riders were told to hold a little in reserve, so that the match could be kept alive and betting would continue while the race was being run.

As it happened, the only thing that went wrong was that the horses, trained to the peak of fitness and eager to go, set off at such a pace that they could not be restrained, and covered the first four miles in nine minutes, thus achieving a speed of nearly 26 miles an hour. Thus Taaffe and Sprowle knew that they had lost their wager before a quarter of the course had been covered, and the betting was brought to a standstill. The full distance of nineteen miles was covered in 53 minutes, 27 seconds.

The result did far more than win William Douglas a handsome wager. It established his reputation in Mayfair as an outstanding sportsman and a king amongst gamblers, even though he was not yet 25. When he returned to London from Newmarket, he was welcomed as a hero and accepted as a leader of the fast set. Now everyone knew him, and all sportsmen admired and respected him. He was delighted. He probably made very little out of the event, because his expenses were so heavy, but in this instance he knew that the money had been well spent. His reputation was made. The time would come soon enough when he would make much more money for a much smaller outlay.

Within the year his reputation for astuteness had been increased, but so also had his reputation for sharp practice. It has already been remarked that this was an age of cheating, even amongst gentlemen, and now William Douglas went a little too far.

One of the most important apsects of the racing ceremonial is the weighing out and weighing in of a jockey. Whatever the race, each horse is allocated a certain weight; and if the jockey is lighter than this allotted weight, lead is added to his saddle to bring the total weight carried by the horse to the required amount. Nothing is calculated to cause more consternation on a racecourse than for a jockey to weigh in at less than he weighed out. When this happens, he is at once disqualified, and he loses the race. It has happened that a jockey has contrived to rid himself of some of the lead in his saddle before the race and to return it to the saddle after he has won, so that he has been able to weigh in satisfactorily.

This was just the sort of artifice to delight William Douglas's astute and inventive mind. One day at Newmarket, when he ran a horse against one owned by a certain short-tempered Irishman, he arranged for his jockey to throw out some of the lead in his saddle. An accomplice picked up the lead and returned it to the jockey after he had won. The Irishman, who was no fool, spotted this piece of trickery and accosted the jockey as he left the weighing room. The jockey was so frightened that he admitted the offence, whereat the Irishman turned his wrath upon William Douglas. Here was a matter of honour, and it could only be settled in one way—by a duel to the death. He invited William Douglas to name his weapons and to appoint his seconds.

Nothing was more offensive to William Douglas than the suggestion that arguments might be settled by acts of violence. Unfortunately, the Irishman was in no mood to be bribed. He was a well-known duellist, and he asked for one of two things—satisfaction, or an abject apology.

William Douglas was in a quandary. His reputation as a sportsman demanded that he at least put on a show, and so he appeared on the duelling ground at dawn, accompanied by a second and a surgeon. The Irishman knew his man, and he also had a rather macabre sense of humour. So he arrived at the duelling ground a few minutes late, accompanied by a lackey who staggered under a heavy burden hidden by a cloth. When this cloth was removed, the object was revealed as a large oak coffin, on which was a brass plate bearing the Douglas coat of arms and the date of William's death—this being the day in question.

William apologised abjectly. He would probably have done so in any case, but the sight of the coffin confirmed him in his natural reluctance to become involved in duelling. He was determined to live as long as he could, and in the greatest possible ease and luxury.

His friends at White's were shocked by this behaviour, and for a time he lost face, but William smiled enigmatically and offered no comment. He knew that a fool and his life are soon parted. But he decided to re-establish his reputation by setting a new record and by once again displaying his ingenuity.

He now claimed that he would send a message a distance of 50 miles in one hour. His opponents were becoming wary of his ingenuity, but this claim seemed impossible. No man had ever achieved such a speed, unless it were a tobogganist flying down a steep hill over hard snow, and so the bets were struck and the members of White's sat back to see what new trick William Douglas was going to pull out of the hat.

In this case his ingenuity was not greatly taxed. He merely assembled a team of twenty cricketers, each an adept at catching and throwing, and placed them in a wide circle. The letter was then enclosed in a cricket ball, which the cricketers flung from one to the other. So long as no catches were dropped—and none was—the task was comparatively easy. The ball travelled repeatedly round the circle, and the letter travelled the 50 miles in under the hour allotted.

By this time, William had become 'a Newmarket man'. The fascination which this broad and ancient expanse of heath has had for Englishmen for centuries now held him in its grip, and for the rest of his life—or at least until within a few years of his death—his love of Newmarket was almost as great as his love of Piccadilly. He was an expert judge of horseflesh, a student of form, and a fine horseman.

It was his misfortune that racing was not to achieve its modern status—following the founding of the so-called 'Classic' races and the famous handicaps—until after his death. During most of the 18th century a race at Newmarket usually meant no more than a 'match' in which only two horses raced, often ridden by their owners, with the betting carried on between gentlemen, without recourse to professional bookmakers. The professional layer and the professional jockey were only just beginning to appear on the scene.

At Newmarket one afternoon, after racing was over for the day, two young backers, a Mr Pigot and a Mr Codrington, having nothing else to do, decided to 'run their fathers' in a match, betting on which of the two old gentlemen would die first. It could not be a case of even-money betting, however, for Pigot senior was over 70, while Codrington senior was only 50. What represented fair odds?

Lord Ossory was called in to adjudicate and said that the wager should be at 500 guineas to 1,600—slightly more than 3:1 against the elder man. Codrington junior considered these odds unfair, having no great confidence in his father's way of life, despite his relative youth, and withdrew from the match, whereat William Douglas stepped in and accepted the wager, backing himself to win 500 guineas if Pigot senior died first, and to lose 1,600 guineas if the younger Codrington senior pre-deceased him.

No sooner had the bet been accepted and duly entered in the betting-books of both young Pigot and William Douglas, than a messenger arrived post-haste at Newmarket to tell young Pigot that his father had collapsed and died that morning at his family seat at Shrewsbury as the result of a sudden attack of gout in the head. William hastened to commiserate with his rival and then claimed the bet.

Pigot junior refused to pay. He argued that his father had never come under starter's orders, so to speak, and that the bet was void.

It was, as the lawyers say, a 'nice' point. But William would have none of it. He claimed the wager and, when young Pigot refused to pay, took him to court. The action was heard in the King's Bench before Lord Mansfield, and a number of learned witnesses were called to give evidence of the turf and gambling rules governing such an eventuality. Lord Mansfield listened attentively and then ruled in favour of William Douglas on the grounds that at the time the bet was struck both backers had every reason to assume that their 'runners' were alive.

Young Pigot was aggrieved, but he had only himself to blame. Anyway, he should never have allowed the matter to come to court (he had to pay court costs, as well as the bet itself). In the past, others who had felt themselves out-generalled by William's astuteness had more wisely decided to take matters into their own hands, well knowing that William was always ready to listen to reason if physical violence was threatened. There had been an incident at Renny's gambling hell in St James's Street, when a hot-blooded Irishman named 'Savage' Roche had accused William of cheating and had picked him up by the ears and called him 'a contemptuous little cock-sparrow'. William had taken this assault quietly. He had to die sometime, but he was determined to die in his bed.

The Prince of Wales at Tranby Croft

One of the classic errors of judgment at a gaming table must have been that of an English Army officer who, according to eyewitnesses and later a jury, found him guilty not only of engaging in hanky-panky at baccarat but doing so in the presence of the heir to the British throne.

BY VIRGINIA COWLES

THE EIGHTEEN-NINETIES opened with a scandal. The British public was not shocked by the Prince of Wales' extravagant life, nor by his mistresses, nor by his bets on the race-track. These were British failings. But the rumpus that broke out in the early weeks of 1891 over a game of baccarat caused a sensation. Baccarat had a distinctly foreign flavour; it must be a vice.

The Prince had gone to Doncaster to stay at Tranby Croft, the home of a wealthy shipowner by the name of Arthur Wilson, for the St. Leger races. Mr. Wilson had a large party, and after dinner the guests amused themselves by playing baccarat. A table was improvised by putting three whist tables together. The Prince took the bank. He also produced the counters with which the guests played.

The game was not played for very high stakes. But on the first night the twenty-two-year-old son of the house, A. S. Wilson, who was one of the players, thought he saw Sir William Gordon-Cumming cheating. He seemed to be withdrawing or augmenting the stake he had placed on the table, under cover of his hand, according to the cards he drew. 'When Lord Edward Somerset, who sat immediately to the left of Sir William, was taking up the cards,' young Mr. Wilson later declared, 'I saw that Sir William had one £5 counter at the top of the notepaper (which lay in front of him) and he was sitting with his hands clasped over the counter ... Sir William leant over to see what cards Lord Edward Somerset had got. I was also looking, and whilst doing so I saw something red in the palm of Sir William's hands, which I knew could be nothing else but a £5 counter. Lord Edward had a natural—a nine—and a court card. Immediately Sir William saw this he opened his hands and let drop on to the notepaper three more £5 counters and he was paid £20 for the coup.

'After this I saw him again sitting in the same position as before. I cannot recall who was taking up the cards at this time. The cards were bad, and I think our side were nothing. Sir William was sitting with his hands advanced over the table as before, and when he saw the cards were bad he withdrew his hands and let some counters which were in his palm fall back on his own pile. I could not say how many.

'I was sitting next to Berkeley Levett, whom I knew to be a brother officer of Sir William. Immediately I saw the last incident I turned to Levett and said, "By God! Levett, this is too hot." He said, "What on earth do you mean?" "Why, the man next to me is cheating." He replied, "My dear fellow, you must have made some mistake; it is absolutely impossible!" "Well, just look for yourself." He did so and a few minutes afterwards turned to me and said, "It is too hot!"'

After the game was over, Wilson went to Levett's room to discuss the matter. Levett was much shaken. He was a young man of twenty-seven, and a subaltern in Sir William's regiment. He had always been on friendly terms with the older man, whom he looked up to and admired. He threw himself across the bed and said, 'My God, to think of it. Lieutenant-Colonel Sir William Gordon-Cumming, Baronet, to be caught cheating at cards! He was my captain for a year and a half. For God's sake, don't ask me what is to be done.'

It was a tragedy that such a delicate situation should have been left in the hands of an inexperienced boy of twenty-two, such as Mr. Wilson. There was only one action that might have prevented the incident becoming public—that was, to confront Sir William immediately and tell him he must leave the house in the morning; then to keep quiet.

But Mr. Wilson hurried off to tell his mother all about it. She was not very helpful. Her only comment was 'For God's sake, don't let us have any scandal here.' Then he told his brother-in-law Mr. Lycett Green, and Mr. Green told his wife. So five people knew. The first mistake they made was to decide to play baccarat again the following evening. Mr. Wilson felt he could solve the problem by giving instructions to the butler to produce a real baccarat table, around which the usual chalk line could be drawn. The stakes would have to be placed across the line. Under these circumstances he felt it would be impossible for Sir William to cheat.

Mr. Wilson was unsophisticated. Cheating at baccarat is such a well-known failing the French even have a word for it; 'la poussette' it is called. When the guests sat down to play, the Prince once again took the bank. Mr. Berkeley Levett, who was sickened by the whole business, refused to look in Sir William's direction. But Mrs. Wilson, Mr. Wilson and Mr. and Mrs. Green kept a careful eye on the colonel and when the game was over all of them told each other they had witnessed further instances of cheating. 'I saw him push a blue counter over the line (value £3) when the cards had been declared favourable to his side,' Mr. Lycett Green declared. 'The next thing I observed was that he was looking at Lady Coventry's hand, and then after the Prince had declared the card, he gradually pushed a £10 counter over the line. The Prince paid, I think £5, and Sir William said, "There is £10 more" and the Prince said to General Williams, "Pay him £10 more." When I saw this I was horrified, and my first impulse was to jump up and say, "Sir William Gordon-Cumming, you are cheating!" But I did not like to make a scene before ladies, and I retired and sent a note to my mother-in-law, Mrs. Wilson. The note has been destroyed but it contained these words, "I have distinctly seen Sir William Gordon-Cumming cheating twice."

At this point the five people who had seen the cheating told Lord Edward Somerset, Lord Coventry and General Owen Williams. The latter was a close friend of Sir William, and it was decided that he and Lord Coventry should confront the baronet with the evidence against him. Lord Coventry opened the conversation by saying, 'A very un-pleasant thing has occurred; some of the people have objected to your manner of playing baccarat.' 'Good heavens, what do you mean?' re-plied Sir William. 'Yes,' said Coventry, 'it is the case; certain persons in the house have suggested that you caused a foul play at baccarat.'

Sir William heatedly denied the charge, but he did not ask the names of his accusers, or insist on being faced with them. Instead, he said, 'What do you advise me to do?' and begged to see the Prince.

At 10.30 that night the Prince consented to see him. The conversa-tion was brief. 'I have asked for an interview with Your Royal Highness,' said Sir William, 'as I have heard that certain persons have brought a foul and abominable charge against me, and I have to emphatically deny that I have done anything of the kind insinuated. Your Royal Highness can see what a terrible thing this must be for a man who has attempted to live for 25 years the life of an officer and a gentleman.'

'What can you do? There are five accusers against you?'

'My first impulse,' said Sir William, 'is to publicly insult these five people on the first occasion I meet them—if necessary on the race-course tomorrow.'

'What is the use of that as they are five to one?'

'Something must be done,' said Sir William, and left the room.

Something was done. The Prince of Wales and General Williams questioned the five people who accused Sir William, and satisfied themselves that they could not have been mistaken. Then General Williams drew up a pledge for Sir William to sign, promising that he would never play cards for money again as long as he lived.

When Lord Coventry and the General confronted Sir William with this pledge later on in the same evening he again professed his in-nocence. 'Why, this would be tantamount to an admission of guilt,' he exclaimed. General Williams admitted that this was so but earnestly recommended him to sign, saying it was the only way of avoiding a scandal. If Sir William did not sign, the whole story would be told over the race course the next day. If he did sign, everyone who knew about the matter would give his word of honour to maintain absolute secrecy. So Sir William put his name to the pledge and ten people added their names as witnesses, including the Prince of Wales. The paper was then sent to the Prince's secretary, to be filed away among his private papers.

Over a dozen people knew about the dramatic events at Tranby Croft. Although they had all pledged themselves to secrecy, could anyone really believe that no word of the affair would leak out? In a few weeks' time the whole of fashionable London was buzzing with gossip. Sir William, who was in Paris, received an anonymous letter which showed him that the matter was becoming public knowledge. People were beginning to cut him, and he knew it would not be long before the War Office got wind of it. There was only one way in which his ruined reputation could be restored. That was to win a slander suit against his five accusers. It was a desperate gamble, but he decided to take it.

The case opened on June 1, 1891, and lasted seven days. The Prince of Wales was subpœnaed to appear as a witness for Sir William and was present in court every day. Sir William continued to deny his guilt, but under cross-examination could not give any convincing reasons as to why he had not at once demanded to be faced with his accusers, and why, if he were innocent, he had consented to sign the document presented to him. His only excuse was that he wished to protect the Prince of Wales from harmful gossip.

The accusers were all called, and testified to the specific acts of cheating they had seen. Then the Prince was called by Sir William's counsel to testify to a long and close friendship with Gordon-Cumming. Just as he was about to step down from the box a juryman intervened and asked His Royal Highness point blank:

'I understand you saw no foul play?'

'It is difficult for the banker to see the play, and moreover at the house of a friend you are not likely to expect foul play.'

'What was your opinion at the time as to the charges made?' persisted the juryman.

'They seemed so strongly supported—unanimously so—by those who brought them forward that I felt that no other course was open to me but to believe what I was told.'

From that moment on, the case was decided in the minds of the jury. If the Prince, an old friend of Sir William, who knew the background and all the people involved, believed the man guilty, guilty he must be. Certainly the evidence against him was overwhelming. When the jury went out they took only ten minutes to reach their verdict. Sir William lost his case and was ordered to pay the costs.

Needless to say a colossal scandal arose. On the very day the case finished nonconformists all over the country were holding meetings. The Welsh Baptists declared that the Prince was fostering 'immoral habits', and the Wesleyans 'bitterly regretted that the Heir to the Throne should be given to one of the worst forms of gambling ... and that he took about with him counters for the game'.

This was not all; bad enough was the baccarat and the counters and the Prince taking the bank and dealing the cards. But what about the

fact that one of the Prince's most intimate friends was a cheat; and that
his hostess, a woman no one had ever heard of before, had spied on one
of her guests; and that someone who had given his word of honour
to remain silent had blabbed? From start to finish the whole business
was squalid.

Almost every paper in the country lashed out against the Prince.
In the *Review of Reviews* the editor calculated that 880,000,000 prayers
had been said for His Royal Highness since his birth and pointed out
that the only answer from the Almighty seemed to be a baccarat
scandal. *The Times* was more pompous. It was grieved to learn that the
Prince's set was 'a gambling baccarat-playing set'. It was shocked that
His Royal Highness carried counters about with him. It also made it
plain that it did not like his friends or his pastimes, 'If the Prince
of Wales is known to frequent certain circles; and to eschew others
with a greater natural claim upon the notice of Royalty; if he is known
to pursue on his private visits a certain round of questionable pleasures;
the serious public—who after all are the backbone of England—regret
and resent it. Sir William Gordon-Cumming was made to sign a
declaration that "he would never touch a card again". We almost wish,
for the sake of English Society in general, that we could learn that the
result of this most unhappy case had been that the Prince of Wales had
signed a similar declaration.'

Even abroad, the papers blazed forth with acid comment. The
spruce oak which the Prince had planted in Central Park, New York,
was adorned anonymously with a sign saying BACCARAT. The German
press carried a cartoon showing the great door of Windsor Castle
decorated with the Prince of Wales' feathers, and underneath his motto
changed from 'I Serve' to 'I Deal'. Almost the last straw was a letter
from the Kaiser, informing his uncle of his displeasure that anyone
holding the position of Colonel in the Prussian Hussars should embroil
himself in a gambling squabble and play with men young enough to
be his sons.

Way Back Then

When did it all begin? No one knows for sure. Long before 3000 B.C., one authority (Alan Wykes) estimates, or "as soon as people could record their ideas in speech, pictures or hieroglyphics." Were dice the first instruments developed for a game of pure chance? It seems likely, however improbable the form they originally took: the ankle bones of sheep. Every civilization has know a version of backgammon, lotteries, etc. And so to a backward look at some forerunners of entertainments cherished today by students in search of the quick dollar, or franc, or peseta.

◇◇

Egyptians, Greeks, and Romans

Like many another before and after him, the nineteenth-century English scholar Andrew Steinmetz regarded the gaming table with disfavor—but sat down at it, so to speak, with no little zest as a historian and writer.

BY ANDREW STEINMETZ

CONCERNING THE ancient Egyptians we have no particular facts to detail in the matter of gambling; but it is sufficient to determine the existence of any special vice in a nation to find that there are severe laws prohibiting and punishing its practice. Now, this testimony not only exists, but the penalty is of the utmost severity, from which may be inferred both the horror conceived of the practice by the rulers of the Egyptians, and the strong propensity which required that severity to suppress or hold it in check. In Egypt, 'every man was easily admitted to the accusation of a gamester or dice-player; and if the person was convicted, he was sent to work in the quarries.' Gambling was, therefore, prevalent in Egypt in the earliest times.

That gaming with dice was a usual and fashionable species of diversion at the Persian court in the times of the younger Cyrus (about 400 years before the Christian era), to go no higher, is evident from the anecdote related by some historians of those days concerning Queen Parysatis, the mother of Cyrus, who used all her art and skill in gambling to satiate her revenge, and to accomplish her bloodthirsty projects against the murderers of her favourite son. She played for the life or death of an unfortunate slave, who had only executed the commands of his master. The anecdote is as follows, as related by Plutarch, in the Life of Artaxerxes.

'There only remained for the final execution of Queen Parysatis's projects, and fully to satiate her vengeance, the punishment of the king's slave Mesabetes, who by his master's order had cut off the head and hand of the young Cyrus, who was beloved by Parysatis (their common mother) above Artaxerxes, his elder brother and the reigning monarch. But as there was nothing to take hold of in his conduct, the queen laid this snare for him. She was a woman of good address, had abundance of wit, and *excelled at playing a certain game with dice.* She had been apparently reconciled to the king after the death of Cyrus, and was present at all his parties of pleasure and gambling. One day, seeing the king totally unemployed, she proposed playing with him for a thousand *darics* (about £500), to which he readily consented. She suffered him to win, and paid down the money. But, affecting regret and vexation, she pressed him to begin again, and to play with her—*for a slave.* The king, who suspected nothing, complied, and the stipulation was that the winner was to choose the slave.

'The queen was now all attention to the game, and made use of her utmost skill and address, which as easily procured her victory, as her studied neglect before had caused her defeat. She won—and chose Mesabetes—the slayer of her son—who, being delivered into her hands, was put to the most cruel tortures and to death by her command.

'When the king would have interfered, she only replied with a smile of contempt—"Surely you must be a great loser, to be so much out of temper for giving us a decrepit old slave, when I, who lost a thousand good *darics*, and paid them down on the spot, do not say a word, and am satisfied." '

Thus early were dice made subservient to the purposes of cruelty and murder. The modern Persians, being Mohammedans, are restrained from the open practice of gambling. Yet evasions are contrived in favour of games in the tables, which, as they are only liable to chance on the 'throw of the dice,' but totally dependent on the 'skill' in 'the management of the game,' cannot (they argue) be meant to be prohibited by their prophet any more than chess, which is universally allowed to his followers; and, moreover, to evade the difficulty of being forbidden to play for money, they make an alms of their winnings, distributing them to the poor. This may be done by the more scrupulous; but no doubt there are numbers whose consciences do not prevent the disposal of their gambling profits nearer home. All excess of gaming, however, is absolutely prohibited in Persia; and any place wherein it is much exercised is called 'a habitation of corrupted carcases or carrion house.'

In ancient Greece gambling prevailed to a vast extent. Of this there can be no doubt whatever; and it is equally certain that it had an influence, together with other modes of dissipation and corruption, towards subjugating its civil liberties to the power of Macedon.

So shamelessly were the Athenians addicted to this vice, that they forgot all public spirit in their continued habits of gaming, and entered into convivial associations, or formed 'clubs,' for the purposes of dicing, at the very time when Philip of Macedon was making one grand 'throw' for their liberties at the Battle of Chæronea.

This politic monarch well knew the power of depravity in enervating and enslaving the human mind; he therefore encouraged profusion, dissipation, and gambling, as being sure of meeting with little opposition from those who possessed such characters, in his projects of ambition—as Demosthenes declared in one of his orations. Indeed, gambling had arrived at such a height in Greece, that Aristotle scruples not to rank gamblers 'with thieves and plunderers, who for the sake of gain do not scruple to despoil their best friends;' and his pupil Alexander set a fine upon some of his courtiers because he did not perceive they made a sport or pastime of dice, but seemed to be employed as in a most serious business.

The Greeks gambled not only with dice, and at their equivalent for *Cross and Pile*, but also at cock-fighting.

From a remark made by the Athenian orator Callistratus, it is evident that desperate gambling was in vogue; he says that the games in which the losers go on doubling their stakes resemble ever-recurring wars, which terminate only with the extinction of the combatants.

* * * *

In spite of the laws enacted against gaming, the court of the Emperor Augustus was greatly addicted to that vice, and gave it additional stimulus among the nation. Although, however, he was passionately fond of gambling, and made light of the imputation on his character, it appears that in frequenting the gambling table he had other motives besides mere cupidity. Writing to his daughter he said, 'I send you a sum with which I should have gratified my companions, if they had wished to play at dice or *odds and evens*.' On another occasion he wrote to Tiberius:—'If I had exacted my winnings during the festival of Minerva; if I had not lavished my money on all sides; instead of losing twenty thousand sestercii (about £1000), I should have gained one hundred and fifty thousand (£7500). I prefer it thus, however; for my bounty should win me immense glory.'

This gambling propensity subjected Augustus to the lash of popular epigrams; among the rest, the following:

> Postquam bis classe naves perdidit,
> Aliquando ut vincat, ludit assidue aleam.

> 'He lost a sea; was beaten twice,
> And tries to win at least with dice.'

But although a satirist by profession, the sleek courtier Horace spared the emperor's vice, contenting himself with only declaring that play was forbidden. The two following verses of his, usually applied to the effects of gaming, really refer only to raillery (or wrestling).

Ludus enim genuit trepidum certamen et iram;
Ira truces inimicitias et funebre bellum.

[For sport like this brings forth a hurried and passionate protest; Whence spring fierce enmities and deadly war.]

He, however, has recorded the curious fact of an old Roman gambler, who was always attended by a slave, to pick up his dice for him and put them in the box. Doubtless, Horace would have lashed the vice of gambling had it not been the 'habitual sin' of his courtly patrons.

It seems that Augustus not only gambled to excess, but that he gloried in the character of a gamester. Of himself he says, 'Between meals we played like old crones both yesterday and today.'

When he had no regular players near him, he would play with children at dice, at nuts, or bones. It has been suggested that this emperor gave in to the indulgence of gambling in order to stifle his remorse. If his object in encouraging this vice was to make people forget his proscriptions and to create a diversion in his favour, the artifice may be considered equal to any of the political ruses of this astute ruler, whose false virtues were for a long time vaunted only through ignorance, or in order to flatter his imitators.

The passion of gambling was transmitted, with the empire, to the family of the Cæsars. At the gaming table Caligula stooped even to falsehood and perjury. It was whilst gambling that he conceived his most diabolical projects; when the game was against him he would quit the table abruptly, and then, monster as he was, satiated with rapine, would roam about his palace venting his displeasure.

One day, in such a humour, he caught a glimpse of two Roman knights; he had them arrested and confiscated their property. Then returning to the gaming table, he exultingly exclaimed that he had never made a better throw! On another occasion, after having condemned to death several Gauls of great opulence, he immediately went back to his gambling companions and said:—'I pity you when I see you lose a few sestertii, whilst, with a stroke of the pen, I have just won six hundred millions.'

The Emperor Claudius played like an imbecile, and Nero like a madman. The former would send for the persons whom he had executed the day before, to play with him; and the latter, lavishing the treasures of the public exchequer, would stake four hundred thousand sestertii (£20,000) on a single throw of the dice.

Claudius played at dice on his journeys, having the interior of his carriage so arranged as to prevent the motion from interfering with the game.

From that period the title of courtier and gambler became synonymous. Gaming was the means of securing preferment; it was by gambling that [the Emperor] Vitellius opened to himself so grand a career; gaming made him indispensable to Claudius.

Seneca, in his Play on the death of Claudius, represents him as in the lower regions condemned to pick up dice for ever, putting them into a box without a bottom!

Caligula was reproached for having played at dice on the day of his sister's funeral; and Domitian was blamed for gaming from morning to night, and without excepting the festivals of the Roman calendar; but it seems ridiculous to note such improprieties in comparison with their habitual and atrocious crimes.

The terrible and inexorable satirist Juvenal was the contemporary of Domitian and ten other emperors; and the following is his description of the vice in the gaming days of Rome:

'When was the madness of games of chance more furious? Now-a-days, not content with carrying his purse to the gaming table, the gamester conveys his iron chest to the play-room. It is there that, as soon as the gaming instruments are distributed, you witness the most terrible contests. Is it not mere madness to lose one hundred thousand sestertii and refuse a garment to a slave perishing with cold?'

It seems that the Romans played for ready money, and had not invented that multitude of signs by the aid of which, without being retarded by the weight of gold and silver, modern gamblers can ruin themselves secretly and without display.

The rage for gambling spread over the Roman provinces, and among barbarous nations who had never been so much addicted to the vice as after they had the misfortune to mingle with the Romans.

The evil continued to increase, stimulated by imperial example. The day on which Didius Julianus was proclaimed Emperor, he walked over the dead and bloody body of Pertinax, and began to play at dice in the next room.

At the end of the fourth century, the following state of things at Rome is described by Gibbon, quoting from Ammianus Marcellinus:

'Another method of introduction into the houses and society of the "great," is derived from the profession of gaming; or, as it is more politely styled, of play. The confederates are united by a strict and indissoluble bond of friendship, or rather of conspiracy; a superior degree of skill in the "tessarian" art, is a sure road to wealth and reputation. A master of that sublime science who, in a supper or assembly, is placed below a magistrate, displays in his countenance the surprise and indignation which Cato might be supposed to feel when he was refused the prætorship by the votes of a capricious people.'

Finally, at the epoch when Constantine abandoned Rome never to return, every inhabitant of that city, down to the populace, was addicted to gambling.

◇◇

No Way to Win

To go on about the Emperor Claudius as a gamester, Dr. Gilbert Highet, Anthon Professor Emeritus of the Latin Language and Literature, Columbia University, calls to the editor's attention that "after his death Claudius was officially declared by the Senate to have become a god. This was a diplomatic move by the advisers of the young Emperor Nero to cover up the fact he had been murdered. For the amusement of Nero's intimates, one of the advisers wrote a satire on Claudius's deification. It shows Claudius going up to heaven and being turned away with contempt. Instead, he is sent down to hell, and there—" Seneca, in his *Apocolocyntosis*, takes over, as translated by Dr. Highet.

BY SENECA

◇◇

THE TRIBUNAL which sentences sinners decided that a new punishment ought to be invented for Claudius: hard labor without result, desire without satisfaction. So Aeacus the judge decreed that he must play dice with a box lacking a bottom. Claudius kept trying to capture the dice and throw, but without effect.

> For every time he rattled the bones and rolled them,
> both dice escaped through the hole in the base of the cup;
> and when he picked them up and tried to shoot again,
> always attempting to grab them and then to throw them,
> they cheated him: they dodged, and through his fingers
> the tricky cubes dribbled elusively away.
> Just so, as it touches the highest peak of the mountain,
> the stone of Sisyphus rolls back to the bottom in vain.

The Barbarians

They played for keeps in those days, as attested by that scrupulous
reporter-historian, Cornelius Tacitus, in his classic *Germania*.

BY TACITUS

SURPRISINGLY, THEY play dice when sober, in the midst of serious
occupations, so reckless in winning and losing that after everything
else is gone they wager their freedom and their body on the very last
throw. The loser willingly accepts slavery: although younger, although
stronger, he allows himself to be chained and sold. In this they show
their wrongheaded strength of will: they themselves call it honor. Slaves
acquired in this manner they get rid of in trade, to relieve themselves
of the shame of victory.

A Game of Piquet

It was in Corfu that Giovanni Giacomo Casanova, then about twenty, developed a passion for gambling that served him well and ill throughout his life. Here we find him in 1764 at Sulzbach, which provided him with one of the happier capers with the cards, and us with a memorable account of a head-to-head bout with an arrogant army officer whom Casanova must have taken special pleasure in defeating—perhaps because the officer's lady held a certain attraction for that susceptible tourist. The game was piquet (two players, thirty-two cards); the duration of the contest, forty-two hours.

BY GIOVANNI GIACOMO CASANOVA

MADAME SAXE possessed every quality to command the homage of a man given to love; and if she had not had a jealous officer who never let her out of his sight and who looked threateningly at anyone who dared to show his admiration by aspiring to please her, she would probably not have been without ardent admirers. The officer was fond of piquet, but he insisted that Madame should always sit at his side, and she seemed happy to be there.

In the afternoon I played with him, and we went on in this way for five or six days. I got tired of it then, for as soon as he had won ten or twelve louis from me he would get up and leave. The officer's name was D'Entragues, he was handsome, though thin, and lacked neither intelligence nor the tone of good society.

Two days had passed since we had played together, when he came to me after dinner and asked if I would like him to give me my revenge.

"I am not interested," I said, "for you and I do not play in the same way. I play for my pleasure, because play amuses me, whereas you play to win."

"What do you mean? You insult me."

"That is not my intention; but each time we have played together you have left me in the lurch after an hour."

"You ought to be grateful to me, for, not being my equal at play, you would perforce have lost a great deal."

"That may be so, but I do not believe it."

"I can prove it to you."

"I accept; but the first to stop playing shall lose fifty louis."

"I accept, but money on the table."

"I never play otherwise."

I order the waiter to bring cards and I go to my room for four or five rolls of fifty louis. We begin playing at five louis a hundred, each of us first setting fifty louis aside for the wager.

It was three o'clock when we sat down to play, and at nine D'Entragues said we might go to supper.

"I am not hungry," I replied, "but you are free to get up if you want me to put the hundred louis in my pocket."

He laughed and went on playing, but the beautiful lady scowled at me, which I gave no sign of noticing. All the people who were looking on went to supper, then came back to keep us company until midnight; but at that hour we were left alone. D'Entragues, who now saw what he had let himself in for, said not a word, and I opened my mouth only to reckon my points; we played on steadily and quietly.

At six o'clock in the morning the water-drinkers began to pass by, and they all congratulated us on our tenacity, clapping their hands, at which we only scowled. Louis were heaped up on the table; I lost a hundred, yet the game was going my way.

At nine o'clock the beautiful Saxe arrived, and a few moments later Madame d'Urfé with Baron Schaumbourg. The two ladies joined in advising us to take a cup of chocolate. D'Entragues consented first, and, thinking that I was on my last legs, he made bold to say:

"Let us agree that the first who asks for food or who leaves the table for more than a quarter of an hour or who falls asleep on his chair will lose the wager."

"I take you at your word," I cried, "and I accept any other more stringent condition you may be pleased to propose."

The chocolate arrives, we take it, and then go on playing. At noon we are summoned to dinner, but we reply together that we are not hungry. About four o'clock we were persuaded to take some broth. When suppertime came everyone began to think the thing was being carried too far, and Madame Saxe proposed that we divide the stake. D'Entragues, who had won a hundred louis from me, would have been glad to accept her proposal, but I refused it, and Baron Schaumbourg declared that I was within my rights. My opponent could have let the wages go and stopped playing; he would still have been ahead; but avarice kept him from doing so even more than pride. For my part, the amount by which I was behind meant something to me, but very little in comparison with the point of honor. I looked fresh, while he looked like a disinterred corpse, his thinness lending itself to the macabre effect. As Madame Saxe continued to insist, I said that I profoundly regretted my inability to yield to the solicitations of a charming woman who in every respect deserved far greater sacrifices, but that in the present case there was a certain element of nice honor, and so I was resolved either to win or not to yield the victory to my antagonist until I dropped dead.

By speaking in these terms I hoped to accomplish two things: to frighten D'Entragues by my firmness and to anger him by making him jealous; certain that a jealous man sees double, I hoped that his skill would suffer accordingly and that in winning the fifty louis of the wager, I should not have the heartbreak of losing a hundred to his superior skill at play.

The beautiful Madame Saxe gave me a scornful look and left, but Madame d'Urfé, who believed that I was infallible, avenged me by saying to Monsieur d'Entragues, in a tone of the deepest conviction:

"My God, Monsieur, how I pity you!"

The people who had been with us before supper did not come back; we were left to continue our combat alone. We played all night, and I paid as much attention to my opponent's face as I did to my cards. The more I saw that it was becoming troubled, the more blunders he made; he mixed up his cards, he scored incorrectly, and often made wrong discards. I was scarcely less exhausted than he; I felt my strength failing, and I hoped every minute to see him drop dead, for fear that I should be beaten despite my strong constitution. I had won back my money at daybreak, when, D'Entragues having gone out, I took him to task for having stayed away longer than a quarter of an hour. This trumped-up quarrel left him the worse and roused me—at once the natural result of our different temperaments, a gamester's stratagem, and a subject of study for the moralist and the psychologist; and my trick succeeded because it was not planned beforehand and could not be foreseen. The same thing holds true for army commanders: a military stratagem must come to a captain's mind from the existing circumstances, from the concatenation of events and from a habit of instantly grasping the connections and the distinctions between men and between things.

At nine o'clock Madame Saxe arrived; her lover was losing.

"Now, Monsieur," she said to me, "it is for you to yield."

"Madame, in the hope of being agreeable to you, I am ready to withdraw my stake and end the matter."

These words, uttered in a tone of marked gallantry, aroused the

anger of D'Entragues, who added sharply that it was now his turn
to say he would not stop until one of us dropped dead.

"You see, most amiable lady," I said, with a look which, in my
state, must have been more bleary than lovelorn, "that I am not the
more obstinate of the two."

We were served a dish of broth, but D'Entragues, who was in
the last stage of exhaustion, had no sooner swallowed it than
he became so ill that he reeled in his chair, broke into a sweat,
and fainted. He was quickly carried off, and I, after giving six louis
to the marker, who had stayed up for forty-two hours, and putting my
money in my pocket, instead of going to bed made my way to an
apothecary's shop, where I took a mild emetic. Having then gone to
bed, I slept lightly for some hours, and about three o'clock I dined
with the best of appetites.

D'Entragues did not reappear until the next day. I expected a
quarrel of some sort, but night brings counsel, and I was mistaken. As
soon as he saw me he came and embraced me, saying:

"I accepted an insane wager, but you have given me a lesson I shall
remember all the rest of my life, and I am grateful to you for it."

"I am very glad of it, if only the effort has not injured your health."

"No, I feel perfectly well, but we shall not play together again."

"I hope at least that we shall not play against each other."

Horses

As elsewhere noted in these annals, no less an authority than Nick the Greek firmly asserted that only madmen and drunks bet seriously on horses. In that case, we have a staggering population of lunatics. Horse racing is without question the outstanding gambling pastime in America, with over $10 billion bet in any given year. Just as surely, it is the greatest spectator attraction in the nation; 81.9 million people were at the track in 1976 to watch thoroughbred and harness racing, and presumably they were not there to enjoy the fresh air. It provides even the nonbetting stay-at-home with certain rewards, for few sports have produced as much colorful writing, fictional and factual.

The Great Racetrack Caper

If you weren't at the track to see for yourself it wasn't always easy,
back in the Gay Nineties, to find out in a hurry how the nag you had
bet on in your neighborhood poolroom made out in the seventh. Thus,
at one track, Pinkertons versus bookmakers, observers in shaky watch-
towers looking on with binoculars to get the results, pigeons waiting to
carry the winning names to the betting marts, and mayhem in the
offing. All in all, a far cry from old Gravesend to the modern, shiny
Belmonts, Aqueducts, and Hialeahs.

BY RUFUS JARMAN

IN THE entire history of the turf there has probably never been anything
remotely resembling the 1891 spring and fall horse-racing seasons at the
old Gravesend track at Sheepshead Bay in Brooklyn, New York. The
extraordinary events that attended the meetings resulted from an
economic squeeze play on the part of the Brooklyn Jockey Club, which
operated Gravesend. Then, as now, off-track betting was illegal in
New York state, but then, as now, it was a popular form of gambling.
To keep local betting parlors aware of all the pertinent racing data—
post odds, scratches, jockey selections, weights, and results—the Poolsellers Association, a syndicate of Manhattan bookmakers, telegraphed
the information direct from the various tracks to the "poolrooms";
for this privilege, the association paid the management of each track
$1,000 a day. When in the spring of 1891 the Brooklyn Jockey Club
suddenly decided to quadruple the rate, the bookies refused to pay.
Somehow they would bootleg the information out of the track; the
Jockey Club could go hang.

The conflict stemmed indirectly from the Ives Law, passed in 1877,
which restricted legal betting in New York state to racetracks. Naturally,
the law made betting with bookies more popular. In 1877 Manhattan
had only four or five poolrooms, which operated behind barricaded
doors equipped with peepholes. By 1891, however, about sixty betting
joints were running wide open. So popular had the poolrooms become,
in fact, that the crowds at the tracks declined sharply; by 1891, the
daily fee the tracks collected from the Poolsellers Association did not
make up for the loss in attendance.

The Brooklyn Jockey Club was controlled by Philip J. Dwyer and his brother, Michael, former butchers who had become interested in swift horses when they operated "the fastest meat delivery wagons in New York." Now they owned a celebrated stable of race horses. Phil Dwyer, the club's president, had a droopy mustache and a greater interest in money than in sport. Operating a racetrack in the red made no sense to him, and so, shortly before Gravesend opened its 1891 spring season, he met with poolroom representatives and upped the daily fee to $4,000. The syndicate would not go higher than $1,600.

"The Poolroom King," Peter De Lacy, a top gambler who dressed like a banker, said he considered all betting evil, but if people were going to gamble, it was no worse to do it in poolrooms than at racetracks.

"If Phil Dwyer bars Western Union's operators from the track, as he threatens to do," De Lacy told the press, "we'll send in messengers to bring out news of each race. But I don't take any stock in Dwyer's bluff. We defy the Dwyers."

Dwyer was not bluffing. As the spring meeting began, he disconnected all telegraph wires out of Gravesend except one that served the newspapers.

Western Union then rented the old Sleight's Hotel just outside Gravesend's entrance and strung in lines. Once a well-known inn, Sleight's was now a rickety, three-story shell with an old-fashioned cupola overlooking Gravesend's starting post and home stretch. With what they could see from this vantage point, supplemented by the reports of De Lacy's messengers shuttling in and out of the gates, Western Union telegraphers managed to meet their clients' needs with few delays.

The Jockey Club president countered by transforming the track into a fortress garrisoned by 130 private policemen under the personal command of Robert A. Pinkerton, who with his brother, "Big Bill," headed Pinkerton's National Detective Agency. Until now, newspaper accounts had featured fleecy prose hailing Gravesend's racing as "spirited," "delightful," "splendid," "positively brilliant." Then, on the season's fifth day, the news from the track shifted dramatically from the sports pages to page one. "TRACK A PRISON," screamed the New York World. "THOUSANDS PENNED UP ON BROOKLYN RACE COURSE. PINKERTON SLUGGERS CLUB INOFFENSIVE CITIZENS."

The Pinkertons locked the gates, according to the World, after some eight thousand people had passed in "as guileless as the wide-mouthed shad which the Spring tides sweep into the fishermen's nets." The World and the Herald castigated the Jockey Club president as

"King Philip, The First" and called the Pinkertons "hybrid policemen" and "chuckle-heads." Both newspapers recounted in horrendous detail the pitiful appeals of patrons to be let out of the track. "I must get to New York," one old gentleman shouted. "I have an important engagement."

"I don't care a damn about your engagement. Nobody can leave this track," said the guard. "Them's my orders."

The *Herald* quoted one "big fellow" who begged, "I am ill; I need a doctor. I've just had a hemorrhage." The Pinkertons were unmoved. A woman with a sick baby pleaded to get out, "but the guards were merciless."

Said an outraged Englishman to an American friend: "You call this a free country, do you? And yet I'm told when I come in here that I can't leave until a certain hour. That's not liberty. It's tyranny. We wouldn't stand it on the other side." The *World* told of a Kentuckian who drew a big horse pistol and walked out grandly while "every Pinkerton in sight sought shelter." The newspaper added that "the hammering of Pinkerton clubs on other men's heads sounded like the popping of firecrackers on the Fourth of July."

The New York Times and the *Sun*, which were against gambling, called these charges "absurd." The persons most eager to leave the track, the *Times* said, "were almost without exception employees of the gambling syndicate or Western Union," which company "ought to be called to account for violating anti-gambling laws."

When the locked gates halted direct smuggling of information, the syndicate undertook fancier measures. Its telegraphers in the hotel cupola had a clear view of the paddock but not of the finish line, so operatives inside the gates performed as "horses": each one held a placard bearing a number corresponding to an entry in each race; after the official results were posted, they galloped across the paddock in the order in which the horses had finished. The watching telegraphers duly transmitted the results. The Pinkertons soon began chasing the horses, who in their scramble to escape were not always able to flee in the proper sequence: transmitting correct results was a problem. Some poolroom agents now equipped themselves with hollow wooden balls; they stuffed these with papers on which were scribbled odds, jockeys, and results: then they flung the balls over the fences, hoping that associates outside would retrieve them. But the Pinkertons patrolled so vigilantly that few balls fell into the hands for which they were intended; some of them struck bystanders on the head, the *Times* reported, and at least one man was knocked insensible.

The track remained in a state of siege during the rest of the spring meeting. Fighting flared now and then at the gates. The Pinkertons roped off the paddock and continued to chase ball throwers. When the gamblers' telegraph lines suddenly went dead, the bookmakers claimed sabotage and offered a $5,000 reward for capture of the saboteur.

During that summer, while the track was idle, Dwyer had a sixty-five-foot-high wooden fence built, which completely blocked the view from the hotel's cupola.

At 3 A.M. on opening day, heavy wagons loaded with lumber, men, and tools rolled up to Sleight's Hotel. The lumber was carried to the hotel's cupola and the carpenters went to work. The *World* described their efforts:

> No circus tent ever went up faster. Ten feet into the air, then a staircase and a landing. Ten feet higher, another staircase, another landing. Another ten feet, another staircase and landing. The carpenters paused for breath.
>
> It was daylight now and the Dwyer forces rallied in a hurry. A group of carpenters set to work to raise the fence still higher. Ten feet more, and the huge structure began to tremble with the weight of the workers. A breeze blew in from the bay and the men's hats flew off. They climbed down, glad to be on earth again. They looked across at the Western Union tower.
>
> "Give her another story," commanded the [tower] foreman. The carpenters hammered and knocked together another staircase and ten more feet of altitude. The tower was now forty-two feet above the cupola and its top platform seventy-seven feet from the ground.

Western Union installed four wires and a half dozen operators in the new tower, the *World* reported, and stationed a guard at the door. In the gamblers' camp an air of triumph prevailed.

But Sleight's Hotel was so situated that, even from their tower, telegraphers could not see the track's finish line; in close races they had to guess the winners. Nor could they observe odds and scratches, which the management was now posting under the judge's stand. When Western Union offered twenty-five dollars to the first person to get the information for each race through to the hotel, racegoers having no connection with either the syndicate or the telegraph company began to fling rubber balls filled with racing data over the fences.

By the time the second day's racing began, telegraph lines had been strung from barns and trees, with sending stations on some flat-topped stumps. The syndicate was reportedly paying $100 a day to a farmer named Young for the use of his two big locust trees as observation posts.

That night the Jockey Club's carpenters increased the height of the fence that stood in front of Farmer Young's trees. Next day the telegraphers climbed still higher, and the Gravesend carpenters appeared with more lumber. Lowering his binoculars, the man in the nearest tree shouted down to his telegrapher, "The horses are going to the post for the second race, and the Dwyers are building another fence!"

Meanwhile, at one entrance the gatemen were challenging a woman. One grabbed at her clothes and a pigeon squawked. "Why," said a detective, "she's got enough pigeons on her to stock a good-sized loft. That dress has pockets all the way down. We know too much about shop-lifters to be fooled by a game like that."

Nevertheless, the poolsellers' lawyers estimated that fully a hundred pigeons were smuggled into the track that day. The Jockey Club reportedly hired "Snapper" Garrison, an unemployed jockey with a reputation as a champion pigeon shot.

The track management further confounded the poolroom forces by concealing the names of entries until twenty minutes before post time for each race. A printer named Eagan was employed to run the information off on slips of paper, using a portable press set up at the track. "The crowd lay in wait for the messengers who distributed the slips and rushed upon them with much scrambling," the Herald reported.

Gradually, it seemed, the cops were beating the robbers. Conditions at the betting places in Manhattan were dismal. Crowds melted, and the bettors who did come complained loudly of the poor service. At De Lacy's own place, the announcer said at 2:42 P.M., "They're at the post at Brooklyn." It was thirty-two minutes later when he got the word, "They're off at Brooklyn!" One place had the horses running in the stretch for two minutes. Some betting rooms posted signs, "Not Responsible For Errors In Weights And Jockeys." All this encouraged the antigambling Times to headline its lead story: "POOL MEN BEATEN AT LAST."

Still there was a leak somewhere. "By some mysterious means," said the World, "whether by necromancy, juggling or what, the 'pool rooms' yesterday seemed in their normal condition. Betting was in full swing on all the events at Brooklyn. Jockeys, with the exception of the first race, were listed. No one seemed to know how the information from Brooklyn had been obtained."

Robert Pinkerton and his men managed to unravel the mystery before the fall meeting ended. What they discovered was proclaimed in these World headlines: "ELECTRICITY IN THE HAT. THE MOST INGENIOUS SCHEME YET FOR OBTAINING RACING NEWS."

"Every afternoon," the *Herald* explained the next day, a "handsome barouche, drawn by a pair of spirited horses, whirled a party of ladies and gentlemen to the lawn just above the betting ring. The driver parked his vehicle at a spot near the track, and the party seemingly turned themselves to enjoying a holiday. They had lunch and wine and cigars in plenty and seemed bent on nothing but enjoying the sweets of life...."

Had the Pinkertons scrutinized the barouche more carefully, they might have noticed that the coachman [Pearsall] wore an unusually tall silk hat and that he kept his seat on the box while members of the party visited the betting ring or viewed the races. They returned to the carriage now and then, ostensibly to refresh themselves. This continued daily until five days before the season ended, when Pinkerton and his men raided the coach. The picnicking group was headed by Joseph W. Frost, an electrician and president of the Automatic Fire Alarm Company, 317 Broadway.

It developed that Joseph Frost had arranged with the syndicate to supply complete racing information from Gravesend to Western Union for $1,000 a day, and he had succeeded in doing so for six days. Pearsall's tall coachman's hat had a hole in the center of its top the size of a half dollar. Inside the hat was a small electric light powered by batteries concealed in the coach. Under his clothing Pearsall wore a network of wires that connected the light with the batteries and with a telegraph key hidden on the coach floor.

Members of the party brought him information on odds, jockeys, and the like from the betting ring. The finishes Pearsall observed himself, simply by standing up in the carriage. He sent a running story by operating the key with his foot, causing the light in his hat to go on and off in Morse code. The telegraph operator in the hotel tower could not see the finish line or the posted odds, but he had a fine view of the top of the coachman's hat. Somehow or other the Pinkertons were tipped off, and suddenly one afternoon Robert Pinkerton himself leaped into the carriage and dragged Frost from it.

The bookmakers left their stands and shouted in excitement. Bettors abandoned the ring and shouted encouragement to Frost. One man jumped over the fence, snatched off his coat, and, directing his ire at the Pinkertons, yelled, "Come on and hang 'em!" The crowd in the ring shouted, "Lynch 'em! Lynch 'em!"

Fortunately, nobody was lynched, and the carriage episode became the final act of "the Great Battle of Gravesend" as public spectacle.

A Story Goes with It

For many a Broadwayite in his day (which ended in 1946), Damon Runyon *was* Broadway: sportswriter, superlative trial reporter, story-telling historian of the Great White Way. Praising "the sensitivity of the ear of Damon Runyon," his contemporary Heywood Broun once noted that "like any artist, he has exercised the privilege of selectivity. But he has not heightened or burlesqued the speech of the people who come alive in his short stories." He had a special fondness for the sport that allegedly improves the breed.

BY DAMON RUNYON

◇◇◇

ONE NIGHT I am in a gambling joint in Miami watching the crap game and thinking what a nice thing it is, indeed, to be able to shoot craps without having to worry about losing your potatoes.

Many of the high shots from New York and Detroit and St. Louis and other cities are around the table, and there is quite some action in spite of the hard times. In fact, there is so much action that a guy with only a few bobs on him, such as me, will be considered very impolite to be pushing into this game, because they are packed in very tight around the table.

I am maybe three guys back from the table, and I am watching the game by standing on tiptoe peeking over their shoulders, and all I can hear is Goldie, the stick man, hollering money-money-money every time some guy makes a number, so I can see the dice are very warm indeed, and that the right betters are doing first-rate.

By and by a guy by the name of Guinea Joe, out of Trenton, picks up the dice and starts making numbers right and left, and I know enough about this Guinea Joe to know that when he starts making numbers anybody will be very foolish indeed not to follow his hand, although personally I am generally a wrong better against the dice, if I bet at all.

Now all I have in my pocket is a sawbuck, and the hotel stakes are coming up on me the next day, and I need this saw, but with Guinea Joe hotter than a forty-five it will be overlooking a big opportunity not to go along with him, so when he comes out on an eight, which is a very easy number for Joe to make when he is hot, I dig up my sawbuck, and slide it past the three guys in front of me to the table, and I say to Lefty Park, who is laying against the dice, as follows:

"I will take the odds, Lefty."

Well, Lefty looks at my sawbuck and nods his head, for Lefty is not such a guy as will refuse any bet, even though it is as modest as mine, and right away Goldie yells money-money-money, so there I am with twenty-two dollars.

Next Guinea Joe comes out on a nine, and naturally I take thirty to twenty for my sugar, because nine is nothing for Joe to make when he is hot. He makes the nine just as I figure, and I take two to one for my half a yard when he starts looking for a ten, and when he makes the ten I am right up against the table, because I am now a guy with means.

Well, the upshot of the whole business is that I finally find myself with three hundred bucks, and when it looks as if the dice are cooling off, I take out and back off from the table, and while I am backing off I am trying to look like a guy who loses all his potatoes, because there are always many wolves waiting around crap games and one thing and another in Miami this season, and what they are waiting for is to put the bite on anybody who happens to make a little scratch.

In fact, nobody can remember when the bite is as painful as it is in Miami this season, what with the unemployment situation among many citizens who come to Miami expecting to find work in the gambling joints, or around the race track. But almost as soon as these citizens arrive, the gambling joints are all turned off, except in spots, and the bookmakers are chased off the track and the mutuels put in, and the consequences are the suffering is most intense. It is not only intense among the visiting citizens, but it is quite intense among the Miami landlords, because naturally if a citizen is not working, nobody can expect him to pay any room rent, but the Miami landlords do not seem to understand this situation, and are very unreasonable about their room rent.

Anyway, I back through quite a crowd without anybody biting me, and I am commencing to figure I may escape altogether and get to my hotel and hide my dough before the news gets around that I win about five G's, which is what my winning is sure to amount to by the time the rumor reaches all quarters of the city.

Then, just as I am thinking I am safe, I find I am looking a guy by the name of Hot Horse Herbie in the face, and I can tell from Hot Horse Herbie's expression that he is standing there watching me for some time, so there is no use in telling him I am washed out in the game. In fact, I cannot think of much of anything to tell Hot Horse Herbie that may keep him from putting the bite on me for at least a few bobs, and I am greatly astonished when he does not offer to bite me at all, but says to me like this:

"Well," he says, "I am certainly glad to see you make such a nice score. I will be looking for you tomorrow at the track, and will have some big news for you."

Then he walks away from me and I stand there with my mouth open looking at him, as it is certainly a most unusual way for Herbie to act. It is the first time I ever knew Herbie to walk away from a chance to bite somebody, and I can scarcely understand such actions, for Herbie is such a guy as will not miss a bite, even if he does not need it.

He is a tall, thin guy, with a sad face and a long chin, and he is called Hot Horse Herbie because he nearly always has a very hot horse to tell you about. He nearly always has a horse that is so hot it is fairly smoking, a hot horse being a horse that cannot possibly lose a race unless it falls down dead, and while Herbie's hot horses often lose without falling down dead, this does not keep Herbie from coming up with others just as hot.

In fact, Hot Horse Herbie is what is called a hustler around the race tracks, and his business is to learn about these hot horses, or even just suspect about them, and then get somebody to bet on them, which is a very legitimate business indeed, as Herbie only collects a commission if the hot horses win, and if they do not win Herbie just keeps out of sight awhile from whoever he gets to bet on the hot horses. There are very few guys in this world who can keep out of sight better than Hot Horse Herbie, and especially from old Cap Duhaine, of the Pinkertons, who is always around pouring cold water on hot horses.

In fact, Cap Duhaine, of the Pinkertons, claims that guys such as Hot Horse Herbie are nothing but touts, and sometimes he heaves them off the race track altogether, but of course Cap Duhaine is a very unsentimental old guy and cannot see how such characters as Hot Horse Herbie add to the romance of the turf.

Anyway, I escape from the gambling joint with all my scratch on me, and hurry to my room and lock myself in for the night, and I do not show up in public until along about noon the next day, when it is time to go over to the coffee shop for my java. And of course by this time the news of my score is all over town, and many guys are taking dead aim at me.

But naturally I am now able to explain to them that I have to wire most of the three yards I win to Nebraska to save my father's farm from being seized by the sheriff, and while everybody knows I do not have a father, and that if I do have a father I will not be sending him money for such a thing as saving his farm, with times what they are in Miami, nobody is impolite enough to doubt my word except a guy by the name of Pottsville Legs, who wishes to see my receipts from the telegraph office when I explain to him why I cannot stake him to a double sawbuck.

I do not see Hot Horse Herbie until I get to the track, and he is waiting for me right inside the grand-stand gate, and as soon as I show up he motions me off to one side and says to me like this:

"Now," Herbie says, "I am very smart indeed about a certain race to-day. In fact," he says, "if any guy knowing what I know does not bet all he can rake and scrape together on a certain horse, such a guy ought to cut his own throat and get himself out of the way forever. What I know," Herbie says, "is enough to shake the foundations of this country if it gets out. Do not ask any questions," he says, "but get ready to bet all the sugar you win last night on this horse I am going to mention to you, and all I ask you in return is to bet fifty on me. And," Herbie says, "kindly do not tell me you leave your money in your other pants, because I know you do not have any other pants."

"Now, Herbie," I say, "I do not doubt your information, because I know you will not give out information unless it is well founded. But," I say, "I seldom stand for a tip, and as for betting fifty for you, you know I will not bet fifty even for myself if somebody guarantees me a winner. So I thank you, Herbie, just the same," I say, "but I must do without your tip," and with this I start walking away.

"Now," Herbie says, "wait a minute. A story goes with it," he says.

Well, of course this is a different matter entirely. I am such a guy as will always listen to a tip on a horse if a story goes with the tip. In fact, I will not give you a nickel for a tip without a story, but it must be a first-class story, and most horse players are the same way. In fact, there are very few horse players who will not listen to a tip if a story goes with it, for this is the way human nature is. So I turn and walk back to Hot Horse Herbie, and say to him like this:

"Well," I say, "let me hear the story, Herbie."

"Now," Herbie says, dropping his voice away down low, in case old Cap Duhaine may be around somewhere listening, "it is the third race, and the horse is a horse by the name of Never Despair. It is a boat race," Herbie says. "They are going to shoo in Never Despair. Everything else in the race is a cooler," he says.

"Well," I say, "this is just an idea, Herbie, and not a story."

"Wait a minute," Herbie says. "The story that goes with it is a very strange story indeed. In fact," he says, "it is such a story as I can scarcely believe myself, and I will generally believe almost any story, including," he says, "the ones I make up out of my own head. Anyway, the story is as follows:

"Never Despair is owned by an old guy by the name of Seed Mercer," Herbie says. "Maybe you remember seeing him around. He always wears a black slouch hat and gray whiskers," Herbie says, "and he is maybe a hundred years old, and his horses are very terrible horses indeed. In fact," Herbie says, "I do not remember seeing any more terrible horses in all the years I am around the track, and," Herbie says, "I wish to say I see some very terrible horses indeed.

"Now," Herbie says, "old Mercer has a granddaughter who is maybe sixteen years old, come next grass, by the name of Lame Louise, and she is called Lame Louise because she is all crippled up from childhood by infantile what-is-this, and can scarcely navigate, and," Herbie says, "her being crippled up in such a way makes old Mercer feel very sad, for she is all he has in the world, except these terrible horses."

"It is a very long story, Herbie," I say, "and I wish to see Moe Shapoff about a very good thing in the first race."

"Never mind Moe Shapoff," Herbie says. "He will only tell you about a bum by the name of Zachary in the first race, and Zachary has no chance whatever. I make Your John a stand-out in the first," he says.

"Well," I say, "let us forget the first and go on with your story, although it is commencing to sound all mixed up to me."

"Now," Herbie says, "it not only makes old man Mercer very sad because Lame Louise is all crippled up, but," he says, "it makes many of the jockeys and other guys around the race track very sad, because," he says, "they know Lame Louise since she is so high, and she always has a smile for them, and especially for Jockey Scroon. In fact," Herbie says, "Jockey Scroon is even more sad about Lame Louise than old man Mercer, because Jockey Scroon loves Lame Louise."

"Why," I say, very indignant, "Jockey Scroon is nothing but a little burglar. Why," I say, "I see Jockey Scroon do things to horses I bet on that he will have to answer for on the Judgment Day, if there is any justice at such a time. Why," I say, "Jockey Scroon is nothing but a Gerald Chapman in his heart, and so are all other jockeys."

"Yes," Hot Horse Herbie says, "what you say is very, very true, and I am personally in favor of the electric chair for all jockeys, but," he says, "Jockey Scroon loves Lame Louise just the same, and is figuring on making her his ever-loving wife when he gets a few bobs together, which," Herbie says, "makes Louise eight to five in my line to be an old maid. Jockey Scroon rooms with me downtown," Herbie says, "and he speaks freely to me about his love for Louise. Furthermore," Herbie says, "Jockey Scroon is personally not a bad little guy, at that, although of course being a jockey he is sometimes greatly misunderstood by the public.

"Anyway," Hot Horse Herbie says, "I happen to go home early last night before I see you at the gambling joint, and I hear voices coming out of my room, and naturally I pause outside the door to listen, because for all I know it may be the landlord speaking about the room rent, although," Herbie says, "I do not figure my landlord to be much worried at this time because I see him sneak into my room a few days before and take a lift at my trunk to make sure I have belongings in the same, and it happens I nail the trunk to the floor beforehand, so not being able to lift it, the landlord is bound to figure me a guy with property.

"These voices," Herbie says, "are mainly soprano voices, and at first I think Jockey Scroon is in there with some dolls, which is by no means permissible in my hotel, but, after listening awhile, I discover they are the voices of young boys, and I make out that these boys are nothing but jockeys, and they are the six jockeys who are riding in the third race, and they are fixing up this race to be a boat race, and to shoo in Never Despair, which Jockey Scroon is riding.

"And," Hot Horse Herbie says, "the reason they are fixing up this boat race is the strangest part of the story. It seems," he says, "that Jockey Scroon hears old man Mercer talking about a great surgeon from Europe who is a shark on patching up cripples such as Lame Louise, and who just arrives at Palm Beach to spend the winter, and old man Mercer is saying how he wishes he has dough enough to take Lame Louise to this guy so he can operate on her, and maybe make her walk good again.

"But of course," Herbie says, "it is well known to one and all that old man Mercer does not have a quarter, and that he has no way of getting a quarter unless one of his terrible horses accidentally wins a purse. So," Herbie says, "it seems these jockeys get to talking it over among themselves, and they figure it will be a nice thing to let old man Mercer win a purse such as the thousand bucks that goes with the third race to-day, so he can take Lame Louise to Palm Beach, and now you have a rough idea of what is coming off.

"Furthermore," Herbie says, "these jockeys wind up their meeting by taking a big oath among themselves that they will not tell a living soul what is doing so nobody will bet on Never Despair, because," he says, "these little guys are smart enough to see if there is any betting on such a horse there may be a very large squawk afterwards. And," he says, "I judge they keep their oath because Never Despair is twenty to one in the morning line, and I do not hear a whisper about him, and you have the tip all to yourself."

"Well," I say, "so what?" For this story is now commencing to make me a little tired, especially as I hear the bell for the first race, and I must see Moe Shapoff.

"Why," Hot Horse Herbie says, "so you bet every nickel you can rake and scrape together on Never Despair, including the twenty you are to bet for me for giving you this tip and the story that goes with it."

"Herbie," I say, "it is a very interesting story indeed, and also very sad, but," I say, "I am sorry it is about a horse Jockey Scroon is to ride, because I do not think I will ever bet on anything Jockey Scroon rides if they pay off in advance. And," I say, "I am certainly not going to bet twenty for you or anybody else."

"Well," Hot Horse Herbie says, "I will compromise with you for a pound note, because I must have something going for me on this boat race."

So I give Herbie a fiver, and the chances are this is about as strong as he figures from the start, and I forget all about his tip and the story that goes with it, because while I enjoy a story with a tip, I feel that Herbie overdoes this one.

Anyway, no handicapper alive can make Never Despair win the third race off the form, because this race is at six furlongs, and there is a barrel of speed in it, and anybody can see that old man Mercer's horse is away over his head. In fact, The Dancer tells me that any one of the other five horses in this race can beat Never Despair doing anything from playing hockey to putting the shot, and everybody else must think the same thing because Never Despair goes to forty to one.

Personally, I like a horse by the name of Loose Living, which is a horse owned by a guy by the name of Bill Howard, and I hear Bill Howard is betting plenty away on his horse, and any time Bill Howard is betting away on his horse a guy will be out of his mind not to bet on this horse, too, as Bill Howard is very smart indeed. Loose Living is two to one in the first line, but by and by I judge the money Bill Howard bets away commences to come back to the track, and Loose Living winds up seven to ten, and while I am generally not a seven-to-ten guy, I can see that here is a proposition I cannot overlook.

So, naturally, I step up to the mutuel window and invest in Loose Living. In fact, I invest everything I have on me in the way of scratch, amounting to a hundred and ten bucks, which is all I have left after taking myself out of the hotel stakes and giving Hot Horse Herbie the finnif, and listening to what Moe Shapoff has to say about the first race, and also getting beat a snoot in the second.

When I first step up to the window, I have no idea of betting all my scratch on Loose Living, but while waiting in line there I get to thinking what a cinch Loose Living is, and how seldom such an opportunity comes into a guy's life, so I just naturally set it all in.

Well, this is a race which will be remembered by one and all to their dying day, as Loose Living beats the barrier a step, and is two lengths in front before you can say Jack Robinson, with a thing by the name of Callipers second by maybe half a length, and with the others bunched except Never Despair, and where is Never Despair but last, where he figures.

Now any time Loose Living busts on top there is no need worrying any more about him, and I am thinking I better get in line at the pay-off window right away, so I will not have to wait long to collect my sugar. But I figure I may as well stay and watch the race, although personally I am never much interested in watching races. I am interested only in how a race comes out.

As the horses hit the turn into the stretch, Loose Living is just breezing, and anybody can see that he is going to laugh his way home from there. Callipers is still second, and a thing called Goose Pimples is third, and I am surprised to see that Never Despair now struggles up to fourth with Jockey Scroon belting away at him with his bat quite earnestly. Furthermore, Never Despair seems to be running very fast, though afterwards I figure this may be because the others are commencing to run very slow.

Anyway, a very strange spectacle now takes place in the stretch, as all of a sudden Loose Living seems to be stopping, as if he is waiting for a street car, and what is all the more remarkable Callipers and Goose Pimples also seem to be hanging back, and the next thing anybody knows, here comes Jockey Scroon on Never Despair sneaking through on the rail, and personally it looks to me as if the jock on Callipers moves over to give Jockey Scroon plenty of elbow room, but of course the jock on Callipers may figure Jockey Scroon has diphtheria, and does not wish to catch it.

Loose Living is out in the middle of the track, anyway, so he does not have to move over. All Loose Living has to do is to keep on running backwards as he seems to be doing from the top of the stretch, to let Jockey Scroon go past on Never Despair to win the heat by a length.

Well, the race is practically supernatural in many respects, and the judges are all upset over it, and they haul all the jocks up in the stand and ask them many questions, and not being altogether satisfied with the answers, they ask these questions over several times. But all the jocks will say is that Never Despair sneaks past them very unexpectedly indeed, while Jockey Scroon, who is a pretty fresh duck at that, wishes to know if he is supposed to blow a horn when he is slipping through a lot of guys sound asleep.

But the judges are still not satisfied, so they go prowling around investigating the betting, because naturally when a boat race comes up there is apt to be some reason for it, such as the betting, but it seems that all the judges find is that one five-dollar win ticket is sold on Never Despair in the mutuels, and they cannot learn of a dime being bet away on the horse. So there is nothing much the judges can do about the proposition, except give the jocks many hard looks, and the jocks are accustomed to hard looks from the judges, anyway.

Personally, I am greatly upset by this business, especially when I see that Never Despair pays $86.34, and for two cents I will go right up in the stand and start hollering copper on these little Jesse Jameses for putting on such a boat race and taking all my hard-earned potatoes away from me, but before I have time to do this, I run into The Dancer, and he tells me that Dedicate in the next race is the surest thing that ever goes to the post, and at five to one, at that. So I have to forget everything while I bustle about to dig up a few bobs to bet on Dedicate, and when Dedicate is beat a whisker, I have to do some more bustling to dig up a few bobs to bet on Vesta in the fifth, and by this time the third race is such ancient history that nobody cares what happens in it.

It is nearly a week before I see Hot Horse Herbie again, and I figure he is hiding out on everybody because he has this dough he wins off the fiver I give him, and personally I consider him a guy with no manners not to be kicking back the fin, at least. But before I can mention the fin, Herbie gives me a big hello, and says to me like this:

"Well," he says, "I just see Jockey Scroon, and Jockey Scroon just comes back from Palm Beach, and the operation is a big success, and Lame Louise will walk as good as anybody again, and old Mercer is tickled silly. But," Herbie says, "do not say anything out loud, because the judges may still be trying to find out what comes off in the race."

"Herbie," I say, very serious, "do you mean to say the story you tell me about Lame Louise, and all this and that, the other day is on the level?"

"Why," Herbie says, "certainly it is on the level, and I am sorry to hear you do not take advantage of my information. But," he says, "I do not blame you for not believing my story, because it is a very long story for anybody to believe. It is not such a story," Herbie says, "as I will tell to any one if I expect them to believe it. In fact," he says, "it is so long a story that I do not have the heart to tell it to anybody else but you, or maybe I will have something running for me on the race.

"But," Herbie says, "never mind all this. I will be plenty smart about a race to-morrow. Yes," Herbie says, "I will be wiser than a treeful of owls, so be sure and see me if you happen to have any coconuts."

"There is no danger of me seeing you," I say, very sad, because I am all sorrowed up to think that the story he tells me is really true. "Things are very terrible with me at this time," I say, "and I am thinking maybe you can hand me back my finnif, because you must do all right for yourself with the fiver you have on Never Despair at such a price."

Now a very strange look comes over Hot Horse Herbie's face, and he raises his right hand, and says to me like this:

"I hope and trust I drop down dead right here in front of you," Herbie says, "if I bet a quarter on the horse. It is true," he says, "I am up at the window to buy a ticket on Never Despair, but the guy who is selling the tickets is a friend of mine by the name of Heeby Rosenbloom, and Heeby whispers to me that Big Joe Gompers, the guy who owns Callipers, just bets half a hundred on his horse, and," Herbie says, "I know Joe Gompers is such a guy as will not bet half a hundred on anything he does not get a Federal Reserve guarantee with it.

"Anyway," Herbie says, "I get to thinking about what a bad jockey this Jockey Scroon is, which is very bad indeed, and," he says, "I figure that even if it is a boat race it is no even-money race they can shoo him in, so I buy a ticket on Callipers."

"Well," I say, "somebody buys one five-dollar ticket on Never Despair, and I figure it can be nobody but you."

"Why," Hot Horse Herbie says, "do you not hear about this? Why," he says, "Cap Duhaine, of the Pinkertons, traces this ticket and finds it is bought by a guy by the name of Steve Harter, and the way this guy Harter comes to buy it is very astonishing. It seems," Herbie says, "that this Harter is a tourist out of Indiana who comes to Miami for the sunshine, and who loses all his dough but six bucks against the faro bank at Hollywood.

"At the same time," Herbie says, "the poor guy gets a telegram from his ever-loving doll back in Indiana saying she no longer wishes any part of him.

"Well," Herbie says, "between losing his dough and his doll, the poor guy is practically out of his mind, and he figures there is nothing left for him to do but knock himself off.

"So," Herbie says, "this Harter spends one of his six bucks to get to the track, figuring to throw himself under the feet of the horses in the first race and let them kick him to a jelly. But he does not get there until just as the third race is coming up and," Herbie says, "he sees this name 'Never Despair,' and he figures it may be a hunch, so he buys himself a ticket with his last fiver. Well, naturally," Herbie says, "when Never Despair pops down, the guy forgets about letting the horses kick him to a jelly, and he keeps sending his dough along until he runs nothing but a nubbin into six G's on the day.

"Then," Herbie says, "Cap Duhaine finds out that the guy, still thinking of Never Despair, calls his ever-loving doll on the phone, and finds she is very sorry she sends him the wire and that she really loves him more than somewhat, especially," Herbie says, "when she finds out about the six G's. And the last anybody hears of the matter, this Harter is on his way home to get married, so Never Despair does quite some good in this wicked old world, after all.

"But," Herbie says, "let us forget all this, because to-morrow is another day. To-morrow," he says, "I will tell you about a thing that goes in the fourth which is just the same as wheat in the bin. In fact," Hot Horse Herbie says, "if it does not win, you can never speak to me again."

"Well," I say, as I start to walk away, "I am not interested in any tip at this time."

"Now," Herbie says, "wait a minute. A story goes with it."

"Well," I say, coming back to him, "let me hear the story."

◇◇

And See How They Run

It would seem that what Nick the Greek had in mind in his dictum mentioned earlier included little refinements like these, as related in *Oswald Jacoby on Gambling.*

BY OSWALD JACOBY

◇◇

THERE IS also the story of the jockey who was riding a particular horse for the first time. He was instructed to hold the horse back at the start, let him move up to fifth or sixth at the halfway point, and then keep him in that position the rest of the way. He was also instructed to observe the horse carefully to determine how well the horse could have done if encouraged.

The jockey followed instructions and brought the horse in fifth. At the first opportunity after the race the trainer asked, "Could he have won?" The answer was, "Sure! One or two cracks of the whip and we would have passed those four horses like a breeze." At which the trainer commented, "Then I guess there is no question that he can win when we race him against the same horses next Thursday." "Well," replied the jockey, "there is no question that we can beat those four that were in front of me, but there were a couple of horses behind me that I feel could have beaten all of us!"

* * * *

Another story in this area concerns two men at the $50 window. (Some tracks have $100 windows for big bettors but at most tracks the largest single bet that you can make is $50. Of course you can buy as many $50 tickets as you wish—as long as you pay cash. The tracks offer no credit and take no checks!) The first man bought ten tickets on the favorite, number seven. The second man bought two tickets on each of the other four horses in the race. As they walked away from the window the second man said to the first, "I'm sorry to tell you that you just threw $500 away. I own number seven and we are just running him for the exercise." The reply was, "Well! It's going to be a mighty slow race. I own the other four horses."

Well, Why Not?

Since time out of mind, the denunciations of gambling have been high-mindedly ferocious, as when one Charles Caldwell, lecturing at Transylvania University in 1834, found that "a vice more nefarious in principle, more foul in its associations, has scarcely an existence . . . a practice identical with knavery in its hatefullest form, allied to theft, pocketpicking, and not unfrequently the source of murder." Somehow, though, there have always been those whose blood was not chilled by such fearsome excoriations. Here is a quintet of them.

A Natural Evil

One of the most remarkable of Renaissance figures was Girolamo Cardano of Milan, physician and mathematician, whose *Book on Games of Chance* is now believed by scholars to have anticipated Pascal's theory of the laws of probability by about a century. In that classic sixteenth-century book, from which an excerpt appears below, he noted appreciatively that when he once thought death to be close at hand, constant playing at dice did much to bring him around.

BY GIROLAMO CARDANO

EVEN IF gambling were altogether an evil, still, on account of the very large number of people who play, it would seem to be a natural evil. For that very reason it ought to be discussed by a medieval doctor like one of the incurable diseases; for in every evil there is a least evil, in every infamy a least infamy, and similarly in loss of time and fortune. Also, it has been the custom of philosophers to deal with the vices in order that advantage might be drawn from them, as for example in the case of anger. Thus it is not absurd for me to discuss gambling, not in order to praise it but in order to point out the advantages in it, and, of course, also its disadvantages, in order that they may be reduced to a minimum.

◇◇

How to Win While Losing

How can you make gambling pay even when you are losing at it? A good deal depends, of course, on such talent as you have to fall back on—the talent, say, of William Saroyan. Even he admits in this autobiographical fragment that it doesn't always work out, but when it does . . .

BY WILLIAM SAROYAN

◇◇

ONCE YOU have messed with gambling, winning or losing, once you have gone into a gambling house, your goose is cooked, you are no longer good for anything else, except more of the same order of derangement, of total dismissal of time and sequence, for that is basically what gambling is. For the true gambler, that is. For the kind of gambler I was, and probably still am, I certainly would be that kind of gambler if I went back to gambling at all, as I probably shall. Money ceases to be money. A thousand means nothing, ten thousand means nothing, whether it is dollars, francs, lire, beans, or points. The only thing that means anything is the right or the wrong of it, and myself in relation to right and wrong. The theory is that if I am right I can do no wrong, and I have all too frequently demonstrated the validity of the theory. But I have even more frequently had it brought home to me that if I am wrong, I can do no right, either. And by that time there is some arithmetic to do, which I tend to do with the sobriety I knew as a newsboy, counting the coins in my hand, and then counting my papers, and then counting the coins again, and then the papers again, because a nickel was missing. The arithmetic might reveal, over the years of gambling, beginning on Third Street in San Francisco, that a dollar was missing, five dollars were missing, ten, twenty, fifty, a hundred, a thousand dollars, two thousand, three, five, ten, twenty thousand dollars were missing.

Now, of course, if you lose money at gambling, you haven't got the money any more.

As a losing Presidential candidate once said, "Under our great democratic system, the losing candidate does not win." Everybody understood what he meant, though, and rather admired him for not crying. He meant that the losing candidate offers his congratulations to the winning candidate, but somewhere in the midst of the thought, his loss troubled him, confused him, astonished him, proved to be not yet totally acceptable. He was still in the midst of disbelief. How could it be possible that he had lost, especially in that he had come so near to winning? And so, in his befuddlement, and with an unmistakable courage, perhaps even bravery, and certainly with a good deal of charm, his language became garbled. In an instant, though, he corrected the garbling, speaking off the cuff and quickly, awfully tired, as gamblers who have stopped gambling always are, too, and hoping that the pathos of his position, and of what he had said, might not have been noticed, as losing gamblers hope the real extent of their losses will not become known.

I am not mentioning the names of Presidential candidates, or Presidents, winners or losers, because when they write their lies I don't expect them to use my name. I don't know them and they don't know me. They gamble and I gamble. They win and they lose, and I win and I lose.

But in the end I stop, and I do the necessary arithmetic. If it tells me I have won, I try to find out how much. If it tells me I have lost, I try to decide how I am going to get the lost money back.

Well, you never do. You never get anything back. You always get something, but it isn't back. Getting something back is part of the fantasy of the gambler, and for all I know of Presidential candidates who have lost, who run again, who lose again, but in having lost twice get something, surely something very valuable, too. And finally they don't run again. They decide not to, or they are not permitted to, but again they get something. They certainly get older, as I have gotten older getting various things but not getting back anything, not getting back the money, the time, the abandoned sequence, or anything else I may have lost. I have gotten other things, some of them better than the things lost.

Now, as a poor illustration of this, but not as an apology for folly, for foolishness, for aberration, for illness, for anything we want to call it, I may say that every time I have lost enough money to be deeply annoyed by the enormity of it, which has always been picayune, even when it has been fifty thousand dollars, I have gotten something I could not otherwise have gotten. My money losses are picayune, because there are billions of dollars. If a man has a million or two he remains entirely the same as anybody else in the basic involvement with time, sequence, and the human experience. Money itself is picayune. Even so, every time I have lost, and have been annoyed about the difference between right and wrong, with the edge of the wrong moving to me, I have made up my mind to somehow right the wrong, to balance the imbalance, to earn more than the sum lost.

What's more, I have done so, and it has always been by means of writing.

But the point I am trying to make is that I believe all such writing is writing I would *not* have done had I not lost at gambling.

Hence, while I have not always won back the money lost, I *have* gotten a number of things from *having* lost.

I have sat down and written steadily for a month, and of course *that* is something. The writing has been published, and of course *that* is something, too. I have sometimes been paid more for the writing than I lost at gambling, and *that* is also something.

But most important of all, my annoyance has *conditioned* what I have written. Consequently, I have a new book, a new novel, or a new play, with a style I could not have otherwise put into it. The annoyance about the loss of money, of time and sequence, gave the work its style, and now and then that style has been rare enough to please me.

A lame explanation? More than lame—cripple. But maybe it's the truth, too. How should I know? In the meantime, the facts, as they're called. Las Vegas 1942. Five thousand dollars lost. *The Human Comedy* written. Two hundred and fifty thousand dollars earned. Las Vegas again, 1949. Fifty thousand dollars lost. *Tracy's Tiger, Rock Wagram,* and *The Laughing Matter* written. No dollars and no cents earned, but I *have* the books, they are there, they are going, they will soon be gone perhaps, but until they are, they are being read and readers are getting something out of them.

The Pleasures of Gambling

Now and then a foe of gambling suggests that a gambler, even if he wins, isn't going to hold onto his profits long enough to enjoy them. One would like to be present if such a one tried to convince Mrs. Nellie McGrail of this doleful notion. A jackpot of $574,658 for an investment of two pence? Has anyone heard lately of a bank that rewards its thrifty clients that way?

FROM ESQUIRE'S BOOK OF GAMBLING

AMONG THE pleasures of gambling, certainly the greatest is winning. Anyone who has ever had a two-dollar bet pay off or the contents of the pot shoved his way knows that special exaltation that comes from a combination of pride in skill and joy at the sense of accomplishment. To beat the system with your own system—that is a fulfilling experience.

Of course, there is nothing wrong with winning even if you don't have a system. Pure luck, when it descends on you of all people, can give you a feeling of gratified self-importance comparable to few other delights. Recall those sweepstakes winners that occasionally grin out at you from the newsreels. "Just lucky, I guess," they say, their wet smiles threatening to crack the cheeks. And there is not a soul watching who wonders why fortune does not shine on him so brightly, so suddenly and so easily.

There are comparable experiences. Finding a serial number on your dollar bill for which some mad newspaper pays you $5,000 is one. Brigitte Bardot calling you up to beg for a date is another.

If such are your dreams, this book cannot help you.

In fact, if we knew how to get Bardot on the phone we would hardly be putting out a book on it.

There are, of course, some contests where one can win big big money for little initial expenditure, but these usually involve a bit of skill as well. England's great football pools, for instance, take a little guesswork on the part of the entree, but luck is more than a small factor. The euphorious bliss of the winners is an unassailable argument for gambling, if one is needed.

One evening early last November, little Mrs. Nellie McGrail, a thirty-four-year-old widow of Reddish, England, was finishing up her supper dishes when a knock came on the door. Mrs. McGrail, who had two young daughters and worked as a fifteen-dollar-a-week mail-order clerk, dried her hands on her apron and went wearily to the door.

"Prepare yourself for a shock, Mrs. McGrail—a pleasant shock," said one of the two men standing outside.

It proved a pleasant shock indeed, for they brought news that she had won over half a million dollars in one of Britain's weekend football pools.

By correctly forecasting eight football games which ended in ties, little Mrs. McGrail had won the staggering sum of $574,658, tax-free, with a bet of two pence (a little over two cents). It was the biggest jackpot in the thirty-five-year history of the pools. (Three months later a young warehouse man topped Mrs. McGrail's windfall by a mere $2,220. And two months after that, a twenty-two-dollar-a-week London lamplighter lifted the all-time record to $585,421.20 when he hit with a thirty-five cent bet.)

In recent years, taking bets on the results of big-league football (soccer) games has become Britain's seventh biggest industry. One-fifth of the entire population has a bet of some sort on the weekly football games, and a total of more than $200,000,000 is won and lost in the course of the season.

For eight months of the year (August through April), it is as though the whole of Britain had been turned into one vast, extremely well-organized and surprisingly honest betting den. In clubs and pubs, on buses and trains, at meal tables at home and in washrooms at work, ten million Britons spend their spare time filling in the gaily colored betting slips. They queue up in post offices for postal orders to mail with their forecasts. On Saturday nights they huddle tightly round radios and TV sets to check off the results of the day's games. On Tuesday those who have come close to correctly forecasting the games discover whether they have won merely a few cents or a top jackpot running into hundreds of thousands of dollars.

News of a big win affects people in different ways. Little Mrs. McGrail for instance, bought herself a new hairdo, a $75 evening gown, a $270 fur stole and a new house. She bought her young daughters new school uniforms and a $140,000 trust fund. She gave $112,000 to her parents, another large sum to her grandparents in Canada, and made generous donations to the local hospital and the National Playing Fields Association. What was left she invested for herself.

On the other hand, a man who won $168,000 went on a binge which culminated in his buying the hotel where he did the celebrating. When he sobered up, he advised future winners: "Change your address, lock your doors, stay home, tear up all begging letters and never sign anything."

Worried by the adverse publicity which stems from this sort of thing, Littlewoods Pools, Ltd., one of the largest football betting firms in Britain, now gives each of its big-money winners a booklet on "Safe Investment." In the case of Mrs. McGrail, the firm set up a committee of lawyers and accountants to advise her on what to do with her money and how to keep the con-men and beggars away.

A few cautious winners need no advice, like the Scot who won $180,000. As he listened to the news of his big win, he carefully stubbed out his half-smoked cigarette and tucked what was left behind one ear.

"Mustna waste cigarettes," he said. "It's a fairfu' lot of money a'right. but cigarettes [fifty-five cents for twenty in Britain] are a fair price, too."

Ernest Taylor, a Yorkshire milkman who won $210,000, carried on with his deliveries as usual, except that he bought each of his 240 customers a capon for Christmas.

Asked if he was going to spend any more of the money, he observed thoughtfully, "Well, I might get half a dozen pigs. I can feed them on the surplus milk."

The men who run them claim that Britain's football pools are not gambling. Their advertising refers to the betting slips as "coupons," the stake money as the "investment" and the winnings as "dividends." Clergymen, some politicians and the poorly paid professional football players themselves, however, do not regard it in quite the same rosy light.

But Britain's man-in-the-street sees a big win as his only real chance of escaping the dreary monotony of workaday life. Week after week he sends in his stake money and betting slip, hoping desperately for a correct prediction of next Saturday's games.

One bettor in three gets a win of some sort in the course of the average football season, but only one in forty ends the season with even a small profit. Each week one or two—like Mrs. McGrail—emerge with a big enough jackpot to buy a fleet of Rolls Royces, a Park Lane mansion or a Pacific island.

From the sixty-odd major-league games played each week, the pools' promoters select the most difficult to forecast. You can predict the results of fourteen of them, pick out five teams you think will win their away games, or like Mrs. McGrail, try to select eight games which you feel will end in ties.

Tie games are the most difficult to predict, and for each one he picks successfully the forecaster is awarded three points. A home win brings one point and an away win two. The forecaster who gets the most points can go right out in search of his Pacific island or Park Lane mansion. He's got it made.

For the British government does not regard betting winnings as income in the normal sense of the word, and hence they are not taxable. But the government insures a steady income from this betting gold mine by leveling a special 30 percent tax on the pools firms, while the post office rakes in another $2,503,000 a year in mail charges.

The majority of bettors fill out their coupons according to the advice given by their favorite newspaper sports writer. A few try to do it scientifically, maintaining form books and elaborate graphs showing the games won and lost by each team. Some adopt the relatively simple system of sticking a pin into the list of games.

One woman, who won $2,240, revealed that her system was to sit at a window with her coupon. If a man walked by in the street outside, she marked the next game as a home win. A woman passer-by meant an away win, a child hop-skip-and-jumping along the street, a tie game. The odds against picking eight tie games are astronomical.

Legally, teenagers are barred from playing the pools. But thousands do, and plan to lie about their ages if they have a big win.

One teenager who won a minor jackpot was away from home when the pool's representative called with the winning check. Mom answered the door instead, took one look at the size of the check and exclaimed excitedly, "Now Joe will be able to have a real slap-up party for his twenty-first birthday."

"Is that so?" said the man from the pool. "If he's not twenty-one, he doesn't get it." And back went the check into his pocket.

For the big-money winners, the pools stage lavish presentation ceremonies at swank London hotels. Mrs. McGrail, for instance, was whisked away by a Rolls Royce to a posh Park Lane hotel where a famous television star presented her with the fabulous winning check. She was featured on TV and in the newspapers, all of which caused a big jump in the stake money the following week as thousands of additional Britons sent their pennies in pursuit of one of the biggest pipe dreams in history.

Certainly the soul of a Mrs. McGrail lurks in us all. But there is more to the pleasure in gambling than the winning. There's a great deal to be said simply for the doing of it.

The Sin of Betting

For twenty-four years, from 1943 to 1967, Charles W. Morton, Omaha's gift to Boston and *The Atlantic Monthly*, delighted readers of that magazine with his shrewd and genial essays in its "Accent on Living" department. As you will see, the word sin in his title—as in that of the George Saintsbury work he cites—should really be in quotation marks.

BY CHARLES W. MORTON

"BET WITH him or against him, folks. He's coming out, he's coming out, he's coming and fielding every roll. On every roll he's coming and fielding, he's—THAT'S craps-two-sixes-a-standoff-for-the-checker-players-and-the-don't-bettors...."

There was always a fine overlay of comedy in the chant of the stick-man who was warming up the customers at the craps table. The high-speed chatter included many variations, but little or nothing of artificially built-up lingo. Every word of it had a precise meaning. "He will!" He won't! Bet with him or against him, and THAT'S five-his-point, five-can-he-make-it, five-his-point, AND seven-the-buster."

The spiel would scale down an octave or so, sorrowfully, on the word "buster," and after a moment's pause the monotone would be resumed: "Getcha-money-down, folks, he's coming out...." The only imagery that I can recall came when a field number was thrown and no bets were on the field: "THAT'S four-a-fielder—" and then, in mock sorrow, "and not a child in the ward!" The field, as I recall it, looked a lot more generous than it proved to be.

These nostalgic recollections of public dice in Omaha, Nebraska, in the days of my adolescence are prompted by the recent hubbub in a New Jersey suburb where a high school boy was running a crap game in the basement of his home. Police who raided the place were preening themselves as if they had brought in dangerous criminals. The story made many a Page One, and to judge from the tut-tutting and whither-are-we-drifting tone of the press, the thought of a sixteen-year-old shooting dice against his schoolmates was enough to pale the cheek of even the most seasoned reporter. Police accused the boy of delinquency, and his parents of contributing to it.

The New Jersey boy was hamming it up a bit, it must be admitted. He dressed for his proprietor's role each evening in a white dinner jacket. As head man, his share of the take was 70 percent, and if the news photograph of his layout was complete, his field looked to be short one number, which bespeaks not necessarily crookedness but rather an extreme cupidity for one so young. His odds for certain other bets were less than generous, even by professional standards. It reminds me of the Maine lobersterman who was arrested for taking "shorts," which caused his neighbor to comment, "I expect he was measurin' some of them a mite snug."

The house in the small-time public games of the Middle West was protected by its edge and by limits of a one-dollar minimum and a fifty-dollar maximum, which prevented doubling on any great scale and which exhausted our bankrolls with some rapidity. But these are trivialities. The main point, as we ponder the New Jersey game, is to remember that few experiences are more exciting for an adolescent than winning in a game of chance. The ordinary sixteen-year-olds of my vintage played tenth-of-a-cent bridge or penny ante or, if in funds, five-and-ten. Craps was too fast for our purses; we preferred a game that we could afford throughout an evening. We all played billiards or pool, the loser paying for the time, and Kelly pool when we had the money to gamble on cue games. We stayed away from the professional gambling places simply because we saw no purpose in bucking the extra edge that the house always set up for itself, and it is this last consideration that makes one wonder why the New Jersey boys were not satisfied to rotate the dice among themselves without indulging their schoolmate in per-centages in his favor.

The moralists who had a field day with the New Jersey episode might do well to read the little essay by George Saintsbury called "The Sin of Betting." In no system of ethics or theology could he find even a suggestion that betting was wrong. "Where on earth or out of the earth," he wrote, "is the conceivable wickedness, or even naughtiness, of saying, 'If Pharos wins the Derby you shall give me six shillings, and if he doesn't I'll give you one'?" The same critics might give a thought, too, to the words of one of the New Jersey game's schoolboy customers as quoted in a news story: "Well, it keeps us off the streets. . . ."

The Way to the Dairy

He was Hector Hugh Munro when he worked as a London journalist, but with his first book of short stories, in 1908, he was to become better known by the pseudonym he then adopted. As Saki he remains, these many years after his death in World War I, a favorite storyteller cherished for his sometimes sardonic, sometimes whimsical humor.

BY SAKI

THE BARONESS and Clovis sat in a much-frequented corner of the Park exchanging biographical confidences about the long succession of passers-by.

"Who are those depressed-looking young women who have just gone by?" asked the Baroness; "they have the air of people who have bowed to destiny and are not quite sure whether the salute will be returned."

"Those," said Clovis, "are the Brimley Bomefields. I dare say you would look depressed if you had been through their experiences."

"I'm always having depressing experiences," said the Baroness, "but I never give them outward expression. It's as bad as looking one's age. Tell me about the Brimley Bomefields."

"Well," said Clovis, "the beginning of their tragedy was that they found an aunt. The aunt had been there all the time, but they had very nearly forgotten her existence until a distant relative refreshed their memory by remembering her very distinctly in his will; it is wonderful what the force of example will accomplish. The aunt, who had been unobtrusively poor, became quite pleasantly rich, and the Brimley Bomefields grew suddenly concerned at the loneliness of her life and took her under their collective wings. She had as many wings around her at this time as one of those beast-things in Revelation."

"So far I don't see any tragedy from the Brimley Bomefields' point of view," said the Baroness.

"We haven't got to it yet," said Clovis. "The aunt had been used to living very simply, and had seen next to nothing of what we should

311

consider life, and her nieces didn't encourage her to do much in the way of making a splash with her money. Quite a good deal of it would come to them at her death, and she was a fairly old woman, but there was one circumstance which cast a shadow of gloom over the satisfaction they felt in the discovery and acquisition of this desirable aunt: she openly acknowledged that a comfortable slice of her little fortune would go to a nephew on the other side of her family. He was rather a deplorable thing in rotters, and quite hopelessly top-hole in the way of getting through money, but he had been more or less decent to the old lady in her unremembered days, and she wouldn't hear anything against him. At least, she wouldn't pay any attention to what she did hear, but her nieces took care that she should have to listen to a good deal in that line. It seemed such a pity, they said among themselves, that good money should fall into such worthless hands. They habitually spoke of their aunt's money as 'good money,' as though other people's aunts dabbled for the most part in spurious currency.

"Regularly after the Derby, St. Leger, and other notable racing events they indulged in audible speculations as to how much money Roger had squandered in unfortunate betting transactions.

" 'His travelling expenses must come to a big sum,' said the eldest Brimley Bomefield one day; 'they say he attends every race-meeting in England, besides others abroad. I shouldn't wonder if he went all the way to India to see the race for the Calcutta Sweepstake that one hears so much about.'

" 'Travel enlarges the mind, my dear Christine,' said her aunt.

" 'Yes, dear aunt, travel undertaken in the right spirit,' agreed Christine; 'but travel pursued merely as a means towards gambling and extravagant living is more likely to contract the purse than to enlarge the mind. However, as long as Roger enjoys himself, I suppose he doesn't care how fast or unprofitably the money goes, or where he is to find more. It seems a pity, that's all.'

"The aunt by that time had begun to talk of something else, and it was doubtful if Christine's moralizing had been even accorded a hearing. It was her remark, however—the aunt's remark, I mean—about travel enlarging the mind, that gave the youngest Brimley Bomefield her great idea for the showing-up of Roger.

" 'If aunt could only be taken somewhere to see him gambling and throwing away money,' she said, 'it would open her eyes to his character more effectually than anything we can say.'

" 'My dear Veronique,' said her sisters, 'we can't go following him to race-meetings.'

" 'Certainly not to race-meetings,' said Veronique, 'but we might go to some place where one can look on at gambling without taking part in it.'

" 'Do you mean Monte Carlo?' they asked her, beginning to jump rather at the idea.

" 'Monte Carlo is a long way off, and has a dreadful reputation,' said Veronique; 'I shouldn't like to tell our friends that we were going to Monte Carlo. But I believe Roger usually goes to Dieppe about this time of year, and some quite respectable English people go there, and the journey wouldn't be expensive. If aunt could stand the Channel crossing the change of scene might do her a lot of good.'

"And that was how the fateful idea came to the Brimley Bomefields.

"From the very first set-off disaster hung over the expedition, as they afterwards remembered. To begin with, all the Brimley Bomefields were extremely unwell during the crossing, while the aunt enjoyed the sea air and made friends with all manner of strange travelling companions. Then, although it was many years since she had been on the Continent, she had served a very practical apprenticeship there as a paid companion, and her knowledge of colloquial French beat theirs to a standstill. It became increasingly difficult to keep under their collective wings a person who knew what she wanted and was able to ask for it and to see that she got it. Also, as far as Roger was concerned, they drew Dieppe blank; it turned out that he was staying at Pourville, a little watering-place a mile or two further west. The Brimley Bomefields discovered that Dieppe was too crowded and frivolous, and persuaded the old lady to migrate to the comparative seclusion of Pourville.

" 'You won't find it dull, you know,' they assured her; 'there is a little casino attached to the hotel, and you can watch the people dancing and throwing away their money at *petits chevaux*.'

"It was just before *petits chevaux* had been supplanted by *boule*.

"Roger was not staying in the same hotel, but they knew that the casino would be certain of his patronage on most afternoons and evenings.

"On the first evening of their visit they wandered into the casino after a fairly early dinner, and hovered near the tables. Bertie van Tahn was staying there at the time, and he described the whole incident to me. The Brimley Bomefields kept a furtive watch on the doors as though they were expecting some one to turn up, and the aunt got more and more amused and interested watching the little horses whirl round and round the board.

" 'Do you know, poor little number eight hasn't won for the last thirty-two times,' she said to Christine; 'I've been keeping count. I shall really have to put five francs on him to encourage him.'

" 'Come and watch the dancing, dear,' said Christine nervously. It was scarcely a part of their strategy that Roger should come in and find the old lady backing her fancy at the *petits chevaux* table.

" 'Just wait while I put five francs on number eight,' said the aunt, and in another moment her money was lying on the table. The horses commenced to move round; it was a slow race this time, and number eight crept up at the finish like some crafty demon and placed his nose just a fraction in front of number three, who had seemed to be winning easily. Recourse had to be had to measurement, and the number eight was proclaimed the winner. The aunt picked up thirty-five francs. After that the Brimley Bomefields would have had to have used concerted force to get her away from the tables. When Roger appeared on the scene she was fifty-two francs to the good; her nieces were hovering for-lornly in the background, like chickens that have been hatched out by a duck and are despairingly watching their parent disporting herself in a dangerous and uncongenial element. The supper-party which Roger insisted on standing that night in honour of his aunt and the three Miss Brimley Bomefields was remarkable for the unrestrained gaiety of two of the participants and the funereal mirthlessness of the remaining guests.

" 'I do not think,' Christine confided afterwards to a friend, who re-confided it to Bertie van Tahn, 'that I shall ever be able to touch pâté de foie gras again. It would bring back memories of that awful evening.'

"For the next two or three days the nieces made plans for returning to England or moving on to some other resort where there was no casino. The aunt was busy making a system for winning at *petits chevaux*. Number eight, her first love, had been running rather un-kindly for her, and a series of plunges on number five had turned out even worse.

" 'Do you know, I dropped over seven hundred francs at the tables this afternoon,' she announced cheerfully at dinner on the fourth evening of their visit.

" 'Aunt! Twenty-eight pounds! And you were losing last night too.'

" 'Oh, I shall get it all back,' she said optimistically; 'but not here. These silly little horses are no good. I shall go somewhere where one can play comfortably at roulette. You needn't look so shocked. I've always felt that, given the opportunity, I should be an inveterate gam-bler, and now you darlings have put the opportunity in my way. I must drink your very good healths. Waiter, a bottle of *Pontet Canet*. Ah, it's number seven on the wine list; I shall plunge on number seven tonight. It won four times running this afternoon when I was backing that silly number five.'

"Number seven was not in a winning mood that evening. The Brimley Bomefields, tired of watching disaster from a distance, drew near to the table where their aunt was now an honoured habituée, and gazed mournfully at the successive victories of one and five and eight and four, which swept 'good money' out of the purse of seven's obstinate backer. The day's losses totalled something very near two thousand francs.

" 'You incorrigible gamblers,' said Roger chaffingly to them, when he found them at the tables.

" 'We are not gambling,' said Christine freezingly; 'we are looking on.'

" 'I *don't* think,' said Roger knowingly; 'of course you're a syndicate and aunt is putting the stakes on for all of you. Any one can tell by your looks when the wrong horse wins that you've got a stake on.'

"Aunt and nephew had supper alone that night, or at least they would have if Bertie hadn't joined them; all the Brimley Bomefields had headaches.

"The aunt carried them all off to Dieppe the next day and set cheerily about the task of winning back some of her losses. Her luck was variable; in fact, she had some fair streaks of good fortune, just enough to keep her thoroughly amused with her new distraction; but on the whole she was a loser. The Brimley Bomefields had a collective attack of nervous prostration on the day when she sold out a quantity of shares in Argentine rails. 'Nothing will ever bring that money back,' they remarked lugubriously to one another.

"Veronique at last could bear it no longer, and went home; you see, it had been her idea to bring the aunt on this disastrous expedition, and though the others did not cast the fact verbally in her face, there was a certain lurking reproach in their eyes which was harder to meet than actual upbraidings. The other two remained behind, forlornly mounting guard over their aunt until such time as the waning of the Dieppe season should at last turn her in the direction of home and safety. They made anxious calculations as to how little 'good money' might, with reasonable luck, be squandered in the meantime. Here, however, their reckoning went far astray; the close of the Dieppe season merely turned their aunt's thoughts in search of some other convenient gambling resort. 'Show a cat the way to the dairy—' I forget how the proverb goes on, but it summed up the situation as far as the Brimley Bomefields' aunt was concerned. She had been introduced to unexplored pleasures, and found them greatly to her liking, and she was in no hurry to forgo the fruits of her newly acquired knowledge. You see, for the first time in her life the old thing was thoroughly enjoying herself; she was losing money, but she had plenty of fun and excitement over the process, and she had enough left to do very comfortably on. Indeed, she was only just learning to understand the art of doing oneself well. She was a popular hostess, and in return her fellow-gamblers were always ready to entertain her to dinners and suppers when their luck was in. Her nieces, who still remained in attendance on her, with the pathetic unwillingness of a crew to leave a foundering treasure ship which might yet be steered into port, found little pleasure in these Bohemian festivities; to see 'good money' lavished on good living for the entertainment of a nondescript circle of acquaintances who were not likely to be in any way socially useful to them, did not attune them to a spirit of revelry. They contrived, whenever possible, to excuse themselves from participation in their aunt's deplored gaieties; the Brimley Bomefield headaches became famous.

"And one day the nieces came to the conclusion that, as they would have expressed it, 'no useful purpose would be served' by their continued attendance on a relative who had so thoroughly emancipated herself from the sheltering protection of their wings. The aunt bore the announcement of their departure with a cheerfulness that was almost disconcerting.

" 'It's time you went home and had those headaches seen to by a specialist,' was her comment on the situation.

"The homeward journey of the Brimley Bomefields was a veritable retreat from Moscow, and what made it the more bitter was the fact that the Moscow, in this case, was not overwhelmed with fire and ashes, but merely extravagantly over-illuminated.

"From mutual friends and acquaintances they sometimes get glimpses of their prodigal relative, who has settled down into a confirmed gambling maniac, living on such salvage of income as obliging moneylenders have left at her disposal.

"So you need not be surprised," concluded Clovis, "if they do wear a depressed look in public."

"Which is Veronique?" asked the Baroness.

"The most depressed-looking of the three," said Clovis.